Social Work

(Theory and Practice)

S.K. Murthy

Saurabh
Publishing House
4735/22, Prakash Deep Building,
Ansari Road, Daryaganj,
New Delhi - 110002

Published by
SAURABH PUBLISHING HOUSE

Distributed by:
Lotus Press Publishers & Distributors
Unit No. 220, Second Floor, 4735/22, Prakash Deep Building,
Ansari Road, Darya Ganj, New Delhi-110002
Ph: 23280047, 32903912, 098118-38000
E-mail : loutspress1984@gmail.com
www.lotuspress.co.in

Saurabh Publishing House is an imprint of
Lotus Press Publishers & Distributors

Social Work(Theory and Practice)

ISBN : 978-81-89005-94-8

Printed at : Lotus Press, New Delhi - 110002

Preface

Social work, organized effort to help individuals and families to adjust themselves to the community, as well as to adapt the community to the needs of such persons and families. Modern social work employs three methods of assistance: case work, group work and community organization. Case work is the method by which individual persons and families are assisted. The person in need of case work may be physically, mentally or socially handicapped. Among those regarded as socially handicapped are: the unemployed, the homeless, members of broken families, alcoholics, drug addicts, and neglected or problem children. To determine the cause of maladjustment, the social worker must understand individual psychology as well as the sociology of the community. Physicians, psychiatrists and other specialists may be required to help diagnose the difficulty.

Social group work is exemplified by the social settlement, the supervised playground and gymnasium, and the classroom, where handicrafts may be learned. The community may be called upon to provide the buildings and grounds for such activities; often the services of volunteers and of public groups are utilized; in recent years people living in poverty areas have been employed to work in and direct poverty projects in their own communities.

Social work emerged as a profession out of the early efforts of churches and philanthropic groups to relieve the effects of poverty, to bring the comforts of religion to the poor, to promote temperance and encourage thrift, to care for children, the sick, and the aged, and to correct the delinquent. Orphanages and homes for the elderly were typical results of these activities. The word *charity* best describes the early activities, which were aimed at the piecemeal alleviation of particular maladjustments. In such charitable work the principal criterion in determining aid to families was worthiness, while the emphasis in later social work was on restoring individuals to normal life both for their own sake and for the sake of the community.

Entry-level social workers are trained as generalists and are expected to provide service to a broad range of clients, maintain a wide scope of knowledge, and practice a great diversity of skills. Advanced practitioners with graduate-level training may specialize in areas such as clinical, medical, or school social work, as well as planning and development, aging, mental health or corrections.

In the public health arena, social workers are a valuable resource for the development of treatment plans for patients, for locating supportive resources, and in facilitating referrals. Under the auspices of government and non-government public health organizations and institutions, social workers often provide behavioural and social assessments along with mental health assessment, treatment, and short-term or ongoing case management. Social workers may also work in the community as planners or community organizers capable of engaging groups of people, neighbourhoods, or entire communities to address social problems such as drug abuse or teen pregnancy. Social work is a distinct profession, requiring college training, and a masters degree is often a necessity. Many states license social workers, and in those states only those holding such licenses may legally provide social work services. The possibilities of employment vary widely and include federal, state, and local government agencies; hospitals; and public health and not-for-profit organizations.

S. K. Murthy

Contents

1

Social Work: Definition and Meaning

Introduction

Social work is a professional and academic discipline committed to the pursuit of social welfare, social change and social justice. The field works towards research and practice to improve the quality of life and to the development of the potential of each individual, group and community of a society. Social workers perform interventions through research, policy, community organizing, direct practice and teaching. Research is often focused on areas such as human development, social policy, public administration, program evaluation and international and community development. Social workers are organized into local, national, continental and international professional bodies. Social work, an interdisciplinary field, includes theories from economics, education, sociology, medicine, philosophy, politics, psychology, and as well as anti-oppressive and anti-racist discourse.

History of Social Work

Social work has its roots in the struggle of society to deal with poverty and the problems associated with it. Therefore, social work is intricately linked with the idea of charity work; but must be understood in broader terms. The concept of charity goes back to ancient times, and the practice of providing for the poor has roots in all major world religions.

Pre-Modern History

In the West, when Constantine I legalized the Christian Church, the newly legitimized church setup poor houses, homes for the aged, hospitals, and orphanages. These were often funded, at least in part, from grants from the Empire.

By 590 AD the church had a system for circulating the consumables to the poor: associated with each parish was a *diaconium* or office of the deacon.

As there was no effective bureaucracy below city government that was capable of charitable activities, the clergy served this role in the west up through the 18th century. During the Middle Ages, the Christian church had vast influence on European society and charity was considered to be a responsibility and a sign of one's piety. This charity was in the form of direct relief (for example, giving money, food, or other material goods to alleviate a particular need), as opposed to trying to change the root causes of poverty.

The practice and profession of social work has a relatively modern (19th century) and scientific origin.

Modern History

Social work, as a profession, originated in the 19th century. The movement began primarily in the United States and England. After the end of feudalism, the poor were seen as a more direct threat to the social order, and so the state formed an organized system to care for them. In England, the Poor Law served this purpose. This system of laws sorted the poor into different categories, such as the able bodied poor, the impotent poor, and the idle poor. This system developed different responses to these different groups.

The 19th century ushered in the Industrial Revolution. There was a great leap in technological and scientific achievement, but there was also a great migration to urban areas throughout the Western world. This led to many social problems, which in turn led to an increase in social activism. Also with the dawn of the 19th century came a great "missionary" push from many Protestant denominations. Some of these mission efforts (urban missions), attempted to resolve the problems inherent in large cities like poverty, prostitution, disease, and other afflictions. In the United States workers known as "friendly visitors", stipended by church and other charitable bodies, worked through direct relief, prayer, and evangelism to alleviate these problems. In Europe, chaplains or almoners were appointed to administer the church's mission to the poor.

During this time, rescue societies were initiated to find more appropriate means of self-support for women involved in prostitution. Mental asylums grew to assist in taking care of the mentally ill. A new philosophy of "scientific charity" emerged, which stated charity should be "secular, rational and empirical as opposed to sectarian, sentimental, and dogmatic." In the late 1880s, a new system to provide aid for social ills came in to being, which became known as the settlement movement. The settlement movement focused on the causes of poverty through the "three Rs" — Research, Reform, and Residence. They provided a variety of services including educational, legal, and health services. These programmes also advocated changes in social policy. Workers in the settlement movement immersed themselves in the culture of those they were helping.

Contemporary Professional Development

The International Federation of Social Workers states, of social work today, that

"Social work bases its methodology on a systematic body of evidence-based knowledge derived from research and practice evaluation, including local and indigenous knowledge specific to its context. It recognizes the complexity of interactions between human beings and their environment, and the capacity of people both to be affected by and to alter the multiple influences upon them including bio-psychosocial factors. The social work profession draws on theories of human development, social theory and social systems to analyse complex situations and to facilitate individual, organizational, social and cultural changes."

A hopeful development for bridging this gap is the compilation of collections of "best practices" which attempt to distill research findings and the experience of respected social work practitioners, educators and researchers into effective interventions. Another important contemporary development in the profession is overcoming suspicion of technology and taking advantage of the potential of information technology.

Qualifications

Professional social workers are generally considered those who hold a professional degree in social work. In a number of countries and jurisdictions, registration or licensure of people working as social workers is required and there are mandated qualifications. In other places, the professional association sets academic and experiential requirements for admission to membership.

India

A social worker, practicing in India, usually requires a doctoral degree (Ph.D or DSW), master's degree (MSW) or a bachelor's degree (BSW or BASW) in social work from a Council on Social Work Education (CSWE) accredited programme to receive a license. In some areas, however, a social worker may be able to receive a license with a bachelor's or even associate's degree in any discipline.

Depending on the university, the four year degree may be structured in different ways and draws upon many fields, including social work theory, psychology, human development, sociology, social policy, research methods, social planning and social administration.

A person with a BSW is considered a "generalist" and the MSW is considered "a specialist or advanced generalist"; a Ph.D. or D.S.W. (Doctor of Social Work) generally conducts research, teaches, or analyzes policy, often in higher education settings.

Various states in India "protect" the use of the title social worker by statute. Use of the title requires licensure or certification in most states. The pass rate for the Master's level licensing exam is around 74%. A range of products and services exist to assist students in preparing for the exam including practice tests, study guides, private tutoring and prep classes.

Canada

A four-year Bachelor of Social Work (BSW) is required for entry into the field. A Masters Degree in Social Work (MSW) is usually required to provide psychotherapy treatment. In Canada social workers may provide treatment but cannot diagnose. Some provinces require registration in order to legally use the title "social worker". Some provinces also require an exam prerequisite for certification through the Association of Social Work Boards (ASWB).

United Kingdom

The main qualification for social work is the undergraduate Bachelor's degree (B.A., B.Sc. or BSW) in social work, offered at British universities from September 2003 onwards. There is also available a master's degree (M.A., M.Sc. or MSW). These have replaced the previous qualifying award, the postgraduate Diploma in Social Work (DipSW), which was first awarded in 1991 and will be phased out across the UK by 2009. Prior to this, the recognized qualification was the Certificate of Qualification in Social Work (CQSW), awarded between 1975 and 1991.

Purporting to be either a social worker or a student social worker without registering with the Social Work Register and holding or undergoing training for the recognized qualifications is now a criminal offence. Social workers must renew their registration every three years. These regulations offer protection to vulnerable people by guaranteeing the professional regulation of people working as social workers. They also promote workforce development, as all social workers must participate in at least fifteen days of professional training over a three year period in order to be eligible for renewal of their registration.

Lay practitioners in the United Kingdom, often referred to as Social Services Assistants or Care Workers, are unregistered social workers that often do not hold any formal social work qualification. This is not the case in Scotland where the scope of registration for social service workers is more advanced. Within the mental health sector in the United Kingdom, social workers can train as an Approved Mental Health Professional. With the implementation of the Mental Health Act 2007, this had replaced the previous Approved Social Worker role and is open to other professionals such as community psychiatric nurses, psychologists and occupational therapists, whilst maintaining a social work ethos. AMHPs are responsible for organizing and contributing to assessments under the Mental Health Act 1983, as amended by the Mental Health Act 2007.

After qualifying, social workers can undertake further training under the social work 'Post-Qualifying Framework'. Before 2007, there were four awards available under this framework:

- Post-Qualifying Award — for advanced social work practice and management.
- Mental Health Social Workers in England and Wales can now train to become an Approved Mental Health Professional or AMHP.
- Child Care Award — qualification to work with children and young people.
- Practice Teaching Award — qualification to work as a tutor, supervisor and assessor for social work students on their work placement.

In 2007, the General Social Care Council and UK partners implemented a new framework which unified these awards in a simpler structure allowing broader study to count towards three levels of social work award: specialist, higher specialist, and advanced.

Australia

A four-year Bachelor of Social Work (BSW) is required for entry into the occupation of Social Worker in Australia, although some universities also offer a two-year, accelerated, graduate-entry BSW. Whilst there are no legal registration requirements, most employers stipulate that applicants must be eligible for membership of the Australian Association of Social Workers (Australia) (AASW). Only graduates of courses recognised by the AASW are eligible for membership. Continuing Professional Education (CPE) is an ongoing requirement of accredited membership of the AASW and must incorporate accountability, gaining new knowledge and information & skill development. A person with overseas qualifications can apply for consideration of recognition of their qualifications via a formal application for assessment by the AASW.

Role of the Professional Social Worker

The main tasks of professional social workers are case management (linking clients with agencies and programmes that will meet their psychosocial needs), medical social work, counseling (psychotherapy), human services management, social welfare policy analysis, community organizing, advocacy, teaching (in schools of social work), and social science research.

Professional social workers work in a variety of settings, including: non-profit or public social service agencies, grassroots advocacy organizations, hospitals, hospices, community health agencies, schools, faith-based organizations, and even the military. Other social workers work as psychotherapists, counselors, or mental health practitioners, normally working in coordination with psychiatrists, psychologists, or other medical professionals. Additionally, some social workers have chosen to direct the focus of their efforts on social policy or academic research towards the practice or ethics of social work. While the emphasis has varied among these task areas in different eras and countries, some areas have been the subject of controversy as to whether they are properly part of social work's mission.

United States

In the United States of America, leaders and scholars in the field of social work have debated the purpose and nature of the profession since its beginning in the late 19th century. Workers, beginning with the settlement house movement, have argued for a focus on social reform, political activism, and systemic causes of poverty. Social workers of the Settlement House Movement were primarily young women from middle-income families and chose to live in lower-income neighbourhoods to engage in community organizing. These workers sometimes received stipends from charitable organizations and sometimes worked for free. In contrast to the settlement house movement, the friendly visitors were women from middle-income families who visited (but did not reside among) families in lower-income neighbourhoods. Friendly visitors emphasized conventional morality (such as thrift and abstinence from alcohol) rather than social activism.

Others have advocated an emphasis on direct practice, aid to individual clients and families with targeted material assistance or interventions using the diagnostic and statistical manual of mental diseases DSM-IV. While social work has been defined as direct, individual practice in the last quarter of the 20th century, there is a growing resurgence of community practice in social work. Of broad and growing significance are the relationship counseling and Relationship Education movements which seek to assist in interpersonal social skill building which can be of great societal value in promoting marriage and family stability. Relationship education and counseling primarily aid the majority of individuals who are free of pathology or who have found that DSM-IV based services are ineffectual. This majority can benefit from education and exposure to relationship skills that have not otherwise been discussed and distributed by social services in this time of weakened family, church, and societal conventions. Another new development in social work is the focus on informatics. For many social workers, the use of any online technology is problematic due to persistent concerns about privacy. However, other social workers recognize that clients are going on line for many purposes. Some schools of social work, such as University of Southern California are offering courses to build informatics skills at the graduate level.

Community practice is the new term of art for what used to be known as "macro practice" social work. Community practice includes working for change at the systems level, including human services management (administration, planning, marketing, and program development); community organizing; social policy and politics; and international social development.

The National Association of Social Workers (NASW) is the largest and most recognized membership organization of professional social workers in the world. Representing

150,000 members from 56 chapters in the United States and abroad, the association promotes, develops and protects the practice of social work and social workers. NASW also seeks to enhance the well-being of individuals, families, and communities through its work and advocacy.

Although membership is generally not required for licensure, NASW survey data give a rough idea of how social workers are employed in the US. According to NASW:

Nearly 40% of NASW members say that mental health is their primary practice area. The health sector employs 8% of NASW's members, and 8% practice in child welfare or family organizations. Six percent of NASW members say school social work is their primary practice area, and another 3% work primarily with adolescents. These figures are significantly confounded by the fact that NASW members are primarily licensed practitioners working in the clinical arena, and the fact that many social workers in the field do not actually hold a degree in social work. NASW is usually concerned with issues like licensing, reimbursement, etc., that are not relevant to child welfare practice, for instance.

Within the mental health field, social workers may work in private practice, much like clinical psychologists or members of other counselling professions often do. Social workers are often in the position of recommending the use of psychopharmaceutical agents, though not prescribing them. The increasingly widespread usage of these agents in the U.S. has received little scrutiny by the NASW, despite that fact that these drugs are prescribed far more heavily in the U.S. than anywhere else in the world. Social workers in private practice may take direct payments from clients and may also receive third-party reimbursement from insurance companies or government programmes such as Medicaid. Insurance reimbursement for mental health services involves the designation of the recipient of services as mentally ill, or more specifically a label is assigned from the DSM-IV, the diagnostic and statistical manual of mental illness. This assignment, when recorded to an individual's medical history can prove to be a significant impediment to future pursuits. It can raise the cost to the individual for health or nursing home insurance; it can be the basis of denial for life insurance; and it can limit an individual's professional choices, such as in health care, motor vehicle operation, or airplane piloting.

Private practice was not part of the social work profession when it began in the late 19th century. It has been controversial among social workers, some of whom feel that the more lucrative opportunities of private practice have led many social workers to abandon the field's historic mission of assisting disadvantaged populations. The private practice model can be at odds with the community development and political activism strains of social work.

Social workers in mental health may also work for an agency, whether publicly funded, supported by private charity, or some combination of the two. These agencies provide a range of mental health services to disadvantaged populations in the US.

Some social workers are child welfare workers, a role that looms large in the public's perception of social work. This role contributes to a negative view of social work in the U.S., since child welfare authorities can remove abused or neglected children from the custody of their parents, a practice that is fraught with controversy and sometimes with scandalous incompetence. Many child welfare workers in the US do not in fact have social work degrees (though all caseworkers in most states have at least a Bachelor's degree in a related field).

Some states restrict the use of the title social worker to licensed practitioners, who must hold a degree in the field. Such restrictions are a high legislative priority of NASW.

2

Social Work for Gender Justice

Introduction

Gender identity, of course, is not entirely separable from biology. In obvious ways, the sexual organs that we are born with contribute to what we learn and the way we are treated in the earliest stages of our lives   the ways in which we are diapered or toilet trained illustrate this point. You may think that it is equally obvious that there are readily identifiable ways in which, right from the beginning, we are taught and learn to express ourselves to others as gendered persons, as social beings who happen to come in bodies with specific sorts of parts. In fact, examples such as the effects of what or how we are taught to play are now so commonplace that pointing them out has become pretty close to unnecessary. But the development of the gender identity of "woman" consists of far more subtle and effective influences than whether or if we learn to like playing with dolls or cars.

In order to get a handle on some of these deep and sometimes hidden influences, I will introduce a list of terms that will help us to start taking notice of some of the significant things that can contribute to the way any particular woman becomes a woman. This list is *not* meant to be rank ordered, nor is it meant to cover everything that is important in this process, but it is meant to help us start thinking about factors that many people may not have thought about as crucial to an appreciation of a woman's identity as a woman.

My philosophical training has taught me to appreciate both the value of carefully dividing up a complicated topic and the risks of doing so. It is possible to confuse a modest attempt at a clarification of complications with a fixed (and false) formula for successfully reducing something that just is complicated, and cannot or should not be oversimplified. No individual human or cultural group can or should be oversimplified or treated formulaically; and if someone tries to tell you otherwise, you should examine their assumptions or' motivations. With this in mind, in the next five sections I will try to convince you that if you want to understand the cultural identification of women, it is wise to consider the many ways in which women are effected by: (1) ongoing support units, (2) ethnic or racial focuses, (3) contexts of sexuality, (4) exposure to moral instruction or value-defining situations, and (5) abilities and disabilities (and how they are balanced). After the specific values and complications of these five areas have been discussed, we will go on to address the question with which I opened this section: Is there some basic set of things that women from all cultural contexts share?

Ongoing Support Units

It is arguable that the term "family" could be used to characterize what actually needs to be considered in this section. In United States, today there is a renewed interest in the importance of the family. In choosing the title there is no way dismissing the importance of this renewed interest. What this section draws to our attention is the presence or absence of continuing, supportive people during the period that leads up to a female child becoming identified as a woman a period that think probably lasts from birth to death, but how long it takes is not the issue here.

The 20th century philosopher Simone de Beauvior offered a number of reasons why a female person is not born a woman, but becomes one. She wrote insightfully about the defining importance of the significant people in our lives who see us, and in whose eyes we see ourselves. She was particularly interested in how women have come to see themselves, through the eyes of men, as "the other," that is, how women have not been separately defined, but defined in terms of how they differed from men. This focus on the role played by significant people in the way women learn to understand themselves easily opens up to thinking about the interaction between family members. The term "ongoing support unit" is introduced to get us thinking about a wider set of significant people than is traditionally associated with the concept of a family. This wider designation can but does not necessarily involve genetic relatedness or providing food, shelter, and clothing. Instead, it draws our attention to the influences of various people in whose eyes we come, over time, to see ourselves, and who are continuous enough in our lives that, in large part, we decide or become who we are in response or in relation to them, for example, a long-time friend who may seem more of a sister than does a biological sister, to whom to provide unqualified support and with whom we identify with so strongly that if she experiences a life-altering event.

It is important to take note that people who are "there for us" can be not only traditionally or untraditionally related to us, but they can "support" our identity formation in positive or negative ways. A supportive person can be well-meaning but miss the mark entirely, or end up providing support that has effects they never intended as for example, with overprotective or heavy-handed parents who pass on lessons of familial dependency relations or intrusiveness to their daughters, or religiously motivated friends who cite doctrine that does not inspire, but elicits shame in a young woman, perhaps deeply lowering her self-esteem. In addition to being an inspiring grandmother or a friend who helps us to grow, an influential person in a support unit could be a neighbor, nanny, nemesis, or an unavoidable nameless nitpicker whose focus on the apparently small details of our lives makes us self-conscious in some lasting way. Such people somehow make it easy or, over time, force us to open or to close up in ways that later can become characteristic of how we see ourselves as women. The amount of time we spend with such people need not be as significant as the impact of whatever time we do spend with them. We need not even remember their names to internalize their influences.

Labelling and appreciating this complex source of input into the development of a woman's identity teaches us to ask the question: "Can we identify specific ongoing support groups that have contributed to women's identities?" In some cases the answer will point us in the direction of looking at the influences of traditional family units but, given the decreasing numbers of such units, in very many cases that will not be the most likely direction in which to look.

To the extent that the concept of "a family" currently is being enlarged to include nontraditional support units, it will become more likely that examinations of family relations will provide insight into women's gendered identities. There is, for example, a growing body of literature on African-American women about the "mother-centred" families in which many grew up-where the mothering was frequently not done by biological mothers, or even by individual women, but rather in a shared, nurturing unit in which some variable cross section of women cared for others in the unit who needed caring for, whether or not any genetic link was present. Patricia Hill Collins, for example, distinguishes between "blood mothers" and "other mothers," and discusses the important role played by this latter category in many families.

What counts as "the" unit in such a creatively expanded family is apparently very open-ended, with biologically unrelated people unofficially (that is, not through legal actions) being adopted as fathers, mothers, brothers, sisters, cousins, aunts, grandparents, etc., who can continue to be so identified, not just for many years, but through subsequent generations. It is important to note that this is not some new definition of family, but that it is a description of a practice that can be traced back through many generations of African-American families. Recently a African-American students told me that she believed that being raised this way had given her a much larger sense of what it could mean for her to be a woman or a mother. Such practices are, of course, not exclusive to just this ethnic group, but this illustration suggests that a wide variety of experiences in the support units with which women are identified for some significant period of time impact their sense of just who they are and what they can be in relation to others. In discussions of articles about various historical examples of creative extensions of the concept of "family," people from many different backgrounds do recognize analogous lessons.

Regardless of how a family is defined, some people will claim that among the basic set of things that it is to be a woman is being (or being somehow programmed to be) a mother, or a nurturing member of a family. Often this is thought to be a very simple point about women being defined by having the physiological capacity to give birth and to establish a "natural" support unit for children (e.g., through breast-feeding). But the points raised in this section allow us to begin to see just how socially impacted concepts such as mothering and family can be, and how important it is to appreciate the many ways in which particular women have had significant variations of such concepts contribute to their self-definition. In some support units women have seen models of women who nurture alone, or together, or who designate nurturing to some specific people (perhaps some women and men), and not to others (perhaps the biological parents). What comes naturally to these women may vary greatly.

Ethnic or Racial Focuses

The preceding section supplies us with a bridge to a second source of influences on women's gender identities. If concepts as seemingly basic as "family" and "mother" can be interpreted and enlarged within ethnic groups, reason suggests that such groups could alter any number of concepts which would influence the gender identities of their women members. In obvious ways gender identity overlaps racial or ethnic identity women can come from every sort of background, and their gender and ethnic interests often bump into each other in very difficult ways. But these overlapping interests are not easy to generalize about.

While we can learn a lot from the discussions of specific ethnically identified writers about their experiences and their proximity to or study of the practices of others within their ethnic group, no writer can (and few will want to) speak for all members of any group, regardless of how identified they are with that group. Alice Walker can get us thinking about "our" mothers' gardens, Amy Tan can introduce us to a cross section of women of Asian-American descent with whom we can identify, Annie Dillard can create a familiar vision of growing up female in America, and we can draw insights from all of them. But who draws what insight and how they draw it may or may not have anything to do with whether readers are ethnically identified with these women writers, or how accurate their remarks are, in general, about members of the ethnic group that they represent.

Ethnic identity is acquired unevenly, running the gamut from persons having deep, sustained exposure to having little or no sense at all about the facts or values of their ethnic heritage. Cases of mixed or obscured ethnicity abound. For example, European Americans (after the first generation) sometimes are identified ethnically and sometimes not (Italian-Americans, often; German-Americans, not quite as often; British-Americans, rarely). For the most part, the students that I encounter who consider themselves European Americans are only nominally inclined to identify themselves in terms of any specific ethnic/cultural heritage; and if pressed, they tend to identify with European culture in general, even if they are pretty sure, for example that their family, has no, e.g., French or Italian background. And, of course, there are European Americans of all racial groups, which complicates the problem even more.

What gender lessons have impacted the identities of European American women? Surely more than those directly attached to their specific (biologically licensed) ethnic, or racial cultures. In addition to a long history of activism for women's rights, women from European American cultural groups also have inherited extremely influential male-headed or "patriarchal" legal and religious institutions that have directly and indirectly codified what women can or cannot, should or should not, do. Can or should women fight in the front lines in battle? Can or should women who have children out of wedlock receive support? Although our inherited legal and religious institutions come from many different cultural groups and differ on such issues, they have addressed and continue to try to answer these questions in ways which imply that women's role in society needs specific and separate rules and regulations.

Are all women of the African American, Asian American, Native American, or Hispanic American categories in significantly different situations? Some of the specific laws and lessons that they have inherited may differ, but the effects of their ethnic heritage is similarly complicated. As Americans, they inherit all of the institutionalized (sometimes conflicting) lessons and practices of this country, and perhaps even more from their particular ancestors. They may or may not have had easy access to their own (biologically licensed) ethnic identity and its cultural lessons. Such information could have been intentionally or unintentionally blocked. Although there is a widespread, active attempt to appreciate the vast historical and cultural values associated with ethnic and/or racial groups, some people who acknowledge the value of ethnic identities continue to argue for a "melting pot" American mentality.

A version of this "melting pot" thinking frequently is raised in reference to women, for, despite the American inheritance of European patriarchal practices (and probably because of historical writers like Mary Wollstonecraft and American counterparts like Susan B. Anthony), there is the popular notion that American women have more possibilities to expand their identities than women who remain deeply linked to some ethnic or racial groups from other parts of the world. All American women have to decide for themselves whether or not this is true, and all of us have to wade through the stated values and devalues of our ethnic or racial backgrounds, to the extent that we can become aware of them, or we risk missing the ethnic influences passed on to us through the people who raised us, and the people who raised them. Labeling and appreciating this ongoing and important source of input into the development of women teaches us to ask the question: Can we identify specific ethnic or racial focuses that have contributed to women's identities? And when we do ask this question, we have to be prepared for a time consuming search for the answer.

Before going on we should pause on a complication that has been suggested in this section, but warrants closer attention. More and more American women are of mixed ethnic and racial backgrounds. If this is not already true of the great majority of American women, it is hard to imagine a future in which it is not true. There are students with all sorts of mixed ethnic backgrounds, and nearly all of them have expressed disappointment that they have not been given the societal room to deeply identify themselves with all of the parts of their heritage, but instead have been pressed to identify with one group over another. Literature on biracial experience is just becoming available which promises to give a huge percentage of women insight into how to deal with the parts of their background that previously may have been minimized.

So the choices are not just whether to find our identity as women within an ethnic group or in an ethnic melting pot, but also whether we can affirm a number of distinct backgrounds at once. Reason suggests that, like the choices of finding one's identity as a woman through identification with one group, or discovering it in a homogenization of all groups, the third option of finding it by affirming specific links to different ethnic groups is not only available to persons of biologically identified ethnicities, but to any woman raised in or strongly influenced by some ethnic groups.

Establishing a gender identity in an ethnically complicated "ongoing support unit," can result in deep tensions between the various lessons that are internalized. When such units are ethnically rich, we can come to see ourselves in and through the eyes of people with dramatically different sorts of sensibilities about concepts such as "family" and "mother." But working through such tension, and having a wide variety of close and inspiring role models, also can be exciting and liberating. When we do identify ourselves as women we find our own way through whatever complex mix of sensibilities we have encountered.

Contexts of Sexuality

For some, adding sexuality to this already very complicated picture of how one becomes a woman may risk making the project of understanding women's culture in general seem almost delusional. For others, women's sexual development may seem to be such a "given," that they might think that a common form of sexuality is a binding factor. This latter group is probably assuming what Adrienne Rich has called "compulsory heterosexuality". In fact, traditional notions of "family" and "mother" frequently assume women's heterosexuality as part of her gender identity. For example, it often is assumed that a woman is "built" to have intercourse with a man, and to bear "his" children. But just how good the assumption of women's basic cultural heterosexuality is depends on the extent to which options in sexual identity have become real options for women.

Most (if not all) women know that there are other historically common sexual practices beyond heterosexual practices, but a good number of women do not understand these practices as "live" or real options. The various social contexts in which women participate may or may not contain viable models of homosexual, bisexual, transsexual, or celibate practice. For many women the word designations for these various sexual possibilities might be available, but there has been no context in which to see these alternatives at work in identity-defining "on-going support groups." When this is the case, the over generalized cultural practice of heterosexuality among women is probably a fairly safe assumption. Whether or not biological factors (hormones, etc.) "determine" sexual preferences in women, or preferences follow from acquired tastes and a strong will, if such preferences are not understood as realistic possibilities, women (inner turmoil notwithstanding) will not be able to choose them and at the same time maintain some realistic goals and expectations. How many women today are in such a situation? While heterosexual practice is surely the dominant, socially reinforced, and most widely celebrated form of sexual identity, for many women a variety of "live" options are emerging. Many examples can be cited of "ongoing support units" that extend family and mothering practices to include women who are sexually identified as other than heterosexual. Film depictions of these options are especially far-reaching. It is even arguable that these options have become "live" options not through immediate support units, but through media representations of such units. Sexual practices often, if not mostly, remain implicit in more traditional families, but frequently get very explicit exposure in the movies, not to mention the nightly news.

One might ask what worries people who believe that other forms of sexual practice are not properly identified with the concept of "woman," and who also believe that women's heterosexuality is part of what really defines women's culture. For if this is the case, even when "live" options are present, it would logically follow that "real" women would not be inclined to pursue them. Such people are in a bind, of course, if more and more adult females do chose other options. Statistics on this possibility will continue to be collected, but in the meantime, if we want to understand the cultural dimensions of being a woman in America in the latter part of this century or the beginning of the 21st century, we must learn to ask: *Can we identify specific and different contexts of sexuality that have contributed to women's identities?*" That is, we need to look not only at heterosexual modeling, but whatever sexual options were opened by the people who effectively contributed to the way any particular woman came to see herself.

But women who breathe life into "dead" options also need to be considered. Alternative forms of sexuality with different sorts of partners is not the only category here. Women, for example, who choose to live celibate or to be artificially inseminated can be seen as choosing options that may not have been modelled for them in any viable way. The first women to engage in artificial insemination were, in many ways, sexual pioneers. It may have seemed an interesting idea, but until fairly recently it was only an idea. It always has been possible for women to engage in sexually self-gratifying behavior, but now it has become possible for women to define a very singular form of sexual existence that can be extended to include childbirth without ever having had "sex."

Learning to put the concept of "sex" in quotation marks is part of what is necessary to begin to understand how many ways women can be defined in contexts of sexuality. When I grew up I understood having "sex" in only one way. It was also euphemistically called "going all the way," and specifically referred to a penis penetrating a vagina. It took me an embarrassingly long time to recognize that this was only the tip of the sexual iceberg, so to speak, and that remaining focused on only this could be roughly analogous to being stuck on the tip of an iceberg. Doing "it," as we thought of "it" then, was to do a very limited act or, to be a bit more to the point, something extremely goal-oriented and not very time-consuming. The late 1960s and early 1970s served to stretch the imaginations of many young women on this score mainly through an emphasis on small-group subcultures (e.g., communes, love-ins like the famous "summer of love" in San Francisco in 1967, as well as in more politically defined groups). Whether or not people really succeeded in challenging the hypocrisy of the day or in raising people's consciousness about sexual issues in this period (which were expressed goals) is beside the point. What did happen was that many young women began thinking about their sexuality in expanded ways, particularly in regard to learning to experience sexual pleasure themselves, regardless of what kinds of partners they had or whether they had one.

Today, having "sex" can mean any number of things, although this may be somewhat more true for women than for men. Still, our task is to try to understand women's cultural identity, and to do so we must examine the ways in which women's sexual self-understanding has developed, and be prepared to try to understand the appeal of sexual behaviors and experiences that we might not have personally experienced or considered. This frequently depends on not only a willingness to spend time understanding these things, but also a willingness to recognize and think about one's own sexual preferences and prejudices.

Moral Instruction or Value-Defining Situations

Here we want to learn to pay attention to the way women have learned to assess right and wrong, good and bad, and what counts as an excellent and as a minimally acceptable action. The work of psychologist Carol Gilligan and the responses that people have had to her work have been very helpful in getting me started in this project. Through a series of interviews with young women and a study of theories of moral development that presumably have been focused on men (e.g., Piaget, Kohlberg), Gilligan concludes that women learn to place and affirm value differently than do men. She goes on to discuss the emergence of women's more relational, people-based (and men's more individualistic, rule-based) moral responses.

Without denying the importance of Gilligan's insights, we need to remind ourselves that conventional "wisdom" about how men and women respond in morally sticky situations commonly suggests that women think more about those closest to them while men are supposed to move quickly to more abstract (and allegedly more weighty) considerations. Most of the familiar fairy tales and story lines that I am aware of which are supposed to impart moral lessons seem to underscore these moral gender differences. Snow White is good because she cares for and worries about the dwarfs, and her Prince is good not because he cares about her, but because he rights the wrong done to her, and symbolizes the (princely) power to do so. The murderous young female exec in *Fatal Attraction* is bad because she becomes obsessed with a particular man, and the man is bad, because he breaks his marital vows, and then (eventually) good not because of his feelings or lack of feelings, but because he recognizes that his interests and responsibilities are at issue, and must be separated and reaffirmed, and because he learns (the hard way) the male version of the *Scarlet Letter* lesson (which, arguably, Hester Prynne herself did not learn).

Of course, there are many stories that convey various moral lessons, but which are the ones that have had the most influence on our gender sensibilities? Such stories are at least as effective, and arguably more effective, than other kinds of stories at getting or keeping our attention when we are becoming sexually aware and learning to specify our gender sensibilities. Women audiences are often named as "target audiences" for such stories (consider the marketing of romance novels, romantic "screwball comedies," as well as the marketing of (not to demean their talent) Julio Iglesias, Demi Moore, or Brad Pitt But stories, films, and celebrity images that convey moral and gender lessons are only one source of value-defining influences for women. Instruction sometimes occurs in the real-life episodes at home, in specifically religious settings (e.g., church, temple, or informal gatherings of believers), at school, at work, at play, or wherever we are with people who contribute to the way we come to see ourselves as women. Although all of these value-providing-contexts should be examined, I will briefly discuss only two of them, home and school.

What we are taught at home generally is thought to be a major source of our gender sensibilities. In fact, the first category of analysis of women's gender identity that I introduced ("ongoing support units") was chosen, in a large part, to stress the (human) influences established at home (understood in a wide sense). But when discussing how women's identities are related to lessons learned at home, too often our focus is drawn only to "positive" moral lessons that are said to have been directly modeled for women in this context. Whether or not we think the lessons that have been taught intentionally were positive or not is not the issue so much as whether we think that the lessons that are thought to be positive are the only ones that are taught. For example, if we attend only to what parents *say* to daughters, and not what they *do,* we miss much of what their daughters learn. Similarly, if we attend only to what parents say or do in the presence of their daughters and not to what they say or do when they think their daughters do not hear or see them, we also miss a lot. Or consider what lessons are overlooked if we attend only to what parents say or do in relation to their daughters, and do not consider whether or not their daughters learn that there are significant differences in what their parents say or do with the boys in the family.

Girls and boys can be explicitly taught "positive" values in a thoroughly loving manner and still learn many negative lessons. In order to make sense of this often obscured context of moral learning we must learn to ask the question: *Can we identify implicit as well as explicit moral lessons that have contributed to women's identities?"* Often this requires speculating on lessons that may have remained implicit or internalized and never spelled out by particular women themselves. Each of us can be unaware of the variety of ways that meaningful people and events have effected us. The questions we must learn to ask about implicit and explicit moral lessons, are often just as important and as difficult for women to ask about themselves as they are for others to ask about them. The need for everyone interested in understanding women's gender identity to try to answer these questions cannot be minimized.

There is also no minimizing the importance of appreciating the defining role of school or formal educational contexts in establishing the values associated with women's gender identity. Distinguishing between school and formal educational setting is important because so many kinds of schools are informal. The phrase "school of hard knocks" helps to illustrate this point, as does pointing out things like televised schooling (e.g. "Sesame Street"), "Sunday school," and a variety of kinds of teaching and learning toys that are manufactured to maximize consumer response (e.g., to home school products) and for commercial profit.

The impacts of this more informal variety of education on the development of women's moral identities are complicated in ways similar to the complications of the impacts felt at home. In both cases, the obvious or expressed lessons are not the only ones that are learned. In fact, the casual, relaxed, or informal atmosphere associated with both home and school contexts that are linked with leisure time may be the most effective places for implicit messages to be received. The idea of subliminal learning is based on a similar assumption. Some young women may be on guard and reflective when they know they are being instructed, but isn't everyone a bit more vulnerable to accepting things uncritically when they are presumably simply relaxing, hanging out, or just enjoying the company of friends or family?

Formal education, of course, can also suggest values to women in less than obvious ways. Negative expectations about the mathematical abilities of girls is a well-known example of this point, as are teachers' recorded tendencies to call on and to ask more questions of male students, sending even more subtle messages of their lower expectations of female students. Perhaps even more pernicious is the often unmarked absence of women among the writers to be read or studied in various disciplines. Many of my Women's Studies students have told me that they were not even aware that women writers had not been included in many of their literature courses until they took a Women's Studies course where a majority of women authors were intentionally assigned, and only then recognized the contrast to other classes. Several students have even said that in some classes when one or two women writers were included, they were used as illustrations of "lesser" or limited talent because the sorts of things they concentrated on were too focused on women's interests. What sorts of values does that lesson provide?

Apparently, in a number of formal educational contexts, even today, a "good" woman, or a woman who is thoroughly identified as a spokesperson for woman's sensibilities or women's culture, cannot be understood as both a good woman and a good example of great or unlimited talent if she reveals a woman's interests, she reveals her limitations.

Abilities and Disabilities

There are all sorts of limitations that women perceive themselves to have, and which others take them to have. The importance of understanding perceived abilities and disabilities in women, we think mainly about things that were measurable or widely acknowledged as assets and liabilities women with high IQs, or women who were blind, for example. I soon came to realize that regardless of how measurable such things were, they were only controversially called assets or liabilities. Women with high IQs could perceive themselves as handicapped when dealing with men or women who did not want to work with women who might be smarter (in some measurable way) than they were. Blind women could perceive themselves as having a substantial advantage when confronted with situations in which an expanded reliance on senses other than sight was exactly what was called for being able to read at night during a massive power failure, for example, or, for that matter, if they had a book, being able to read much more readily than could sighted women who depended on glasses that easily could be misplaced or broken.

I came to appreciate the interplay between abilities and disabilities mainly by reading the work of women who were identified as "disabled". A number of these women are particularly interested in how disabilities can impact who they are as women They sometimes contrast themselves to "able-bodied" women or evaluate the way that others have contrasted them to "able-bodied" women. Or they may discuss and illustrate the many ways in which bodily disabilities and other of the most obvious or measurable sorts of disabilities are not simply limitations, but also can be sources of growth, humor, and creative redefinition of everyday life that establish new links to other people.

But despite this ability to put a positive spin on disability, most women who are, in some official way, labelled "disabled" resist the euphemism "differently able." This alternative description is thought to go too far in trying to describe a capable image, and tends to obscure the obvious fact that they live in a world that all too often ignores or dismisses the importance of what they require (e.g., access ramps, specialized educational materials, equal opportunity for employment) if they are to turn limitations into resources. This is an especially sensitive issue for physically disabled women who are ignored or dismissed in regard to what they need to realize their gender possibilities. This should not need to be said, but far too many people fail to appreciate that disabled women have, and need to be given the opportunity to realize, as many possibilities for developing as women as other women have. For example, if conventional assumptions about women as the ones who are the primary care givers are not backed up by a willingness to supply what a physically disabled woman needs (e.g., books in Braille that can be taught to children, kitchens lowered for use from a wheelchair), she is unable to creatively take up this traditional care giving option if she is inclined to do so. Women must find a way to strike a balance between their own disabilities and abilities, but if they cannot get access to what they need to strike this balance, their own creative potential can be deeply damaged.

Despite the importance of attention to measurable or widely acknowledged "disabilities" and the abilities with which they are supposed to contrast, we also need to learn to consider hidden or internalized factors that can be powerfully disabling or enabling. Particularly relevant here are the economic advantages or disadvantages that can enhance ability or deeply hamper not just a woman's sense of who or what she is, but her sense of whether there is anything she can do outside of whatever limited choices she has been shown. Consider the case of a young girl who grows up with only the bare opportunity of going to school, coupled with a life of turmoil and poverty, and perhaps even close observation of domestic abuse. The damage done to her, although perhaps not measurable, could be disabling in such intensely complicated ways that discovering how this affected her gender identity, and what were necessary to help her turn her disadvantages into advantages, would take the deepest sort of commitment. But in this case, if we wanted to understand how she understood herself as a woman, and whether or not others would recognize her as such (or would see her gender development as having been blocked), this sort of commitment is exactly what would be required.

When considering what goes into making a woman a woman we must learn to ask the question: Can we identify abilities and disabilities (and the extent to which they have been balanced or intensified) that have contributed to women's identities? And when we set about asking ask this question, we have to be ready to respond with a commitment that might draw on all of our emotional, physical, intellectual, and material resources. Appreciating disabling as well as enabling factors in a woman's sense of self forces us to accept responsibility for at least trying to make sense of the real or apparent failures and cruelties of others, and perhaps of society in general, which may be very painful for us to even think about, much less to try to understand.

Women from All Cultural Contexts

After having read the five preceding sections, it may be tempting to conclude that what women share is the form of their experiences, but not necessarily the content. That is, one might suggest that the five areas which should be considered when trying to understand women's gender identities are areas in which all women are, in some way or other, affected, and they differ only in specifically how they are affected. It may make you doubt the aptness of these five areas in regard to an analysis of women if I now say that these areas can as easily be thought of as indicating the form (but not the content) of what men have in common, too.

But it is not the form of these five areas of concern that is most important. What is important are the ways in which these forms direct our attention specifically to the great variation in the contents of women's lives. Women are unified only through their diversity. This may seem like a contradictory claim, but it is not. "Women's culture" becomes sensible as a subject of study through a close appreciation of the various overlapping possibilities for living life as a woman.

There are many ways in which women's lives can and do overlap. Women obviously differ significantly, but since the units, focuses, contexts, and situations in which they participate can cut across any particular group of women, the odds are very high that women within different groups will share something with women out of their group. An Asian American woman might not share ethnicity with a Latina but could easily share family similarities, sexual preference, significant value defining experiences, or a sense of abilities and disabilities. One of the reasons that so many women readers identify with Alice Walker *In Search of Our Mother's Gardens* is not that they identify with the lack of cultural history about African-American women, but because they recognize that their own foremothers (biologically related or not) also lived with limitations that forced them to find their own ways of blossoming, or of surrounding themselves with growing things, when little could be grown in the outside world.

Women cannot be grouped into a single culture because there are infinitely many ways for any one of us to be grouped and to differ within our groups. But just as groups can break apart from differences, new groups can reform from cross-group similarities. Like my Grandmother's old lace tablecloth, made many years ago and brought out now for special occasions, threads may continue to break apart, but I can find any number of ways to tie together other loose threads to make sections hold together for awhile. Women's culture holds together in a similar fragile but reinforcing way.

❑❑❑

3

Sociocultural Dimensions and Social Work

Introduction

Wealth and income determine not only an individual's social class but also his or her access to health care facilities. There is a cruel, vicious circle from which few poverty-stricken people can extricate themselves. For example, most low-income children attend inferior schools and, consequently, receive an inferior education. If they graduate from high school or a vocational school, most low-income people who manage to get a job are disproportionately employed as unskilled and semiskilled labourers. Thus, low-income people are likely to work in jobs hazardous to their health. At the end of the circle are inadequate health care systems, which, if used, conflict with lower-class mores. All the chapters in this book touch on social class variables.

Religion is a universal institution. Some religions, including Jewish sects, place considerable emphasis on the family. Human services professionals unaware of this emphasis are likely to engage in nonhelpful behaviour.

Religious differences add complexity to transcultural health care. Equally complex is ethnic similarity. Human services practitioners frequently overlook the problem inherent in identifying too closely with their clients. Language is an integral aspect of culture. The arrogance of economically or politically dominant groups is seen in their failure to learn the languages of subordinate groups. The effect of denying interpreters to clients who speak English as a second language is the subject of research by Luis Marcos and associates. Although they may be difficult for some human services professionals to read, the data generated by Marcos are crucial to bilingual-bicultural health care.

The Nation's Health in U.S.

Each decade ends with a larger number of people of colour living in metropolitan areas of U.S. such as Chicago, Denver, Los Angeles, New York, and San Francisco. The major reason for this relocation from rural areas is the search for jobs. Few well-paying jobs can be found on reservations and in rural areas. Rural or urban people of colour face a special set of health care problems and concerns. The types and multitudes of diseases in any given population have direct correlation to the population's environment, economic status, education level, and traditional values. The health of Native Americans is illustrative. For example, these variables influence Native Americans' health and nutritional status as well as the availability and demand for health services.

Impoverished socioeconomic conditions, limited educational levels, substandard housing, poor sanitation, malnutrition, and inadequate health services all contribute to Native Americans' high incidences of deaths by accidents, suicide, and disease. Diseases that are virtually nonexistent in other populations are still leading causes of death in the Native American population. As noted in the final report on Indian health to the American Indian Policy Review

Commission, "While there has been striking improvement in mortality from diseases of acute and chronic infections as well as cardiovascular disease, these results are overshadowed by the increased deaths associated with accidents, alcoholism, cirrhosis of the liver and suicides".

An examination of the external and internal forces impacting all ethnic groups is vital to understanding their health behaviour. It is a truism that socioeconomic phenomena influence health care. Relatedly, an ethnic group's ability to control or participate equally in community power relationships affects the quality of its health care. Furthermore, health knowledge is proportionally related to an ethnic group's technological advancement. Health care should be viewed in relation to intervening socioeconomic variables because they significantly influence health beliefs and practices. For too long it has been erroneously concluded by some health services professionals that only environmental conditions influence public health. The issue is much more complex than this simplistic analysis. Poor people in particular have less health care knowledge and fewer economic resources to draw on in their battle against illness. However, even knowledgeable poor persons with minimally adequate financial resources or state-subsidized care plans are hesitant to take time from work for long-term treatment.

The phrase "a sound mind in a sound body" reflects an ideal that has remained constant from ancient to modern times, and medical research has brought us closer to this goal. Enormous improvements have been made in diagnostic procedures, surgical techniques, and both prophylactic and therapeutic medicine. Unfortunately, the delivery of mental and physical health services has not kept pace with medical research. This is true despite unusually large government expenditures for health care delivery services. Particularly neglected are low-income communities, where a disproportionate number of people of colour reside.

Effects of Racism in the United States

Although all Americans might justifiably hope for better health care delivery systems, people of colour have even more to wish for. As with many other services, people of colour often receive the least and the last in health care. This difference in delivery of services may be attributed to the pervasiveness of racism in the United States. Drawing on the findings of the National Advisory Commission on Civil Disorders, known as the Kerner Commission, John Norman wrote: "America is, and has always been, a racist society. Bigotry permeates every level of every region of the country, North and South, business, labour, journalism, education, and medicine. The causes of racism are ignorance, apathy, poverty, and above all else a pervasive discrimination that has thwarted each and every citizen in an avenues of life".

There are two kinds of racism: individual and institutional. *Individual racism* refers to the behaviour of individuals that supports the belief of racial superiority of one or more groups over others. *Institutional racism* refers to the systematic oppression of people through institutional policies and practices. It is common for individuals chided for racist conditions to retort: "Don't blame me, I haven't done anything." Civil rights activists say that this is precisely the problem: they have done little, if anything, to understand or abate current conditions of racism. Through their ignorance and inaction, racism remains a destructive force in our nation's health care.

People of colour in particular are handicapped by poverty, discrimination, and sociopsychological barriers to health care. To most low-income people of colour, stories about cancer and drug research, birth control clinics, and government funding for research on vital areas of human medical treatment are akin to *Alice's Adventures in Wonderland*. Low-income people of colour receive the worst type of physical and mental health care. Nonwhite babies die at a rate 92 per cent higher than for white babies, and nonwhite mothers die during childbirth at a rate four times greater than for white mothers. In fact, the American nonwhite deaths at birth and during infancy are worse than the record of most of the world's urbanized nations. Clearly, the major issue for low-income people of colour is not tax reform or welfare checks it is survival. Cardiovascular diseases and malignant neoplasms are the two leading causes of death for all ethnic groups, but they are higher for nonwhites than whites. The next three major causes of death for all groups in rank are cerebrovascular diseases, accidents, and chronic obstructive pulmonary diseases. Cancer is on the upswing in nonwhite communities.

Statistics compiled by the American Cancer Society show that there are striking racial differences in deaths from specific types of cancer. The mortality rate for cancers of the stomach, liver, esophagus, cervix, and uterus is higher for nonwhites than for whites. On the other hand, whites have a greater mortality from leukemia and cancers of the ovary, brain, and skin. Some researchers suspect that the higher cancer toll among nonwhites may stem from the fact that they tend to live in areas of high air pollution and are more likely than whites to be exposed to harmful chemicals on their jobs.

But cancer is not the only major medical problem for nonwhites. High blood pressure also afflicts a large number of them. Commonly known as hypertension, high blood pressure plays a direct role in the deaths of at least 100,000 men and women both white and nonwhite each year by placing severe strain on their hearts. The presence of high blood pressure is most severely felt in African American communities. Numerous studies estimate that at least one in seven African Americans has high blood pressure. Because African Americans get hypertension at a young age, it is more severe among black teenagers than white teenagers. Among black men thirty-five to forty-four years of age, the death rate from hypertension-related heart disease is fifteen times greater than among white men of the same age. Hypertension is seventeen times greater among black women than it is among white women. Finally, hypertension kills more African Americans every year than sickle cell anemia. The nonwhite death rate for hypertension is more than twice the rate for whites.

The "Latin American" health problem has been intensified by large numbers of Spanish-speaking people who have immigrated to the United States. Neonatal deaths are three times as high among Spanish-speaking groups as among Anglos, reflecting less adequate conditions at and following delivery, a lack of prenatal care, and poor nutrition and deficient health care of the mother. Studies show that Puerto Ricans have a higher death rate from tuberculosis than any other country that gathers such statistics. Tuberculosis thrives in poor, overcrowded conditions, which are exactly the conditions in which many Puerto Ricans live, both in Puerto Rico and on the American mainland. These conditions are exacerbated by many Puerto Ricans' ignorance of sound health care and sanitation practices.

Commenting on the health care of American Indians, Vine Deloria noted that although Indians of the 20th century are much better off than they were in earlier times, they still have a long way to go to meet the standards of most white Americans. Cultural conflict is stiff a problem among Indians, and the anomie and feelings of helplessness created by this conflict are still evident. Perhaps malnutrition, brought about in many different ways, is the most common problem among poor people white and nonwhite. Malnutrition occurs when a person's food is inadequate in terms of either quantity or quality. Frequently, low-income living habits and environmental conditions result in a poor appetite, aversion to particular foods, or refusal to eat certain foods. It is not easy to tell whether a person is malnourished. Many malnourished people are fat due to their intake of large quantities of carbohydrates. Medical systems can be fully understood only by knowing a culture's food preferences.

When Cultures Clash

Cultural beliefs are mainly static phenomena; they seldom change, but the people exposed to them do. Thus, culturally stable beliefs are those that an individual maintains, and culturally unstable ones are abandoned. Behaviour is a dynamic phenomenon that people may elect to do or not do. Therefore, an individual repeats dynamically stable behaviour, while dynamically unstable behaviour is extinguished. Simply stated, people exposed to conflicting cultural beliefs and behaviours adopt either stable (traditional) beliefs and behaviours or unstable (nontraditional) beliefs and behaviours. Culturally, the maintenance of a traditional way of life is a static condition, and the change from traditional to nontraditional beliefs and behaviour is a dynamic condition. *Static* does not refer to an inferior situation, nor does *dynamic* denote a superior situation. Rather, the terms pertain to cultural equilibrium and disequilibrium.

The major focus of this analysis is not on the *way* people behave the way they do but, instead, *why* people in certain circumstances believe they must behave the way they do. Thus, attention is given to purposive action and the anticipated consequences of such action. In a broader sense, I am concerned with action that involves motives and a choice between alternatives. A culturally stable person accepts his or her traditional culture's beliefs, whereas an unstable person does not. A behaviourally stable person returns to traditional cultural behaviours, but an unstable person adopts nontraditional behaviours. Traditional beliefs and behaviour are strongest when individuals are unaware of alternatives. Based on the preceding assumptions, I further postulate that cross-cultural interaction produces the following four types of people.

1. Culturally stable—behaviourally stable. These people accept their traditional culture's beliefs and behaviours; and if for some reason they experiment with nontraditional beliefs and behaviours, they will still maintain the traditional beliefs and way of life. Once equilibrium is established, people within a traditional culture are likely to believe there are no "good" reasons to adopt a nontraditional way of life, and there are ample reasons, in terms of group stability, they should not. Adherence to group norms is taught and individuality is discouraged in traditional cultures. Culturally stable-behaviourally stable people are the least conflicted of the four types. Wilbur Moore and Melvin Tumin observed that "all socialization processes operate to reduce curiosity and knowledge about the presumed socially dysfunctional alternative of pursuing individual tendencies. These processes act so effectively in most cases that the matter rarely appears as a matter of choice, much less as a conflict".

2. Culturally stable—behaviourally unstable. These people have internalized traditional beliefs and behaviours; but if they are exposed to compelling nontraditional beliefs and behaviours, they will change to the non-traditional or new way of life. Cultural instability is the opposite of the general *law of assimilation*, which states that the human organism will respond to new situations in the same manner it responded to familiar situations. Statically stable-dynamically unstable people typify individuals who are marginal within their ethnic group.

Being aware of others in the same aggregate and defining oneself as a member may still not guarantee that the individual is involved. Everyone knows people who, although nominally members of a group, nevertheless seem completely uninterested in the group. For them to be real members of a group, they would have to feel kinship or identity with the others—to feel they were significant. Social psychologists would say that these people belong to a *membership group*, since they belong to the group in name only.

3. Culturally unstable—behaviourally stable. These people have not fully accepted their culture's traditional beliefs but continue to act as if they have, even when exposed to attractive nontraditional beliefs and behaviours. This situation typifies many individuals who live in cultural enclaves. Because their survival is dependent upon "fitting in," they maintain traditional behaviours. For example, a college-educated client may elect to speak black English, even though he is uncomfortable with it. When a society or subculture demands adherence to behaviour that is inconsistent with an individual's feelings about it, stress and trauma develop. Fortunately, every culture has its own level of anxiety that its members can withstand without serious psychological harm of maladjustment. Thus the client talks "black" with a minimum of stress.

4. Culturally unstable—behaviourally unstable. These people are sometimes seen as social deviants. Because abnormality refers to descriptive behaviour that deviates markedly from what a group considers to be normal, it is essential that human services professionals understand what the client's culture considers normal. Several studies conclude that social deviance varies across ethnic groups. In a different environment, these people may be quite normal. For example, immigrants who reject the "old ways" and seek identity with a nontraditional culture illustrate this phenomenon.

There is stress in each of the culture types described. When people throughout the world experience conditions of stress, it is natural for them to use defense mechanisms to cope repression, suppression, rationalization, projection, and so forth. Coping mechanisms allow people to adjust to problems. In fact, a client's emotional survival is often dependent on being able to regulate personal feelings, beliefs, and actions so that anxiety remains at a manageable level. While defense mechanisms do not in themselves solve problems, they can allow a client time to cope with them until better solutions are found. When defence mechanisms cease to relieve stress, clients frequently turn to behaviour that is called "maladjustment" or "maladaptive." But a few words of caution are in order. There is a thin line between normal behaviour and neurotic and psychotic behaviour. Except for extreme psychoses, what is normal and what is abnormal are difficult to ascertain. It is even more difficult for human services professionals from different cultures. Within all cultures, most people have periods of maladjustive behaviour, and most maladjusted people have periods of rational behaviour. Poverty or residence in a socially disruptive area is a compounding factor in maladjustive behaviour associated with ethnicity and social class. For example, the fact that African American rates of hospitalization for mental disorders are somewhat lower than white rates in the United States appears to be related to a higher arrest and imprisonment rate for African Americans than for whites of equivalent behaviour. African Americans, in particular, typically receive more severe psychiatric diagnoses (e.g., paranoid schizophrenia) than whites. There is also evidence that social class is linked to the number of incidences of mental illness. The poor are more likely to be more severely diagnosed by practitioners than the affluent. Studies show that neuroses diagnoses are concentrated in middle and upper classes and psychoses in the lower classes. Anxiety and insecurity are common characteristics of poor people in urban societies, but this does not necessarily lead to mental illness. When these data coalesce, it is dear that there are connections among ethnicity, social class, and particular kinds of therapeutic treatment. This raises questions about the efficacy of therapeutic interventions. Doris Mosley identified six barriers to the delivery of health care to the poor:

1. Inability of the poor to pay, including the humiliation of "means tests," which establish physical and mental health care indigence necessary to receive so called free care, greatly restricts health care for people of colour.
2. Fragmentation of health care the depersonalization and confusion of referral to various specialty clinics prevents many clients from receiving health care.

3. Operational features of securing the services, including travel, long waits, unattractive surroundings, and inconvenient hours, discourage client participation. Also included as barriers are lack of two-way communication, trust, and understanding between clients and care providers; and lack of time due to personnel shortages. Understandably, client hostility and isolation often result from these factors.
4. Negative attitudes toward nontraditional health care services result in differing perceptions of the health care system by clients and health personnel. This leads to misinterpretation of clients' behaviour and delay or nonutilization of services.
5. Racial discrimination in the provision of services takes a heavy toll. Some hospitals and clinics are not utilized to maximum potential. Many of them refuse to employ ethnic minority staff.
6. Lack of facilities and manpower are further barriers to health care. Urban slums and ghettos as well as remote rural areas are unattractive to most professional personnel and their families, who choose to live and practice in upper-and middle-class areas. Hospitals and clinics relocate in suburbs to escape deteriorating central city areas, and local politics often prevent establishment of area wide, centralized health care facilities.

Culture Revisited

No two cultures are precisely alike. As noted earlier, culture is the human-made part of the environment. The *material* components of culture are items human beings produce through creative thinking and technology. The *nonmaterial* components of culture consist of intangibles and symbolic abstractions. Because it is not biologically inherited, culture must be learned and transmitted to each successive generation. Optimum health is a cultural value shared by all health care professionals; however, not all clients share this value. Failure to understand this fact can result in defining clients who have values different from those of the care provider as "bad," "uncooperative," or "difficult." The cultural context of a client's (and care provider's) behaviour refers to the implicit and explicit tendencies of subgroups to respond to stimuli according to their learned styles of coping. Each subgroup has its own unique ways of seeing, interpreting, and coping with its environment and the people in it. Human services professionals concerned with the why and what of a specific ethnic minority's health practices can get most of their answers by becoming familiar with the group's history, religion, kinship patterns, and social systems.

America is a nation of great cultural diversity. Although all segments of our population share certain common elements in life patterns and basic beliefs, there are significant differences in subcultural attitudes, interests, goals, and dialects. Clients bring to health care settings cultural differences in perceptions of masculine and feminine roles, in rural and urban backgrounds, in ethnic groups, and in social classes.

Masculine and Feminine Roles. Until recently in our culture, men and women were expected to play different roles. One of the first lessons children learned from those around them was that their behaviour must accord with that generally considered appropriate to their sex. A boy was not expected to take on feminine characteristics; a girl was handicapped if she was not feminine in dress, speech, and aspirations. "Good boys" and "good girls" were those who engaged in sex-appropriate behaviour. For example, Hispanic females tend to respond to stress by crying (*lorando*), praying (*rezando*), and enduring (*aguantando*). Gradually, sex stereotyping is disappearing.

Rural and Urban Backgrounds. Although they are not as striking as they used to be, differences in language, attitudes, and interests between rural and urban dwellers still exist. Few graduate programmes acquaint students with clients who live in rural areas.

Ethnic Groups. Nearly every American can trace his or her ancestry back to some country across the seas. Each ethnic group has enriched our culture with its own particular types of music, food, customs, and dress. It usually takes two or more generations for the members of a new ethnic group to become sufficiently absorbed into the life of the community that they lose their separate identity. Some ethnic groups mainly those of colour—never achieve assimilation. The assimilation of the more recent immigrant groups seems to be unlikely; most of them are of the lower socioeconomic classes, and they tend to maintain their traditional beliefs, attitudes, and behaviours.

Social Classes. The United States has rather clearly defined social classes. The social class to which the parents belong determines to a great extent a child's educational and occupational attainments. Numerous studies have documented how difficult it is for an individual to advance from one social class to another on the basis of ability and effort. Although more than half of 1990 white high school graduates had clerical jobs, less than one-third of nonwhite graduates held such jobs. Furthermore, proportionately more nonwhites than whites are employed in service occupations. African Americans, Latinos, and American Indians are disproportionately represented in the lower socioeconomic classes.

Rural-Urban Dichotomies

Romantic conceptualizations assign different values to rural (folk) and urban (scientific) communities. Some individuals maintain idyllic images of rural life. "Rural" conjures up the smell of freshly mown fields, herds of cattle or sheep, fields of crops, a country store, and farmers in blue jeans. From this perspective, the Third World indigenous curer is the prototype of the sturdy, independent person in a natural, unspoiled environment. On one hand, urban life is viewed by some critics as unnatural and, indeed, bad. On the other hand, there are people who view the city as the center of civilization, the epitome of progress and the good life. From this perspective, the urban dweller is the prototype of a truly civilized person. Unlike Rousseau, who viewed rural people as "noble savages," critics of rural life label rural people as "country bumpkins" who do not share the richness of culture found in urban areas. Even the urban Third World curer is viewed as someone slightly removed from the Neanderthal people.

Somewhere between these two extremes is a more accurate picture of rural and urban life. In terms of life-styles, there is much similarity between urban-oriented and rural-oriented people. Both share and are influenced by the products of urbanization. Both have been enculturated in a country that has strong folk cultures, but folk cultures do not yield willingly to technology. Before the introduction of rapid transportation, mass communication, and other intrusions of urban culture into rural communities, villages and small towns were isolated, very much like Washington Irving's *Sleepy Hollow*. There was an overriding sense of independence, on one hand, and ethnic solidarity, on the other. The range of interaction was restricted primarily to the rural community. This set of circumstances resulted in community efforts to retain folk beliefs and practices while fueling prejudice against outsiders and new medical beliefs and practices. Contact with the outside was intermittent and slow in coming, but once contact was established through explorers, exploiters, and churches, folk beliefs and practices were altered forever.

Ethnicity

There is ample empirical evidence that ethnic values and identification are retained for several generations after people migrate from their native land, and these values and identification are central in family life and development throughout the life cycle. Indeed, second, third, and even fourth generation immigrants tend to maintain traditional culture values, lifestyles and behaviour. Ethnicity subsumes group commonality that is crystallized over generations by the community and reinforced by the family. It incorporates conscious and unconscious processes that characterize group identity and historical continuity. Psychological studies document that ethnicity shapes an individual's thinking, feelings, and behaviours in both overt and covert ways. A cursory survey of related literature reveals that ethnicity plays an important role in determining an individual's diet, work habits, religious beliefs, philosophy of life, and methods of coping with illness and death.

Ethnic groups differ in their inclination to seek help outside the family. They also differ in the kind of help they will accept. For example, Italians generally rely on family members and turn to outsiders as a last resort. African Americans tend to mistrust social services agencies staffed by non blacks. Some groups, including Puerto Ricans and Chinese, are culturally conditioned to somatize when they are under stress and prefer medical rather than mental health treatment. Furthermore, members of some groups are taught to define their problems in terms of their own inadequacy, action, or sin; while other groups tend to see their problems as a result of somebody else's inadequacy, action, or sin. It is helpful for practitioners to determine which of these perspectives is operative for each client.

Poverty

Poverty is characterized by conditions of not enough not enough money, food, clothes, adequate housing, prestige, or hope. Generally, when affluent people go without soap, hot water, light, food, medicine, and recreation, it is because they elect to do so. When poverty-stricken people go without these things, it is because they have no choice. Therein lies the major difference between the poor and the affluent. The former are controlled by the economic system, and the latter control it. Poverty has a familiar smell a smell of rotting garbage and sour foods. It is the smell of children's urine and unwashed bodies. Above all else, it is the smell of people wasting away physically, socially, and psychologically. Urban poverty is much more visible than rural poverty. Dilapidated buildings, garbagestrewn alleys, and rats are the dominant characteristics of urban slums. These conditions blur the memory of clean, well-kept buildings that also characterize many urban poor neighborhoods. Although it is difficult to change the negative image of the urban slum, it is almost impossible to erase the idyllic picture of rural poverty frequently called "quaint," "picturesque," or "Americana." Nearly one-third of rural Americans are poverty-stricken.

Problems that characterize low-income, inner-city residents also include unequal access to public services, inadequate police protection, and racially segregated housing. Further, inner-city residents are isolated educationally, economically, socially, and politically. Moreover, people of colour are disproportionately found in the lowest income areas of cities, and female-headed families are the largest number of povertystricken people who live in cities. Low-income people have been referred to as the *underclass* by Gunnar Myrdal, Ken Auletta,, Ronald Mincy, Isabell Sawhill & Douglas Wolf and Gary Rolison. African Americans with low incomes and low educational achievements are more likely to live in racially segregated neighborhoods than Hispanic Americans or Asian Americans. Beyond the statistics is the stark reality that the underclass are America's throwaway people they are economically, socially, and physically expendable when community rehabilitation and therapy plans are drawn up.

These social forces must be considered within the framework of health care delivery. No one can seriously dispute the fact that environment plays a very important role in maintaining and improving the health of any group.

Poor housing is only one cell of a cluster of adverse conditions affecting people of colour. Nutritional deprivation caused by inadequate or nonexistent sanitary facilities, lack of adequate social services, geographic isolation, lack of transportation, low income, and unemployment are also cells that contribute to ill health. If human services professionals understand the impact of these social forces, they can be in a better position to assist clients who are affected by them.

Social Pathologies

The social pathologies that accrue to poverty-stricken people of colour are vividly seen in the following 1990 census in U.S. demographic, education, and employment data. Compared with their white peers, people of colour are less likely to graduate from high school and college but are more likely to be functionally illiterate. Inadequate education, in turn, negatively affects employment and income. Therefore people of colour are more likely than whites to be unemployed and underemployed. The African American, Hispanic, and Native American unemployment rates are consistently 50 per cent above the white rate regardless of the economic condition. Further, people of colour are disproportionately employed in low-skill, low-wage jobs. Consequently, people of colour are about three times as likely as white families to be poor. In 1990, 50 per cent of Native Americans, 45 per cent of African Americans, and 35 per cent of Hispanics under the age of eighteen were poverty-stricken. Almost half of children of colour in female-headed households were poor, compared with 13 per cent of white families.

People of colour often are relegated to marginal jobs in which workers are vulnerable to seasonal layoff and displacement. They are less likely than whites to be employed as highly skilled, highly paid managers, professional workers, and technicians. Instead, they are more likely to be employed as labourers, farm workers, fabricators, and operators. They are the bulk of the working poor. Human services professionals must be careful not to unrealistically advise these clients to pull themselves up by their nonexistent bootstraps; or that if they only applied themselves, they could become anything they want. To raise a client's level of aspiration without providing needed skills or opportunities for success is a proven way to demoralize a client.

White Americans tend to live in nuclear families, alone, or with nonrelatives; people of colour tend to live in extended families or with nonrelatives. The number of single-parent households is increasing for all ethnic groups. Even so, the rates for people of colour particularly African Americans (42 per cent) and Hispanics (24 per cent) greatly exceed the white rate (13 per cent). However, single parents within Third World cultures tend to be considerably more dependent on their parents and other kin than whites. As a result, helping strategies designed to foster client independence are likely to be met with great resistance. To be without interdependent family relationships is perceived by many people of colour as a condition worse than being without an adequate income. More than 50 per cent of Third World female-headed households were poor in 1990, compared with 27 per cent for white families. Sadly, a disproportionate number of the 60 per cent of the federal and state prison inmates who are people of colour come from poverty-stricken homes. Thus they move from one kind of extended family in the "free" world to another in prison.

Rural Poor

Hired farm workers illustrate the plight of the rural poor. Hispanics comprise approximately 30 per cent of the more than 885,000 farm workers, whose median annual income is less than $10,000 per year. Migrant workers are even worse off. Life for the migrant is seasonal: a day here, a week there. For example, migrants pick citrus fruits in California and Florida, beans and tomatoes in Texas, cherries and blueberries in Michigan, sugar beets in Kansas, cucumbers in South Carolina, and potatoes in Idaho and Maine. Most migrants sleep in dilapidated structures that lack adequate heat, refrigeration, and sanitation facilities. They play on garbage-strewn grounds and drink polluted water. Communities in which migrants work tend to lack minimally adequate medical care and health services. Most migrant workers and their families are infected with intestinal parasites and have chronic skin infections and dental problems. Many have chronically infected ears that can result in partial deafness.

Because in America the norm is affluence, to be poor in America is to be among the most economically deprived people in the world. All health care workers should understand this phenomenon. Telling an economically poor client how well off he or she is compared with the poor in Latin America or Africa will have little positive effect. The comparisons that reveal an ugly health picture for the poor in the United States were succinctly captured in the following statement by Richard Lyons:

> No finer medical treatment in the world may be found than what is now available at the Mayo Clinic in Minnesota, Johns Hopkins Hospital in Maryland, Methodist Hospital in Texas, Columbia-Presbyterian Medical Center in New York, or Stanford University Hospital in California. Yet only a few miles from these great humanitarian institutions, large segments of the nation's population receive hit-or-miss health care, with infrequent visits to doctors or public health nurses and virtually no dental treatment. The poor customarily enter a hospital only when they are very ill, often beyond help.

The foregoing summary of statistics and practices characterizes the state of the nation's health and substantiates the assessment of experts that the United States has reached a crisis situation in health care. This situation can be summarized in the ideographs of the

Chinese language, in which two characters are used to write the single word *crisis*—one is the character for "danger" and the other is the character for "opportunity." One of the first requisites for a solution is culturally competent professional helpers.

Immigrants

A large number of immigrants come to America as sojourners people who do not plan to settle here permanently. Their motives differ greatly from those of other ethnic people who are forced to sever ties with their home country. Most African and Asian immigrants are temporary residents in a strange land, who set out to get a college education or earn a sizable amount of money and then return to their homeland. To accomplish this mission, the sojourners tend to select occupations that do not tie them to a territory for long assignments. Instead they seek jobs that allow them to be mobile. Relatedly, they are willing to endure short-term deprivations to achieve their long-term goals. They often work excessively long hours and spend little money on conspicuous consumption. They come to save money or send some of it home, not to spend it.

Because they plan to return home, many sojourners have little motivation to develop intimate, lasting relationships with host country people. Ethnic and regional associations are maintained within ethnic enclaves that resist marriage to nonethnic group people. These enclaves also perpetuate residential self-segregation and the sojourners' native language. Further, the enclaves encourage traditional religions and family institutions. Of course, enclave residents are insulated against local politics except those that directly affect their group members.

In some ethnic groups family members staff businesses. For example, in Chinese restaurants and Korean stores, it is common to see unpaid family labour. If wage labour is needed, members of the extended family or ethnic group associates are hired for wages lower than the market standard. Employees work long hours for no or minimum wages, and they are extremely loyal to the enterprise owners. In return, the workers become partners in the business or receive assistance in starting their own business. In large urban areas sojourners do not have to deal with labour unions. The net result has been ethnic groups' carving out niches for themselves in business and industry (i.e., Jews in clothing manufacturing and retail outlets; Japanese in fruit and vegetable growing and wholesale in California; and Chinese in restaurants and laundries). This kind of industriousness often leads to antagonism and conflict when sojourners compete with U.S. citizens.

Some sojourners earn enough money and return to their homeland; many of them do not, however. The dream to return home is sometimes not feasible because of conditions that make the sojourners' return a situation of imminent danger political, economic, or religious oppression. Yet other sojourners return to their homeland only to immigrate back to the United States, where life is economically better for them. Those who remain in America tend to keep love for their homeland alive by occasional visits and sending funds to family members "back home." This kind of sojourner often becomes "the person who comes today and stays tomorrow. He is, so to speak, the *potential* wanderer; although he has not moved on, he has not quite overcome the freedom of coming and going". These immigrants truly become strangers in strange lands. A growing number of immigrants are refugees.

Refugees

The first large wave of Cuban refugees were called the "golden exiles" because they were members of the upper economic class. Sixty-four per cent of them had held white-collar positions, 31 per cent left professional managerial jobs, and 33 per cent had clerical-sales positions. Their departure constituted a Cuban "brain drain." The 1962 Cuban missile crisis caused an additional decrease in Cuba's population. Most of the Cuban refugees who immigrated to the United States between 1962 and 1965 used various methods of subterfuge to leave. For example, some of them went to Mexico or Spain and then to the United States. In 1965, the United States and Cuba signed an agreement allowing refugees to be airlifted to Miami. The two daily "freedom flights" brought more than 340,000 refugees to the United States between 1965 and 1973. The Mariel boat lift in 1980 brought the last significant flow of Cuban refugees. A large number of them were detained in U.S. government camps because they were suspected of being mental patients or convicts.

The new immigrants were opposed by diverse groups of American citizens, including nativists, political conservatives, union members, and a few political liberals. There was fear that the new immigrants would take away jobs that traditionally were filled by non immigrants. On one hand, political conservatives feared the immigrants would destroy the cultural values and moral fiber that have made America great. On the other hand, political liberals believed the new immigrants would adhere too closely to right-wing political philosophies and, thus, would tilt local American voting patterns in that direction. In 1990 the U.S. Cuban population had grown to more than 1 million, and they represent all Cuban socioeconomic classes and ethnic groups. The promise of refuge and political asylum, the lure of economic opportunities, the yearning for family reunification, and, above all else, the quest for personal freedom have been powerful Cuban migrational inducements.

Unlike the Cubans, who were welcomed as refugees from communism, the Haitians were unwanted refugees from hunger. One of the factors that preceded the "boat people migration" was the closing of the Cuban, Dominican, and Bahamian markets to Haitian workers. Like most immigrants, when the Haitians finally decided to leave home, they searched for the best opportunity and right time to leave in order to maximize their gains. In the early 1970s, the boat people started reaching the shores of Florida. Many of them were Haitian peasants who fled drastic rural poverty or, in some cases, the harassment of Tontons Macoutes, the secret police force of the Duvalier government. When the Creole-speaking illegal immigrants landed, they were interrogated by English-speaking officials whom they had difficulty understanding. They were often sent to jail to await eventual deportation.

The early Haitians who chose New York City as a place to live settled primarily in three boroughs: 30 per cent moved to Manhattan, 50 per cent to Brooklyn, and 20 per cent to Queens. This reflected their desire to live near relatives and friends and also their need to find inexpensive housing. The majority of early immigrants were members of the upper and middle class. During the turbulent 1960s, with mixed emotions, Haitians started to look to the United States for refuge. They not only remembered the barbaric treatment under the Duvaliers but also were afraid of being drafted by the United States to fight in Vietnam. As a matter of fact, several young immigrants were drafted, and some were killed in action. The latest immigrants have come directly either from Haiti or from the Bahamas, and they have elected to settle in the Miami metropolitan area.

Wherever they settle, the key determinants of the Haitians' economic position in the United States are their immigrant status and educational qualifications. Haitian immigrants now can be found in almost every state, and they tend to form separate cultural enclaves. They prefer to establish their own churches, restaurants, social and literary clubs, newspapers, stores, and health care systems. Such social closeness has helped them to maintain their cultural traditions. One reason for problems with U.S. citizens who take offense to Haitian immigrants is the practice of voodoo. "Voodoo had always suffered from a bad press: reports of grave robbers arrested with skulls headed for 'Voodoo rites,' 'Voodoo ladies' blessing the guns and drugs of heroin dealers; chicken carcasses in Riverside park; bloody bits of goat by a Central Park transverse road; a decapitated rooster in Prospect Park; a ram's head drifting in Harlem Meer". These are examples of "offense taken."

Many Central American refugees who seek residence in the United States claim to be fleeing political repression and the accompanying violence of their own government, but some of them also emigrate from very poor countries. Consequently, the Immigration and Naturalization Service has had to make classification distinctions in order to establish priorities for admission. People who wish to immigrate to get better economic status have been refused entry on the grounds of political persecution. Some potential refugees want to escape countries whose governments the United States fully supports politically. To admit a large number of these refugees would be an embarrassment to U.S. foreign policy. It is difficult sometimes to make a distinction between economic privation and political persecution in Central America. As in Haiti, politics and economics in Central and South America are not always easily separated, since the one strongly influences the other.

The great majority of Central American immigrants have chosen to live in cities, particularly cities in the New England, Middle Atlantic, Great Lakes, Gulf Coast, and Pacific Coast states. The rate of immigration from Central America was very low for almost the entire period when there were no immigration restrictions governing the entry of people from the Western Hemisphere to the United States. There was a dramatic increase, however, after the Immigration Act of 1965. There is also a gender difference in immigrants from Central America, with women outnumbering men by about one-third perhaps because of job opportunities. There has been little change in occupational characteristics in the last two decades: 30 per cent to 40 per cent of people who come from Central America are professionals and white-collar workers. Agricultural and industrial labourers, domestic servants, housewives, and children account for most of the other immigrants. Mexico is the country of first asylum for Central Americans, and, like many other countries in the world today, it increasingly resents having to bear that burden.

More than 200,000 Vietnamese have immigrated to the United States since the defeat of the Saigon government in 1975. Beginning in 1979, thousands of "boat people" who fled Southeast Asian countries in decrepit boats and were denied asylum in neighboring countries also came to America. In the 1980s and 1990s, large numbers of Cubans and Haitians joined a long list of people who came to the United States to gain political and economic relief. As the new immigrants have found their way into American communities, incidents of immigrant-bashing have increased. While not as numerous or intense as the nativism and xenophobic bigotry of the 1890s and the period shortly after World War I, immigrant racial and ethnic group hatred continues to trigger heavy tolls. The majority of the new immigrants are nonwhite peoples from Asia, Latin America, and the Caribbean countries. Most of the abuses have been verbal; some have been physical attacks a few of them fatal. For example, two skinheads in Houston stomped to death a Vietnamese boy, Hung Truong, in 1990. The victim cried out before dying: "God forgive me for coming to this country. I'm so sorry."

Assimilation

For most nonwhite ethnic minorities the melting pot has been and continues to be an unreachable mirage. This does not in any way detract from the significance of any group's contributions to the United States. It merely highlights the necessity for placing more emphasis on equalizing opportunities. Throughout this decade, ethnic group immigration histories and examples of cultural contributions have provided explicit data to support the contention that each group is an integral part of the United States. Although Americans of Indian, Mexican, Chinese, African, and other Third World ethnic groups have contributed to American life, they frequently are treated like second-class citizens. Yet, the peoples of the United States are bound together not as separate ethnic groups but as members of different ethnic groups united in spirit and behaviour and locked into a common destiny. Human service agencies and the professionals who run them must reflect this diversity.

The United States is one nation enriched by the contributions of all its ethnic groups. The truth of America's diversity is evidenced in the New York City public schools, where in the 1991-92 school year English was not the first language of more than 133,000 students. Instead, the most common of the 120 languages spoken by the students were Spanish (88,894), Chinese (12,921), Haitian Creole (7,166), Russian (5,332), Korean (3,467), Arabic (1,883), Urdu (1,421), Bengali (1,184), Vietnamese (986), French (928), Polish (862), Italian (732), Hindi (683), Albanian (595), and Farsi (509).

Human service practitioners are likely to observe that generational differences and length of time in the United States are important determinants of immigrants' personal and familial problems. For instance, Mexican Americans and Asian immigrants in different generations vary in terms of their acculturation to American norms; the later generations are more acculturated than the early generation. In fact many of the problems within immigrant families evolve around the deviation from traditional culture values and behaviours by younger family members, especially males. Whether ethnic minority people choose to assimilate or maintain their separate ethnic identities, the effects may not be negative. Some people of colour are happily assimilated into the mainstream society; others are happy in their culture enclaves. The critical factor is whether people have choices and are aware of them.

Fueled by a downturn in the economy, shifting demographics, and worldwide ethnic turmoil, American neighborhoods in several communities have become flashpoints of nativism. African American, Hispanic, Asian, African, Middle Eastern, and Eastern European residents are transforming once-homogeneous, white, middle-class neighborhoods into microcosms of cultural diversity reminiscent of early twentieth century urban population shifts. The new migrants and immigrants gradually move into housing once occupied by descendants of Western European immigrants. During the shift in population, the interim volatile mix usually precipitates blatant racist behaviour. Immigrants in general and refugees in particular are victims of verbal and physical abuse.

Helper Roles

The psychiatrist is a central figure in mental health care. Historically, the profession of psychiatry partly arose out of the practice of wealthy persons' hiring physicians to care for their mentally sick and to assist them to perform tasks that illness prevented them from accomplishing. Many psychiatrists feel that little has changed from those early attitudes regarding the status of psychiatry in medicine. Identified with the history of "crazy" people, especially mind healer roles, psychiatry has found it difficult to shirk culturally demeaning views of abnormal behaviour. Inadequate client care is sometimes a result of the practitioner's role conflict and lower status than "body doctors," rather than of understaffing and ethnic or social class attitudes. Much of mental health care training in America is still accomplished by an apprenticeship that emphasizes obedience to authority. A part of the current strain and unrest within the helping professions derives from physicians who expect automatic and unquestioning response to their directives and orders. The more effective supervisors provide opportunities for care providers to exercise professional judgement. Most human services practitioners seem to prefer situations where they can function more or less on their own, responding directly to clients' needs and deciding when intervention by a supervisor or psychiatrist is appropriate.

How human services professionals administer a health care plan matters as much as the details of the plan. Each practitioner must carefully decide how she or he can best maximize the health care resources available for each client. It is useful to think of professional helpers in this case as guides. They show clients the pathways to the various destinations of socially functional health. As guides, they determine the pace and sequence of the trip; they help decide which route should be taken to achieve the desired end; and it is the practitioner's responsibility to make the journey interesting and enriching for the client traveler. The guide, with his or her own zest for a helping profession, must awaken a desire in the client travelers and instill in them the tenacity to complete the journey.

The professional helper is also a *model* for clients to emulate, an example they can follow. This is one of the greatest responsibilities of the practitioner and one from which she or he cannot escape. This part of the practitioner's job is helped by cultural understanding. The impressions practitioners make remain forever in the minds of their clients.

The role as a *counsellor* bears much responsibility for advising clients, who are continually faced with major personal problems. During times of crisis, some clients turn to human services professionals for guidance. In this capacity a practitioner is able to bend and shape clients into many forms of behaviour. Insensitive helpers fail during these periods, and in doing so they fail to provide optimum health care.

The practitioner is also an actor. She or he fits Shakespeare's definition:

- All the world's a stage
- And all the men and women are merely players.
- They have their own exits and entrances,
- And one man in his time plays many parts.

For example, actors read a script, decide they like it, and study it until they know it. When they are competent, they go on stage and portray the character so that it communicates to the audience, who come to know the content of the character before they leave the theatre. It is much the same with an effective human services professional. She or he learns the subject, goes into an agency setting, acts the role of caregiver, and before the performance ends, the clients come to know the practitioner as a good or bad actor.

When professional helpers guide clients, their chief work is helping them to learn how to take better care of themselves. This means helping clients to define their own interests, needs, abilities, and problems; helping them to understand themselves and others; and otherwise helping them to become more fully functioning. Out of this process emerge specific goals each client will want to achieve. The practitioner's role is to help clients formulate and evaluate health goals in terms of their own values and those of the larger community. It is imperative to involve clients in as much of the health care process as possible. To do this best, each professional helper must be in touch with herself or himself.

One can master the facts, principles, and laws contained in a hundred books on psychology and still understand neither oneself nor others. Selfunderstanding requires integrity rather than mere cleverness. It involves emotion. To know oneself, one must be able to recognize feelings, act on them, and deal with them in constructive ways; and this is something quite different from reading or talking about them with detachment.

An important factor hindering a cooperative relationship between human services workers and clients is the fact that many clients view themselves as uneducated and incapable of understanding the explanations given by professionals, whom they frequently describe as talking among themselves and using "big words." A great many clients feel excluded from their own illnesses, convinced that professional helpers deliberately and needlessly withhold information from them. Embarrassed by their ignorance, clients often fail to ask their questions and instead act out their hostility at being pushed around and ignored as persons.

The job of the professional helper is further complicated by the belief of a significant number of clients in folk medicine concepts that are different from those of modern scientific health care. Such beliefs are particularly pervasive among Third World and poor clients, who are often operating in distinctly different cultural mores. Meaningful relationships between the human services professional helper and the client are further complicated by the marked increase in specialization. The relationship is also fractured by the need of Third World and poor clients being forced by court decrees to use health clinics, which means that clients frequently are cared for by different staff members on each visit.

It appears that the degree to which the qualities ideally defined as essential to the therapeutic relationship, namely mutual trust, respect, and cooperation, will be present inversely with the amount of social distance. Conversely the greater the social distance the less likely the participants will receive each other in terms of the ideal type roles of professional and patient, and more likely they will perceive each other in terms of their social class status in the larger society.

There is fairly general agreement that because of certain attitudes, the low-status client has a markedly lower chance of obtaining optimal care than the high-status client. Several generalizations are given for this discrepancy, including the following: low-status clients give less attention to symptoms, they are less willing to sacrifice immediate for future gain, and they display less initiative. When taken at their face value, these reasons stereotype low-status persons as being shiftless and lazy. Knowing the effect of cultural conditioning on the behaviour of both the care provider and the client can do much to prevent inhumane health care. It can certainly reduce the negative human dimensions of our health care crisis.

Cross-Cultural Helping

Third World peoples who seek health care outside their family do so because neither they nor their families can help them. Ideally, the practitioner will offer care that minimizes cultural conflicts. This type of reality based care giving is built on empathy. Human services professionals who are different from clients in terms of cultures generally have more difficulty communicating empathy, congruence, respect, and acceptance than those who share or understand the client's cultural perspective. To be more specific, non-Third World health care providers who understand the social and psychological backgrounds of Third World clients are better able to work with such clients than their colleagues who lack this knowledge. Indeed, a meaningful relationship with a non-Third World practitioner representing the dominant power society can do much to reduce hostile feelings of Third World clients. The act of providing care to another human being is a rare opportunity for understanding ethnic group similarities and differences. It is in this setting that the social and behavioural sciences concepts discussed in this book are acted out.

Contrary to popular notion, little empirical evidence supports the assumption that race or ethnic group identity per se is related to the level of understanding between professional helpers and Third World clients. Generalizations about race and cross-cultural helping should be made with great care. At best, the literature on the subject is inconclusive. Several seminal studies suggest that cultural barriers make the development of successful cross-cultural interventions highly improbable. Yet, other replicated studies conclude that well-trained, empathic caregivers can establish effective relationships with clients from other racial and ethnic backgrounds.

It seems appropriate here to provide an overview of areas in which it is important for human services professionals to be both knowledgeable and understanding. Bilingualism and biculturalism present a special kind of challenge. Spanish speaking Americans are the largest number of bilingual-bicultural clients in American hospitals and clinics. Human service professionals must be aware that language, culture, and ethnicity play the most important role in the formation of the client's self-concept and in the development of his or her cognitive coping skills. The three concepts are analytically different, yet they are interrelated. Most bilingual-bicultural subcultures have not assimilated into the American melting pot because they prefer not to assimilate. Only African Americans (who are not bilingual-bicultural in the true sense of the terms) have mounted national civil rights campaigns to gain integration and assimilation with white Americans.

Human services professionals must also be aware that Third World clients who live in traditional families usually function according to the norms of their kinship network and also according to the norms of non Third World institutions. This conflict was vividly captured by D'Arcy McNickle, when he summarized the dilemmas of traditional Indians:

The problem of being an Indian, and being obliged to function at two levels of consciousness, for many individuals reduces itself to this: They are aware that their communities, their people, their kinsmen are Indians and are held in low esteem by the general society. The young people especially recognize themselves as Indians, but they do not want the low-status equivalent. They look for some way in which they can share in the status ascribed to middle-class Americans without ceasing to be Indians.

The lack of high status shows up when human services professionals mispronounce Third World names while taking ample steps to learn the pronunciation of equally difficult non-Third World names. Mispronouncing a person's name, whether through carelessness or laziness, can easily be interpreted as a lack of interest. In the case of Spanish, for example, pronunciation is much more consistent than English because each vowel is pronounced the same way in all words. When in doubt about pronunciation, the practitioner should ask the client.

Ethnic group language shapes a client's philosophy of life. Consider the following example: in English the dock runs; in Spanish el reloj anda (the clock walks); and for American Indians it just ticks. The first group is preoccupied with hurrying to be on time, whereas the latter two adopt a slower pace of life. Thus acceptance of the concept of time and structuring relationships around the clock-measured medical appointments vary according to culture.

A male social worker in a mental health clinic gave a thorough explanation of a proposed treatment plan to a female Chinese client. When he finished, he asked the client if she understood. She nodded and said, "Yes." Later the social worker learned that "yes" meant the client was listening. However, she did not understand the therapy plan. But she also did not want to be so impolite as to interrupt (or disrupt) the social worker by saying "no" or by asking questions. This kind of politeness and restraint is more pronounced in Asian women who interact with men than in Asian men because of the former 's inferior status. This is also true in other Third World societies. The social worker should have asked the client to explain her understanding of the treatment in her own words. It is important for professional helpers to determine whether "yes" is being used in the Asian or American sense.

It is helpful to clients when professional helpers phrase questions in such a way that requires more than a "yes" or "no" answer. The use of negative questions should be avoided because of the confusion they generate due to differences in the Asian-English grammatical use of "yes" and "no" when answering negative questions. A "yes" to a negative question in the Asian sense means a "no" in English. For example, the social worker asked, "Haven't you forgiven your sister for hurting you?" The Chinese client answered, "Yes," meaning, "Yes, you are right, I have not forgiven her." The client answered in English, but she used an Asian grammatical syntax.

The net result of ethnic people's living outside their ancestral lands and maintaining their cultural heritage is less than traditional culture. For example, African American culture is not African culture; Mexican American culture is not Mexican culture; mainland Puerto Rican culture is not island Puerto Rican culture; Chinese American culture is not Chinese culture; Japanese American culture is not Japanese culture. These cultures have become a synthesis of their own native and adopted American cultures. The derogatory terms *apple*, used to refer to American Indians who are red on the outside (ethnically) and white on the inside (beliefs), and banana, a term used to refer to Asian Americans who are yellow on the outside and white on the inside, illustrate possible cultural conflicts growing out of assimilation.

Crossing Cultural Barriers

The problem of inadequate health care cannot be attributed solely to lack of knowledge and economic deprivation. Structural differences also produce differences in attitudes and values. Health care providers consciously and unconsciously exclude the poor from active, peer participation in health-related organizations and activities. In turn, negative attitudes and social distance between themselves and affluent people prompt Third World poor people to reject Western health care systems. Instead of narrowing the gap between poor and affluent citizens, increased technology has widened it. Yet, it is imperative for human services professionals to remember that because something has always existed does not mean that it must continue to exist.

Understanding and accepting another person's cultural reality are the beginnings of a helping relationship. Helpful, as opposed to harmful, relationships do not require either party to compromise his or her own values and beliefs. Often a lack of knowledge or understanding leads to individual and group feelings of inadequacy and, ultimately, alienation. Successful transcultural involvement with another person requires considerable empathy. Ethically, human services professionals ought to be committed to protecting their clients' value systems. The therapeutic process includes both delivery of services and protection of ethnic identities. Human relationships automatically involve risk taking, and sharing feelings and testing commitments are part of the helping relationship. Thus, although value conflicts are inevitable, they should not lead to a client's ego or ethnic group destruction. The human relations lesson is quite clear both practitioners and clients can be in the process of becoming more healthy and humane persons.

Human services professionals who do not know the various social class dimensions of ethnic minorities also are unlikely to know that despite common language, colour, and historical backgrounds, all members of a particular ethnic group are not alike. It is presumptuous and counterproductive to talk about *the* African Americans or *the* Indians or *the* Hispanics as if members of these and other groups have only one set of behaviour characteristics. This text focuses on ethnic characteristics, but the reader is reminded that social class differences often are more determinant of a client's behaviour than his or her ethnic background. For instance, middleclass-oriented Third World families tend to be much more ready to fit the Western therapeutic routine.

Additional thought should be given to caregivers who ostensibly have everything in their favor when working with clients from their own ethnic group. Several factors frequently mitigate against their being effective helpers. First and most important, most people of colour who become human services professionals are Anglo-Saxon in terms of their training and professional associations. They are, in short, carbon copies of their white colleagues. Of course, some people of colour are able to maintain their ethnic identities with a minimum loss in credibility. In terms of their verbal and nonverbal communication, however, many people of colour who earn graduate degrees appear condescending to minority group clients. In other instances, ethnic minority practitioners feel quite marginal estranged from their white colleagues and no longer comfortable with members of their own ethnic group. These professional helpers appear cold and detached to both ethnic minority and majority group clients. Another problem is the possibility that minority group clients will displace to these practitioners their hostility toward white people.

A related issue seldom explored in depth is the lack of empathy and sensitivity care providers have for clients other than those of their own ethnic group. American Indians, for example, sometimes display considerable hostility toward African Americans; Mexican Americans frequently reject Chinese Americans. Social agencies are full of other illustrations. It is worth repeating at this juncture that all Americans are products of institutionalized racism, and awareness of this fact will allow the professional helper to better deal with her or his own racism.

White social workers, who constitute the overwhelming majority of members in professional human services associations, are beginning to come to grips with their own racism and that of their colleagues. It is hoped such introspection will not lead to a repression or denial of hostile feelings. Nor should a practitioner who is trying to understand her or his racism be immobilized by guilt. *Proactive* helpers rather than *reactive* helpers are needed if the vicious circle of racism is to be broken. One of the deficits in education in the various helping professions is the lack of systematic transcultural coursework and supervised transcultural experiences. A lack of quality care for culturally different clients is likely to result in human services professionals' feeling incompetent or inadequate when treating people of colour. This feeling is not without foundation optimum care delivery is impossible without cultural understanding. However, each practitioner must be aware of his or her own cultural attitudes and values in order to optimally help clients in other cultures.

One way to gain knowledge of other cultures is to become a participant observer. If this is done, care must be taken not to view all people in other cultures as weird folks who need psychiatric treatment and a drastic change in values. A participant observer should not be a social voyeur. The kind of self a professional helper brings to the relationship will determine the quality of helping that occurs. Ethnicity affects the behaviour of caregivers in both culturally similar and culturally different groups. There is the danger that human services professionals will identify too much with the client. Counter transference, the process of projecting their own values onto the client, must be dealt with by practitioners in order for the therapeutic process to develop. Basic to dealing with counter transference is the need for caregivers to examine their own feelings, attitudes, values, and behaviour.

Helper-Helpee Communication

Language can significantly affect psychopathological assessment of bilingual clients. The responses are cued differently, depending on whether or not interviews are conducted in the client's native language. Factors such as the amount of content and expansion on a particular subject affect pathological assessment. For example, the tense used by a respondent may be incorrectly interpreted as a sign of activeness of his symptoms; or language patterns may be incorrectly interpreted as signs of anxiety or depression. Clearly, language barriers pose special problems for diagnosis when clients are interviewed in a language other than their native one. Only recently have health care researchers noted that cognitive behaviour may be influenced by the semantic structure of languages. People who do not answer questions in ways acceptable to interviewers may be judged as displaying signs of psychopathology by practitioners who are unaware of the clients' cultural norms.

Interventions are carried out every day in almost every kind of health care situation. This exchange may be between a nurse and a patient, a social worker and a client, or another health-related person and a client. The initial health care interview is designed to get and to give information; therefore, the quality of this interaction is crucial to a client's adjustment. People of colour who come to modern health institutions after being treated by traditional curers are likely to be extremely anxious and fearful. As noted earlier, hospitals are especially sensitive places. For example, when a nurse admits a patient for treatment, she or he conducts an interview. This initial interview may result in valuable information that will be helpful in evaluating the patient and planning for subsequent medical care. Often, this opportunity is not used to its greatest advantage. Most nurses, especially those trained in less progressive schools, adhere strictly to the printed interview form, ask direct questions to make sure that all the blank spaces are filled, and usually fail to allow the patient time for self-expression.

If a bilingual client asks a question, a non bilingual interviewer usually gives long, detailed answers, which in most instances serve only to allay the interviewer's fears or feelings of inadequacy, thus leaving the client floundering.

In some clinics the place for admitting a client and conducting the interview is the reception area, where there is a continuous stream of traffic, or the waiting room, with an audience of one or more other persons. Obviously, these situations are not conducive to a good interview; they block the client's desire to ask questions or to talk freely. To conduct a successful interview, human services personnel must familiarize themselves with the purpose of the interview and with methods of conducting interviews, including what to look for during the interview. The first consideration should be to put the client at ease and make him or her as comfortable as possible. This can be accomplished by the care provider's introducing herself or himself and any other agency personnel who are present at the time. If possible, the interview should be conducted in an otherwise unoccupied room or office.

Next, the interviewer should explain to the client what records will be needed to assist in the data gathering. Since the primary purpose of the interview is to elicit information about the client's situation, it is important to let the client do most of the talking. The interviewer may need to direct the interview to a certain extent, but the interview should not be dominated by the interviewer. Nor should self-expression during the interview be dominated by the interviewer. Self-expression on the part of the client may uncover hidden problems and fears. It is important that these are uncovered early in the client's treatment so that needed resources can be brought to bear before additional complications occur. In addition to listening, interviewers must be able to communicate with clients. The most effective communication is two-way. This involves spoken language and body language. Frequently, a client's spoken language is incongruent with his or her body language, and the reverse can be true. Congruence between words and gestures is the key to understanding the messages being sent and received.

Successful communication between human services professionals and clients usually results in the following positive outcomes: (1) trust is formed, and the clients' ego defenses are reduced; (2) validation of the clients' subjective experiences increases their self-reflection and self-processing, and this leads to greater client self-understanding; (3) the professional helper becomes better able to distinguish *what* clients say from *how* they say it; and (4) clients' self-awareness and the professional helper awareness of them facilitate culture-appropriate behaviours by the clients. Most of what can be said about things practitioners should observe in clients are just as important for practitioners to know about themselves. Only by admitting their personal fears, inadequacies, cultural biases, and so forth can practitioners be optimally effective as care providers.

In the end, ethnic and gender similarities are not adequate substitutes for professional helpers who are (1) linguistically compatible with clients, (2) empathic, and (3) well trained. This means that the initial edge human services professionals may have with clients in their own ethnic group will be lost if the practitioners cannot get beyond ethnic history and identity. These considerations should not, however, be interpreted as obviating the need for colleges and human services agencies to recruit and train considerably more people of colour, who comprise less than 10 per cent of all college-trained human services practitioners.

❑❑❑

4

Social Work for Child Education and Development

Introduction

Only professional education for social work practice will be considered and therefore not the associate or doctoral levels. The issues to be discussed are (*a*) how many social work professional degrees there should be and how they should relate to one another; (*b*) what functions each should prepare for and what common content should exist; (*c*) the design of advanced concentrations; and (*d*) an overarching concern, the issue of quality. All of these matters are looked at from the perspective that education cannot be designed without careful attention to practice, and that practice in turn is equally affected by and concerned with the design of education. The purpose of social work practice is to deliver service, and the purpose of professional education is to study and teach how to do that.

One Degree or Two

Each of these issues has a long history, and each assumes a particular shape or importance as a reflection of the general societal context of the time. Born in the Progressive Era, social work education began with both university and agency-based programmes, offered both baccalaureate and graduate degrees, and lasted for varying amounts of time. Moving entirely to the campus after World War I, the focus shifted to developing methodology and away from social reform, raising the issue of *cause or function*, in Porter Lee's famous phrase. By 1951, the uneasy coexistence of baccalaureate and graduate programmes was ended by the Hollis-Taylor report, which declared that only 2-year graduate study prepared professional social workers. The rapid expansion of publicly funded social services, begun with the Social Security Act amendments and continued with the Great Society programmes initiated in the 1960s, revealed enormous numbers of jobs named or claimed as social work but filled by persons with no social work education. This led in 1971 to the restoration of the baccalaureate degree as an accredited professional social work degree and its insertion into a policy of educational continuum. These decisions were made without any data or consensus as to the functions for which each degree was to prepare nor of how, perhaps even if, an educational continuum should be shaped. *Webster's New World Dictionary* defines continuum as "a continuous extent, succession, or whole no part of which can be distinguished from adjacent parts except by arbitrary partition." Gross says that an educational continuum must have the following four characteristics:

1. Each level has its own educational integrity and objectives.
2. Each level builds on, without repeating, the preceding segments, and prepares for the next level.
3. Each successive level is different, more advanced, and more complex in educational content than the prior one.
4. A planned relation exists between the educational continuum and the operational practice continuum.

A formidable task confronted social work education, given the turbulent history, of trying to create a coherent first professional degree as part of a continuum with a preexisting second professional degree that had been the only game in town for 20 years. The task was not made easier by strong feelings on the part of some that there should only be one professional degree—a graduate one or by equally strong feelings by others that there was a desperate need for persons with social work preparation to fill the many positions not likely to be filled by MSWs and then held by totally untrained personnel.

In addition to ambivalent acceptance of the BSW, there was also no clarity about what functions this degree should prepare for or what functions should be assigned to the MSW degree. There are, by now, several studies which suggest that in the real world of employment, patterns of differential use of BSWs and MSWs are emerging. Kolevzon and Biggerstaff reviewed all existing studies and then carried out one of their own in one state. They examined BA, BSW and MSW workers at the direct service level. In summary, all the studies showed few significant differences in knowledge or skill as reported by workers. Those with BAs were more often found in public sector agencies than BSWS, and BSWs more often than MSWS. The reverse pattern was true for private agencies. The MSWs spent more time providing therapy, supervising, in intra-agency conferring and in programme planning. The BSWs spent more time on home visits, in consultation with other agencies, in information and referral, eligibility, case management and in recording. However, the more powerful predictors of who did what were agency setting and experience, not educational degree. A recent study suggests that BSWs do a good deal of case management and that their generalist preparation seems a good fit for these tasks. Also, BSWs are found in larger numbers in the public sector social services than are MSWs at the client-facing level.

The labour market seems well able to use two levels of professional social workers and also technicians and doctoral personnel. There is one widely accepted policy: MSWs may practice autonomously and BSWs only under supervision. If further research, clearly needed, confirms patterns described here, then both educational levels will need to consider whether to design their programmes to prepare graduates more effectively for the functions the labour market demands or to try to change the labour market patterns so as to fit better with educational design. At present, BSWs may offer the best hope of filling many jobs which demand considerable social work knowledge and skill in the public sector but are now filled by persons without any social work education. If that route is taken, there will also be a need for MSWs to fulfill the supervisory and training roles as backup to the BSW staff.

Relating the Two Degrees

There have been some 20 years of experience by now of the coexistence of the accredited BSW and MSW degree programmes. In 1991, there were 375 accredited BSW programmes and 103 MSW programmes in the United States. These graduated, respectively, 8,778 BSWs and 10,969 MSWS. More than 70% of all students accepted into MSW programmes entered with any kind of baccalaureate degree except a BSW. However, some BSWs did decide to gain an MSW degree. This is where the policy of continuum ceases to be an abstraction. How should BSWs be treated when they apply to MSW programmes? How should MSW programmes deal with applicants who lack BSW preparation?

Of all the BSW graduates extant, 3,853 applied to MSW programmes for a shortened programme which recognized their prior social work education, called advanced standing; 1,976 were accepted into graduate social work programmes. These numbers do not reflect an unknown number of BSWs who applied to the 36 graduate programmes that did not offer any advanced standing status to BSWs. Several mechanisms exist to manage articulation so as to avoid redundancy and create an educational continuum. Forty-four graduate schools offered a blanket exemption of a term or a year for all admitted graduates of accredited BSW programmes, called advanced standing, in 1990. Only non-social work baccalaureates must take the standard 2 years of study. This is an administratively simple device to employ. However, 36 of the 103 MSW programmes treated all applicants the same, regardless of the kind of baccalaureate degree held. This approach to a continuum is, first, inequitable as it treats a student differently depending upon the programme to which application is made. Second, there may not be enough time and curricular room to prepare a truly advanced practitioner in the 1 year assigned to that task, yet a one-term reduction may not avoid all redundancy nor bring the BA in-anything to the same level as the BSW graduate who has had perhaps 30 to 40 undergraduate credits in his or her social work major. Advanced standing is a common device to operationalize the continuum.

A few graduate programmes that also administer undergraduate ones admit their undergraduates into graduate classrooms for the foundation courses that both levels of students must take. At the end of this year of overlap, the BSW degree is granted to those students. Should they wish to earn an MSW, 1 added year is required, in effect a 3-2 pattern of study. Such a pattern meets all of Gross's criteria for continuum except perhaps the last. It is not a pattern usable in dealing with students from independent BSW programmes, which constitute 289 of the 375 BSW programmes. The advanced standing pattern described above divides the same 5-year span into a 4-1 pattern to create a continuum between the BSW and MSW degrees.

Thirteen programmes give a test to all students before they may enter the advanced component of the MSW programme and use this to allow BSWs to test out of any aspect of the introductory curriculum. Some programmes grant credits and some only waivers of courses. This approach permits the student to test out upon demonstrating mastery over the content in question and thus may be the best way to articulate the two levels into a true educational continuum. This approach builds a continuum on demonstrated knowledge learned rather than record of courses taken. Particularly if the exams are designed to test broad knowledge and the ability to think like a social worker, it may be possible to combine such tests into a national placement exam (comparable to the ACSW exam) which can serve both as an articulation device for graduate programmes and also as the knowledge component of a competency exam for BSW graduates.

Seven programmes use an individualized assessment of each BSW's preparation and waive students from duplicative courses. This is a more discretionary approach and is also very labour-intensive, so most programmes eschew its use. This method requires the same credits of all students but more courses of some, and does avoid redundancy.

There is another difficulty in building a proper educational continuum among the many programmes under diverse auspices. For example, one BSW programme may teach about the present organization of social services in its social policy course, but graduates may be waived from the first graduate social policy course, about the history of social work and social welfare, and be required to take the second course, which addresses the present organization and delivery of social services. This kind of problem can be found across the curriculum.

The usual conception of continuum in higher education is a cumulative one, a series of building blocks with some content clearly perceived as introductory or foundational, to be followed by later content of a more sophisticated, advanced kind. In this model, students can freely exit upon completion of all the foundation work or can go on to the next higher level. Only social work has created a model that also allows people to enter at a more advanced level without having covered the beginning level first. Given the data on the high proportion of students who in fact do enter the continuum in the middle without the earlier work, the practicalities of this decision to replicate the foundation at the higher level are evident. Academic disciplines like chemistry require the coverage of foundation prior to entry into advanced levels of study. Professional programmes like engineering or nursing require the first degree for admission into graduate levels of advanced study in the field. Social work's approach to continuum creates a kind of limbo for holders of baccalaureate degrees other than in social work. They are post-baccalaureate yet have not covered the foundation content needed prior to entry into the advanced component of graduate education. This necessary foundation could be provided by MSW programmes but could also be provided by referral to a BSW programme which covers the foundation content. Graduate programmes fear asking more time of their applicants yet also wish more curricular space to prepare a truly advanced MSW graduate. It remains to be seen if social work can have its cake and eat it, too—that is, can claim continuum and still permit entry at either of two levels without adding time.

Common Foundation

In addition to the mechanics of articulating the two degrees, there is also the question of what, if any, content is needed by both degrees. Another way of putting this is to ask if there is a common core or foundation for all professional social work education and of what it consists. Some would argue that no common foundation is needed, as the two degrees have such different functions. Harold Lewis suggested that the BSW is a technician, "one who fixes television sets," while the professional MSW is one who "designs television sets." He said that the public is much clearer about which kind of social worker to go to for what kinds of problems than is the profession. Kolevzon argues against a common foundation for pedagogical reasons, saying that it overstuffs the graduate curriculum and does not allow beginning where the graduate student is. He also says that the same foundation cannot serve equally to prepare for the different objectives of the two levels. If we are one profession, however, one must ask what there is in common that links us together. However defined, that common content must be provided to all would-be professional social workers.

There is also an educational dispute. One pole assumes that the first time some content is taught, especially when using the same text, the same topics and so on, similar learning outcomes result, regardless of educational level. The opposite pole assumes that learning outcomes differ with level, in part because the students are more educated and more mature, in part because teacher expectations are different and do depend on educational level. There are no clear empirical data to support either view. There is anecdotal evidence that some BSWs in graduate foundation courses report much repetition and some new content. Other anecdotal reports by teachers describe visible and notable differences among students by level, even when in the same classroom, but also note wide variability unrelated to level. It is evident that no two people teach given content in exactly the same way, which further confounds this debate.

Some argue that a true graduate programme should not teach content that is assigned and designed for an undergraduate programme. The question remains as to whether there is something that all professional social workers, regardless of level, must know, must value and must be able to do. And the question remains, also, of where we teach that common content.

We have said since about 1941 that all professional social work education must contain the same broad content areas. These have appeared in successive Curriculum Policy

Statements of the Council on Social Work Education or its predecessors under slightly varied labels and emphases, starting with *The Basic Eight* in 1941. That curriculum required courses on:

1. Casework, group work and community organization—what we would now call practice, if of a very broadly conceived kind.
2. Social welfare administration—which we might now identify as the social environment part of Human Behaviour in the Social Environment (HBSE).
3. Research.
4. Medical and psychiatric information—which we would now see as the Human Behaviour part of the HBSE component.
5. Public welfare—which we would now call Social Welfare Policy and Services.
6. A field practicum.

We have obviously modified and shifted emphasis and focus in each of these areas and more recently have added content on values, on diversity, on oppression and the groups at particular risk of oppression. In effect, this may be a working definition of the common social work foundation: the knowledge, values and skills that under gird the profession—its common core. Current curricular policy requires that both BSW and MSW programmes cover these areas and MSW programmes must go well beyond. To maintain that there is no common foundation for all social work greatly weakens any claim that social work is indeed one profession, especially in the light of the great diversity in the tasks that it states are its domain.

At a less abstract level the agreement breaks down. What form(s) of practice, if any, must all social workers have? The Basic Eight said all, with more emphasis on one. We now appear to be moving toward a generalist formulation. Most would agree that the values of the profession are an essential element. After this, agreement lessens. Some claim, others dispute, a social work model of problem solving. Most agree that the central focus of social work is the interaction between persons and their environment.

Other Professions

It may be useful to examine how others deal with these same issues. Academic disciplines such as history or chemistry require students entering their graduate programmes to have either an undergraduate major or a bulk of courses in that discipline. Graduate work then builds on that foundation, pursuing greater depth of knowledge and sophistication in ever more specialized aspects of the area.

Engineering and nursing are professional programmes that consider the baccalaureate level the first professional degree. Nursing is the profession perhaps closest to social work in its curricular dilemmas. The holder of an associate degree in nursing is considered a technician. The first professional degree is the BSN, and the holder of an associate degree in nursing can transfer into a BSN programme. A BA not in nursing must take a second, if shorter, baccalaureate programme in nursing in order to earn the BSN degree. Entry into a master's programme in nursing, which is the advanced and specialized level, requires a BSN. There are a few specially designed master's programmes tailored to the needs of the non-BSNs to catch them up to the holder of the BSN, and these offer advanced content and take longer. Similarly, an applicant to a graduate engineering programme must have a baccalaureate degree in engineering to be considered.

There is agreement that the nursing content in an ADN programme is a subset of the nursing content in the BSN programme. Such agreement makes articulation between the two levels simpler. Criterion #17 for accrediting baccalaureate and higher degree nursing programmes reads: "The master's curriculum builds on the knowledge and competencies of baccalaureate education in nursing and provides for the attainment of advanced knowledge and practice in nursing". Nursing has gone a step further. It has developed a model of differentiated practice for each level which allows for a career ladder within each but eliminates overlap of functions. The ADN prepares for entry into technical nursing practice to work mainly with individuals in secondary care settings under the supervision of a professional nurse. The BSN prepares a generalist professional. A master's level nurse has further advanced and specialized knowledge in a particular area such as psychiatric, public health, managerial or interpersonal practice. Most important, this focus on practice outcomes allows for clarity in the design of curricula to attain those outcomes.

As McClure points out, if educational design determines practice, then the issues of how the various differentiated forms of practice fit together into one whole arise. If practice, on the other hand, determines the educational design, these issues do not arise.

Can social work ever establish the requirements such as those in nursing and other professions, that one must complete the first professional degree before entering the more advanced one? Should we continue to offer the catch-up content at the graduate level for those who lack it? And are the complaints valid that 1 year is not sufficient time to prepare an advanced graduate when nursing and engineering have managed with a 1-year master's degree? None of the answers is easy to find. One approach is to claim far more credits in the baccalaureate level, as do nursing or engineering, and thereby abandon adherence to the liberal arts base of social work education. Another is to wait until there are both more data and more agreement as to the functions and therefore the curricular design of both BSW and MSW programmes. The former faces opposition from the university; the latter is politically easier to maintain.

Advanced Concentrations

In the master's programmes, students who have completed the foundation content, whether through BSW or MSW study, then choose which of the advanced concentrations offered by their programme they will enter. In 1991, of the 22,932 students in MSW programmes who had chosen their concentration, 13,607 were in one based upon a field or practice, a social problem or a population group. Most often, this was combined with a method or combination of methods of intervention. There were 9,325 in purely method based concentrations. The largest number of students in field-of-practice concentrations were in mental health, family services, health, or child welfare not a surprising finding. Half of the students choosing among methods of intervention chose direct practice.

At present, the CSWE requires that every MSW programme design and provide advanced concentrations, and the CSWE allows maximum leeway as to how that should be done. Concentrations may be based upon methods of intervention, on fields of practice, on social problems, on population groups, or on a model of advanced generalist practice. There is no consensus within either the education or practice communities about which of these is the better approach. Should one develop interventive skill and techniques of a specialized kind—for example, direct or clinical practice, administration and assume that in the first 6 months on the job one will learn the field-specific knowledge and skills required to perform at an advanced professional level? This is in addition to the agency specifics of forms, rules, culture, and networks of personal relations needed to survive. This question is more difficult to answer since one cannot predict where that first job will be or whether a career in that field will follow. The argument is made that virtually all of the methods, as taught, are of equal application and use wherever the graduate may go; that little of the field-specific knowledge is needed; and that it can be learned relatively easily on the job.

The other side of this argument stresses the extent of specialized, field specific knowledge that is needed to practice at an advanced professional level. It emphasizes that the specialized settings shape and alter the way in which the professional encounters take place and how they proceed. Hence, any given mode of practice may be central or of little use, may be so twisted by the nature of the clients, the auspice, the baggage carried by the staff member and the problem that causes the encounter to begin with, as to bear little resemblance from one setting to another. There is some anecdotal evidence that graduates unprepared for these large differences perform poorly, are unhappy (as are their employers) and leave such jobs soon—a waste for all parties.

Some illustrations may be useful. A model of direct practice based upon the assumptions of a voluntary counseling agency that clients come voluntarily seeking help, with a time frame of weekly encounters over 2 or more months does not serve the needs of a health care social worker who must *sell* the patient and family on their need for her services and must accomplish the essential work to be done within the average 6- to 7-day length of stay in a hospital, constrained by the time pressures of medical cost containment policies. The client is not voluntary and has not sought social work help, and the agenda of work to be done is radically shaped by the short time available, then reduced even more by the condition of the patient for part of that time, caused by tests and treatments. Further, a key skill for effective practice in such settings is the skill of working with other disciplines from a position of small power, not often part of the all-purpose model of practice sketched above. Then there is the specialized knowledge of the impact of illness, acute or chronic and of this particular diagnosis—upon patient and family, knowledge of all the special policies and programmes affecting worker and client which constrain and shape practice. This content, too, is not part of a method-for-all-settings concentration.

A different illustration is the social worker in a child welfare agency who must know all of the policies and procedures of a very legalistic sector, including the skills of working in a court/judicial arena. Moreover, this is in addition to the specialized knowledge and skills of assessing a possible abuse situation; dealing with child and family and whether the child stays or is removed; recruiting, training and working with foster parents and the child in their care as well as the biological family looking toward the child's return; assessing potential adoptive parents; and contending with all of these conflicting interests while trying to serve the best interests of the child. Again, this highly specialized knowledge is not likely to be found in a method-oriented concentration. The ability to offer both health care and child welfare content in a method-oriented course is even less likely, yet some students will go on to practice in one arena and some in the other, and some in neither.

To complicate the issue further, a method-based concentration in administration might need to be divided in a somewhat different way, depending on whether the model of practice was that of a voluntary agency, one in the for-profit sector, or one in the public sector. The first of these might stress work with volunteers, a board of directors, fund-raising and relations with the community. A public agency model would not deal with these to any extent but rather budgetary politics at the legislative and hierarchical level, and would stress internal management functions and a very different kind of public relations. A for-profit agency model of administrative practice would need to address promotion and recruitment of customers, public relations and marketing, a still different approach to budgetary processes, and so forth.

There are a few studies which have looked at the fit between education and subsequent social work employment. All agree that between one third and one half of all MSWs were practicing in a method of intervention or an area other than that which they had studied in their MSW programme. The most common shift was from direct practice into administrative practice roles. None of these studies examined the extent to which social workers move across sectors—for example, from health to child welfare—nor have any such studies been found.

According to NASW data, which are the best available source on what MSWs are doing after graduation, 17% are practicing solely as private clinical practitioners. Another 47% are part-time private practitioners in addition to holding other jobs, usually in a clinical agency setting. Some 32% describe themselves as doing agency-based clinical practice only. However, 24% describe their primary functions as doing supervision, management, programme planning and so forth, while 45% say that these are secondary functions. Since most MSWs were trained as direct practitioners, one can only assume that most persons in the last group have little educational preparation for these new tasks.

Responsibility for this may lie in the employer's hands, or with the educational programme, or with the individual social worker who may not have known exactly what kind of social work he or she would face in 5 or 10 years. Few of the people in managerial positions chose that concentration while in school, yet the reward system in social work is such that few can remain at the client-facing level without serious financial loss compared with those who advance. Method-based curricula may be too narrowly focussed to address the commonest path of movement from direct practice into supervisory positions. A brief exposure to generalist practice may not be enough to remedy the problem. It would be helpful to know more about careers in social work in order to inform the discussion of how best to organize curricula at the advanced level. Lacking data, we argue from ideology.

Some kinds of intervention must be taught to students so that they can go forth and practice, however the curriculum is organized. What is at issue is whether some or all are taught in a field-specific fashion or whether a methodological approach both narrows and misses the range of what is needed more than the world of work would suggest. It is also important to stress that whatever the mode of curricular design, all students are placed in one or more agencies for the practicum. Here the student acquires practice know-how that is highly specific to the field, problem and population that the agency and the student's field assignments address. The onus for finding the transferability of such specific knowledge to a different agency and different field/problem/population lies with the student. Too often, the student is not helped to find the theoretical and empirical knowledge that underpins practice in either setting and must hunt out for him- or herself the aspects of practice that are shared and those that are not.

One means of reconciling these dilemmas in curricular design is a matrix model where students opt for a field/ problem/population and an interventive method, perhaps a means for having one's cake and eating it too. Thus a student chooses among direct practice, management and community development for example, and also selects one field/problem/ population area: health care, mental illness, children or aging. It is easy to develop a specialized social policy course, a human behaviour and the social environment course in support of health care or mental illness or children. At issue is how the practice courses are dealt with: all-purpose, field/problem/population-specific, or some mix of the two. The argument being made here is that field-specific practice knowledge is as important as general, all-purpose practice knowledge. Both are needed. Often the answer is determined by the size and resources of the school that may limit the number of highly specialized courses it can mount.

A different approach attempts to reconceptualize the traditional methods—casework, group work, community organization and administration—into broader clusters. For example, direct practice has combined casework and groupwork, but group workers will tell you that it has been at the loss of any real depth of knowledge about how groups work and how to work with them. Some schools have developed micro, mezzo and macro concentrations, the middle one attempting to span some direct service and some management. The argument made above about the desirability of staffing public sector agencies with BSWs also suggests the equal necessity of preparing MSWs to work as supervisors and in-service trainers in support of those BSWS. These persons would need a mix of direct practice and supervisory skills as well as field-specific knowledge. In all of these designs, there is the painful consideration of the cost of adding this new content at the expense of no longer having room for that desirable other content.

In any event, the permissive policies of the CSWE regarding the design of advanced concentration offer the opportunity of a natural experiment. It is a chance to study the interplay of selected concentration and future career, including the effectiveness of the graduate's performance, the employer's and employee's satisfaction and the degree to which career paths by method and by field/problem/ population can be predicted. Another factor that may restrict the present freedom of movement by social workers is the development of advanced certification by the professional association. It is creating credentials for advanced, post-MSW practitioners, beginning with a diplomate in clinical social work and one in school social work. The intent appears to be to try to limit entry into specialized forms of practice to those with the appropriate educational and experiential preparation. It is not clear if this will shape future curricular design or be based upon existing curricular design. And which should determine which? There is much debate as well about whether such advanced certification should be by field of practice or methodology or population or social problem. It is the same argument as that about advanced curricular design. It seems self-evident that these must come into some eventual harmony with one another, that specialized curricula become part of the requirement for the advanced certification. This would require the professional organization that is developing diplomate criteria to work closely with the educational organization that is approving advanced curricula. It is to be hoped that such conversation will have the benefit of some data on career needs, and on what is as well as some discussion of what ought to be. As in medicine, certification may use a number of different organizing concepts, not just one.

Quality in Social Work

Mechanisms to improve quality come in two broad forms: external and internal, with attention here mainly on the latter. Briefly, the external mechanisms are accreditation and efforts of the host institution to support or impede better quality. Accreditation's effectiveness rests upon the usefulness of the standards and processes used and the effectiveness with which they are employed. A central aspect now is the self-study, which is based on the belief that the required self-examination will lead to programme renewal and self-improvement—belief only, as there is no empirical evidence that this is so. There are input standards in social work as in other professions, and these are often couched in terms that leave much room for discretionary judgement. To some degree that may be unavoidable. This makes all the more important the preparation of the expert peers who make those judgements.

There has been an effort in social work both to move toward more precision in the standards and policies and also to frame at least some of them as output or outcome measures. It would seem that the overall quality of an educational programme would best be measured by the careers of its graduates. Such indicators as rates and kinds of employment (first job and career path), activities that show leadership, employer and graduate satisfaction with the graduate's education, scores on state and national tests, and so on are examples of such an approach. It would not be easy but would be most interesting to seek judgements of recipients of the social worker's services, even if only reviewing the rate of premature terminations of service. Some of this data may be costly or difficult to collect, yet most programmes do try to keep in touch with alumni for other purposes, so it seems not beyond reach. Accreditation may never be popular, but there may be ways to make the judgment of peers more objective and more effective as a tool for quality enhancement.

At the institutional level, there is an evident relationship between the degree of support and the kinds of expectations on one hand and the programme quality on the other. Higher education in general is facing very hard times at this writing, and social work is suffering along with other disciplines. Of concern, however, is a base level of support which recognizes the special demands of field placements and other aspects of professional education not encountered in the usual academic disciplines.

The expectations of faculty to be researchers, publishers and grant-getters like other academics may have ultimate benefit as social workers research and find empirical answers to the thorny problems practitioners face in their daily work. This pressure newer to social work than to more academic disciplines—has several hazards, however. One is that new faculty may be coming on board with highly developed research skills but little practice experience, which may in turn limit their ability to be effective practice teachers or researchers into practice. Further, once hired, the pressures are to seek funding for research and to publish rather than develop the missing practice experience, so such deficits are less likely to be corrected. This emphasis also pulls academic social workers further away from practicing social workers, a separation that is cause for concern. Each must learn from the other and each must understand the pressures, needs and contributions of the other for education to thrive and for the profession as a whole to progress. Finally, as public support for higher education and for research shrinks, corporate donors become ever more important. Social work has less access to such resources since so much of its organizational base is public or not-for-profit. Less access to funding for research may mean less research by or for social work and may also reduce the power and influence of social work in the academic world. There are pulls, therefore, in opposing directions.

Even matters of size may be a determinant of quality that is externally shaped. Very small departments with one or two faculty cannot offer a well rounded programme, a matter both of institutional and accrediting concern.

Internal to the programme are a number of factors that affect quality. One of these is the admission process, from recruitment through selection and retention of students, that affects the quality of the products of the programme. Programmes need to specify and operationalize the qualities they seek in their students. Which are most important: leadership capacity, intellectual skills, social commitment, caring? Most applicants are not equally blessed with each of these. Further, a programme must be realistic as to which aspects it can expect to change. For example, attitudes may be less accessible to alteration than are intellectual skills. Students euphemistically called nontraditional may bring both a need for specialized help—for example, differently scheduled classes for mothers—but also a richness of experience and maturity. They may prompt an increased demand for scholarship aid and advisement, not easy to meet in these times of scarcity.

Some programmes have lowered the admission standards of academic performance for certain students because they bring other qualities considered valuable for future social workers. The students have not been insured extra help in acquiring the academic skills necessary to perform in what is, after all, an academic and graduate programme. These extra helps are also not easy to provide in times of budgetary stringency. Without such help we do no favor to these students, admitting them only to failure. On the other hand, most programmes are under pressure from their academic environment always to raise admission criteria based on prior academic performance without regard to what some nontraditional students can contribute.

Policies on student retention also affect quality of outcome. Education serves as a gatekeeper, and we must remember this. Efforts to rescue students who should not be inflicted upon agencies or clients in the future serve no one well. Too often, inadequate students are allowed to graduate because of the lack of quality control mechanisms in place along the way for both class and field. Programmes may wish to consider whether a simple cumulation of passing grades is the best way to assess progress toward the goal of preparing a professional and competent social worker. Arkava and others used clearly stated competency goals and a variety of measurements to test their attainment. A presentation of a piece of practice and a discussion thereof can also serve this end. Other programmes use a thesis or a comprehensive exam which attempts to measure both the attainment of specific components and also their integration. With more attention, other devices may be found to assure the attainment of some level of quality for all graduates. All of these programmes believe that grades alone are not sufficient. It may be time for a stronger effort to make that practice more widespread.

A second internal area important for quality improvement is faculty. The criteria for faculty selection are usually clear and involve some combination of scholarship and research, content competence and teaching skills. One might wish to add role modeling to that list. One function of a faculty member that is often assumed but not addressed is that of teacher. This entails an understanding of the entire curriculum, of the particulars for which he or she is responsible, how these relate to the whole and the skills of using the classroom experience to facilitate the desired kinds of learning on the part of the students. Selection of faculty is often based more on scholarship potential than teaching, and too often neither is addressed in faculty development efforts. Whether good teachers are born or made, teaching effectiveness can be enhanced with efforts directed to that end. Most social work students are motivated to learn at least those parts of the curriculum they feel relevant to their own goals. If all faculty are clear as to the purpose of each of the curricular parts and how they connect, and if all faculty are helped to present their own part as effectively as possible, the quality of the curriculum experienced by the student and the quality of their own learning can only be enhanced.

Programmes can also improve the quality of their curriculum through planned efforts at faculty development geared to those areas that the faculty (some or all) have felt to be weak. This can be done in a wide variety of ways, from using *homegrown* experts from within the programme or other parts of the university to bringing in experts from outside. The choice may best be politically determined as to which is most likely to work better. An alternate approach is to ask some esteemed outsider to come in as consultant to assess, with the faculty, what areas are in need of attention and possible ways to address improvement.

It is likely that many programmes will be addressing a most difficult issue of maintaining quality while going through a sustained period of downsized budgets. How to do the essentials well with less becomes a critical question that few have had experience in answering. It may be a question of designing quality control measures for an ever-increasing number of adjunct faculty; or of finding less expensive, more cost-effective ways to monitor the field practicum; or of offering certain courses and a key question is how to decide which ones—on a large-lecture format with student-led recitation sections; or other devices. It is not a way of thinking that we have been used to, in spite of a general reduction in agency and public funding for social services. Those reductions are now hitting academe as well, and the easy places to cut have been used up on too many campuses. The challenge is to handle downsizing cost in a way that does not equally downsize quality. Let us hope that higher education budgets will grow, making the pursuit of quality improvement both pleasanter and much easier.

Ideas for the Future

The basic curriculum approved for social work education has been largely the same in its general design for some 50 years, with only a few innovations. That fact alone suggests that a more empirical and rigorous examination of some of the issues, as well as some deliberate, planned experimentation, may be overdue. Many of our debates are fueled more by ideology than data, and good data may help to move the discussion forward.

One major innovation in the last couple of decades is the generalist model. There are surely other good ideas out there in need of encouragement to allow them to be tried, with only the one condition that they be rigorously evaluated to see if the product was any improvement and if the resources used were equal to or less than those currently required. As we seem to be well into an era of scarcer resources in higher education, some further experiments may be in order to see if there are more resource-efficient ways of doing what we do, without loss of quality. Improving the articulation devices between BSW and MSW programmes may be one way to make better use of scarce resources. Another may be to shift to a BS degree, allowing for many more social work courses and a more competent first level worker, at the sacrifice of a liberal arts preparation. The rationale for this approach is that it should allow the MSW graduate to reach a higher level of expertise.

Further work is also needed in examining ways to enhance the quality of our graduates. The ultimate test is how well our graduates do social work with their clients, their agencies and their communities. Ways to examine those issues are in need of development and application. It may be that promoting the use of increasingly specific outcome measures as part of the accreditation process may lead in that direction. It seems worthy of trial. This too should be a joint effort of the education and the professional practitioner communities, as both have a stake in how competently our graduates perform.

Advanced concentrations are based on methods, on fields of practice, on social problems or on population groups. Some beginning research suggests that a method model is a good fit for the first job after the degree-not for all students but for a significant number. For many, it is not a good fit for a career. We do not know if a cross-method field-of-practice model or other paradigm works any better over the course of a career. That surely is testable. An alternative means for ensuring a better quality of performance over a career is that which appears to be developing in the profession through advanced certification. How these will be designed, whether by one method or by one field but cross-method, or by yet another method, is not clear at this time but is surely important. The question for us all is whether this task should be jointly designed by the education and practitioner communities or should be left to the practitioners alone. Some partnership between social work education and post degree learning needs to be arrived at by educators, practitioners and employers. Employers also need to be more explicit about what they expect new hires to know and be able to do, and then check to see if the applicant is so prepared. One would hope that the design of future diplomates will be based upon some empirical data as to what is needed, not only in the present job but also in a likely career. One also hopes that there will be a plan for evaluation of whatever pattern emerges.

In examining the field almost 2 decades after writing on manpower needs and the necessity for at least two levels of professional social workers, there is no evidence that this was an erroneous conclusion. There are still large numbers of jobs that should be but are not filled by personnel with the knowledge, values and skills which are central to social work. The public sector, in particular protective services and services for public assistance recipients, as well as neighborhood development should have a major infusion of social work-trained personnel. This will require a change both on the part of public agencies in how jobs are designed and on the part of institutional programmes in how education is designed. So far, BSWs have tended to fill social work kinds of positions in places where MSWs have tended not to go. There is also need for a new pattern of education to prepare the MSW in-service trainer-supervisor who can serve as consultant and backup for BSWs in those public sector jobs. Again, the more we know about the actual patterns of the labour market, the better off we shall be in the way we design educational programmes.

It may be a useful idea to hold a meeting of expert educators in many professions to discuss, share, exchange and debate solutions to mutual problems. To start, a meeting of engineering, nursing, pharmacy and business educators might usefully discuss similar issues of articulation among educational levels and the means to improve competence of graduates, as well as identify anew which competencies are crucial and the most cost effective ways to attain the best results. This should prove of use to all concerned and might spin off some innovative solutions to shared problems. Such an event may also remove some of the more doctrinaire arguments that have impeded our progress. Social work's standing as an admired and valued profession can best be served by seeking as many ways as we can find to prepare more competent, more committed and more courageous social workers to deal with the social problems and social needs of the coming century.

5

Social Work for Solving Problem of Youth

Introduction

Methods of Changing Attitudes and Habits. The most effective and lasting adjustments are achieved through a change of attitudes and habits. But these are difficult to change because they are frequently deeply rooted, have an emotional significance to the person, and have validity and reason for their existence. As Dewey points out:

Habits are arts. They involve skill of sensory and motor organs, cunning or craft, and objective materials. They assimilate objective energies and eventuate in command of environment. They require order, discipline, and manifest technique. They have a beginning, middle and end.

A bad habit suggests an inherent tendency to action and also a hold, command over us. It makes us do things we are ashamed of, things which we tell ourselves we prefer not to do. It overrides our formal resolutions, our conscious decisions. When we are honest with ourselves we acknowledge that a habit has this power because it is so intimately a part of ourselves. It has a hold upon us because we are the habit. All habits are demands for certain kinds of activity; and they constitute the self. In any intelligible sense of the word will, they are will. They form our effective desires and they furnish us with our working capacities. They rule our thoughts, determining which shall appear and be strong and which shall pass from light into obscurity.

Recently a friend remarked to me that there was one superstition current among even cultivated persons. They suppose that if one is told what to do, if the right end is pointed to them, all that is required in order to bring about the right act is will or wish on the part of the one who is to act. He used as an illustration the matter of physical posture; the assumption is that if a man is told to stand up straight, all that is further needed is wish and effort on his part, and the deed is done. He pointed out that this belief is on a par with primitive magic in its neglect of attention to the means which are involved in reaching an end.

To reach an end we must take our mind off from it and attend to the act which is next to be performed. We must make that the end. The only way of accomplishing this discovery is through a flank movement. We must stop even thinking of standing up straight. To think of it is fatal, for it commits us to the operation and established habit of standing wrong. We must find an act within our power which is disconnected from any thought about standing. We must start to do another thing which on one side inhibits our falling into the customary bad position and on the other side is the beginning of a series of acts which may lead into the correct posture. The hard drinker who keeps thinking of not drinking is doing what he can to initiate the acts which lead to drinking. He is starting with the stimulus to his habit. To succeed he must find some positive interest or line of action which will inhibit the drinking series and which by instituting another course of action will bring him to his desired end. In short, the man's true aim is to discover some course of action, having nothing to do with the habit of drink or standing erect, which will take him where he wants to go. The discovery of this other series is at once his means and his end. Until one takes intermediate acts seriously enough to treat them as ends, one wastes one's time in any effort at change of habits. Of the intermediate acts, the most important is the next one. The first or earliest means is the most important end to discover.

Change of attitudes is rarely achieved through scolding, admonition, punishment, but rather through the child's experiences and his desire for change when he is helped to understand the necessity for change. When the social situation is not defined, we resort to the crude and ineffectual method which Thomas calls "'ordering-and-forbidding' that is, meeting a crisis by an arbitrary act of will decreeing the disappearance of the undesirable or the appearance of the desirable phenomena, and using arbitrary physical action to enforce the decree. This method corresponds exactly to the magical phase of natural technique." On the subject of punishment, Healy and his associates observe that while no one can deny the value and the correct psychology of unpleasurable returns as a means of checking misbehaviour, and while One can hardly advocate threats or holding "a big stick" over an offender's head; yet there can be no doubt that in exceptional cases, where the delinquent does not respond to constructive and kindly effort, a vigorous warning may be of great value.

It is of much greater importance, however, that the more constructive but often neglected principle of reward and praise could be generously used to prevent delinquency. Reward and praise represent the positive aspect of treatment stimulus, the encouragement to right-doing rather than to mere repression of wrong-doing.

Undoubtedly reward as a method in reeducation has its disadvantages, since the child may become discouraged over the remoteness of the reward and the losses suffered in relapses of behaviour. Particularly dangerous is the feeling which may arise that every good deed needs to be compensated.

In Aichhorn's opinion the most valuable method of changing attitudes of wayward youth is "talking together and aiding to understand the causes and effects of maladjustments and displaying an attitude of forgiveness toward even the worst offenses. This served us [as psychoanalyst in a house for wayward youth in Austria] well because we had the confidence of the children." He cites the following case as an illustration of one method to be used in reeducation:

The Case of A. An eighteen-year-old boy, expelled from a military school for stealing from his comrades and who had stolen at home and elsewhere. After he had been with us for several months, I put him in charge of the tobacco shop. The employees each contributed a certain amount to buy their tobacco in common. I told the cashier to keep an eye on the boy without letting him know and to report to me when any money was missing. Four weeks later, he reported that about half the sum taken in weekly was missing. This seemed to be the right moment to expose the boy to an emotional shock in order to bring about catharsis, although I had no clear idea how I was going to do this. I inquired how he was getting along and gradually we approached the topic of the tobacco shop. "How much do you take in each week?" He mentioned a certain sum. We continued to dust the books. After a pause, "Does the money always come out right?" A hesitating "Yes" of which I took no further notice.

After another pause, "When do you have the most trade?" "In the morning." Then still later, "I must look in on you some time and go over your cash drawer." The boy was getting more restless all the time but I ignored it, went on working and kept coming back to the tobacco shop. When I felt that I had intensified his uneasiness sufficiently I suddenly brought the crisis to a head. "Well, when we get through here I'll go and take a look at your cash." We had been working together for about an hour and a quarter. He stood with his back to me, took a book from the shelf, and suddenly let it fall. Then I took cognizance of his excitement. "What's the matter?" "Nothing." "What's wrong with your cash?" His face became distorted with anxiety, and he stammered out the sum. Without saying a word I gave him this amount. He looked at me with an indescribable expression on his face and was about to speak. I would not let him talk because I felt that my action must have time to take effect and so I sent him away with a friendly gesture. About ten minutes later, he came back and laid the money on the table, saying "Let them lock me up. I don't deserve your help—I'll only steal again." He was greatly excited and was sobbing bitterly. I let him sit down and I began to talk to him. I did not preach, but listened sympathetically to what he poured out, his thievery, his attitude toward his family and to life in general, and everything that troubled him. The emotion gradually receded, relieved by the weeping and talking. Finally I gave the money back to him, saying that I did not believe he would steal again; that he was worth that much to me. I said too, that it was not a present, that he could smoke less and pay it back gradually. So that no one should know about this, however, he had better put the money back in the cash drawer. I told the cashier that the amount had been returned and that he need take no notice of the affair. In the course of the next two months, the money was actually returned.

It is not improbable that the contrast in emotion from fear to relief brought about the solution. Practically the treatment was effective; in the short time he stayed with us, he conducted himself well. Later he was employed as a draughtsman in a furniture factory and acquitted himself creditably. In this case we had succeeded in arousing a strong emotion in him and in making use of it in his retraining. We must wait for further experience with this method to see in which cases it is applicable as a special technique.

The Case of Arline Watkins. The case of Arline Watkins is a good illustration of how a well-established habit of stealing was overcome in a girl through kindness, confidence, provision of attractive clothes, sweets, wholesome amusements, and particularly those things for which the child had a secret longing; through fostering a sense of responsibility, a feeling of being a grown-up, and by building stronger personality traits through encouragement, response, and recognition. Gaining a new name with its implication of new personality was a powerful motive.

In this case a girl who was well on the road to becoming a "wild child," homeless, living from moment to moment, responding to every possible impulse, sustaining few of the tensions which social living requires, was converted into a responsive, adjusted well-balanced child amenable to the requirements of family life.

Petition filed in August of 1935 by the San Pedro Police Department— Juvenile Bureau. The child had been known to the Bureau on more than five separate occasions, after having been apprehended for burglary, stealing suitcases, and money; and on the occasion of the last theft of $60, her partner, a boy, was also filed on. The parents have been inefficient and disinterested; although repeatedly warned against it, they have allowed the child to roam the streets at all hours; and she had been selling newspapers. She has been described by the San Pedro Police as a "regular bandit." The neighbors have made numerous complaints to the police, who feel that nothing further can be done by their department, as the child needs supervision which cannot be given in that home. She was brought to the attention of the police several times when her uncle reported her missing. The first time she was found at midnight by the soldiers at Fort McArthur, sleeping in a truck. Later, in the company of a boy, she took a suitcase and other articles valued at $31; on the occasion of the $60 theft, she and the boy had seen a ring on a dresser through a bedroom window. He helped her open the screen, and she went in, found a wallet in the top drawer of the dresser, and took it, but did not take the ring. The boy took the wallet from her, and went to his own home. He later spent part of the money, but Arline spent none of it.

Report of Juvenile Hall Clinic

Physical Examination. General physical appearance good. Small denuded area on lower lip, probably a herpes (cold sore). Throat slightly inflamed. Temperature 100 degrees at 11 A.M. Hymen edges inflamed, but no evidences of gonorrhea. Hymen not ruptured. Wassermann negative. Smears U—negative.

Psychological Examination. Stanford-Binet. Physical age 10:6; mental age 8:4. I.Q. 79. Border-line or dull normal. Reads fairly well, but too slowly to pass the ten-year test. Very poor memory. Unable to give the day, month, or year correctly. Fails ninth-year arithmetic problems badly. Poor comprehension, necessary to repeat most questions; follows directions poorly.

Behaviour Report (from Juvenile Hall Hospital). The patient is apparently an untrained child who has grown up without constructive influences, or any environmental advantages. She seems crude and somewhat sophisticated. Has an independent manner, and has no doubt been much "on her own" without supervision. From the child's manner and statements it is inferred that she runs about as she pleases, without supervision or plans for her leisure time. Has been associated with various stealing episodes, but has ready alibis or excuses which show her incidental connection with these escapades. She has in all probability felt much deprivation in the home, has lacked satisfactions, and has reacted to this by unconsciously seeking other compensations, which have proved socially unacceptable.

Social History and Home Conditions (mother's statement). Arline and her oldest brother, Fred, are the woman's children by a former marriage. Their father died after an operation when Arline was two months old. Woman married not long afterwards, and there are three children by the second marriage. Mother's statement and Arline's agree on the stepfather's behaviour. He is continuously drinking, and very often brings drunken men into the home; demands food at all hours for himself and his drunken friends; is very ugly toward woman and children; curses a great deal; is untidy about his person and about the house; is so rough and unreasonable with the children that they dread being at home when he is there. Woman's relatives come only when they do not expect him to be there. He is suspicious of woman and often accuses her of being immoral with other men, and threatening to take the children from her, though she cannot understand why he would want them, when he is so abusive toward them. Woman has several times left her husband, but comes back on promises of good behaviour, which are never kept. She has had him before the San Pedro City Prosecutor on charges of nonsupport, but his contributions to the family's support have always been very irregular, despite his regular $75 per month income from work in the lumber yards. Spends much money on liquor, and some on other women. Mother feels helpless to cope with Arline's stealing and other bad habits.

In September, 1934, Arline was placed on probation in the home of her maternal grandmother in San Pedro, with her mother's home only a short distance away. In December, 1934, she, in company with a seven-year-old boy, entered the Richfield Warehouse, and took from the open safe $35, much of which was recovered. Further contact with all relatives showed none able to assume the responsibility. As the stepfather and mother were again living together, the child was returned to them after the hearing. In July, 1935, Arline was brought to court on a new petition. She had remained away from home the greater part of the night, in the company of three boys, aged twelve and thirteen years. The children had broken into a garage, stolen a rifle valued at $5; the same day they had broken into a store, and took canned goods valued at $5; they then went to a garage at the rear of a court, where they slept all night. However, no physical injury seems to have ever befallen the child at the hands of the boys with whom she played. She herself was more like a boy than a girl in mannerisms and behaviour. When asked once if she wasn't afraid one of the boys would hurt her sometime, she replied that they wouldn't dare so much as lay a hand on her.

At the hearing that followed the last escapades, boarding home placement was recommended and she was placed with Mrs. Florence Jones of Long Beach. She is still there, and making a very remarkable adjustment.

She is happy, and shows signs of improvement in many ways. The school reports that the child is doing as well as she is mentally capable of. The only outstanding trouble has been bed-wetting and soiling clothes, which is gradually being corrected. There has been backsliding at times, but on the whole continuous progress. She still tells some stories, and is a bit careless about her person, but there is a marked improvement. Arline has adopted the name of her foster mother, and calls herself "Arline Jones," and arranged for the school records to be changed accordingly on the approval of Mrs. Jones and the probation officer. Her mother is a little hurt by this change of name, but it seems to have had an excellent effect on Arline. She thinks of herself now as a different person, and occasionally says, "Well, when I was Arline I could do that, but since I am Arline Jones, I can't."

Interviewed Mrs. Jones, boarding mother; also Arline. Mrs. Jones states that she has had Arline with her since August, 1935, and has noticed improvement all along the line. At present, Mrs. Jones has only two girls with her, both aged thirteen years. During the past year, she has had also twò older girls, but they were there only for a short time.

Only once since her arrival has Arline been known to take anything that did not belong to her. Shortly after her arrival, the girl was visiting Mrs. Jones's married daughter, who lives near by. On this occasion, the daughter was making a quilt of some very pretty material. A few days later, a square of the material was found among Arline's personal belongings in the bedroom. When questioned, she repeatedly denied knowing anything about the material, where it came from, and how it had got into the girls' bedroom. After the foster mother had failed to get any response but denials, Mr. Jones talked with her long and earnestly, telling her how much they were trying to help her, and the trouble that comes of stealing. She seemed to be touched by his kindly manner, and cried, but still did not admit the theft. Then Mrs. Jones said, "Now, Arline, we aren't going to say anything more about this mistake that you have made. Just take the cloth and go back to the place where you got it, and lay it down where you found it. You needn't say anything at all to the lady, and she will understand." The daughter reported to her mother that little Arline entered the house and laid the material on the sewing machine, where it had been on the day of the child's visit. The incident was never again mentioned to Arline.

The little girl has been several times taken into stores by Mr. and Mrs. Jones, turned loose and told to look around at things, but to keep her hands in her pockets, if necessary, to keep from picking up things. If she saw something that she felt she had to have, and couldn't get along without, to come to them and tell them about it. If they could possibly afford to get it for her, they would; if not, they would get her as good a substitute as they could afford. On several occasions, they have had to buy for her attractive clothes that had caught her eye in stores, but the urge to steal seems to have been conquered. Temptation is removed in many ways. Fruit and the wholesome candies and sweets are kept in the house at all times, and given in moderation to the children; ice cream is frequently bought. Other things that they desire may be had as rewards of good behaviour and something to work for. The children go to shows once a week, but just recently have they been allowed to go alone in the afternoon. This they consider a great honor, and quite grown-up.

The girls' bedroom opens into the hall, and until a short time ago, it was always kept open. Now the door may be closed at night on good behaviour. If they have misbehaved, it is a sign that they are still just children, and must be watched over at night, so the door is left open. They both feel the disgrace now if the door is left open some night because of what they have done that day. Washing dishes is a special privilege.

The most persistent habit of Arline's has been bed-wetting over the entire period of her stay. Although it has decreased considerably, it has not been stopped, despite the fact that almost everything imaginable has been tried. Her physical examination shows no particular weakness that would account for it, and when she is promised some very special privilege for not wetting the bed for an entire week, she seldom does. Mrs. Jones has tried to shame her, deprived her of privileges, and talked with her about the extra work that she made her boarding mother, who was already very busy. About two weeks before the visit, Mrs. Jones, wearied and discouraged, told Arline that she was tired of continually having to wash out clothing after a thirteen- year-old girl, and that hereafter all clothing soiled by Arline would have to be washed out by Arline, and that the girl would have to take money from her savings to buy her own soap. This was a bitter ordeal, and probably hurt the boarding mother more even than the girl, who cried long and loudly while washing the clothing. But this drastic measure seemed to make her realize the amount of work that bed-wetting did cause, and the soiling of clothing has since been almost nil.

Both children go by the name of "Jones" providing that they live up to the good name of that family. They are told that the Jones family is well known and respected in the community and the children that are known as theirs must be a credit to them. They are very proud of their new name.

Children who have stolen because of an acquisitive impulse not too seriously complicated with other factors should not be deprived of their pocket money, as is frequently done, since the deprivation often gives them an added incentive to steal. It may seem paradoxical to advocate that their allowance be increased. Burt observes that "the readiest way to cure the robber is to use him with unexpected generosity; give him, not only pennies to spend, but sixpences to save and a cash box of his own to lock them in. Ownership is the best school of responsibility and faithfulness."

Older boys and girls may be given opportunities at home to earn more and more as their needs increase. If they work outside the home and earn, definite but reasonable arrangements should be made to their satisfaction as to how much should be saved, how much should be contributed to the family exchequer, and how much retained for pocket money.

Sweets, toys, clothes, amusements, special coveted articles, should be provided by adults, as far as possible, in large enough amounts to overcome any impulse to acquire them illegitimately. Where financial circumstances do not allow purchases of articles not absolutely necessary for maintenance they can be made at home. Though crude in form they may have more meaning, when properly interpreted and made with the assistance of the young, than many ready-made articles.

When a child has made a genuine attempt to conquer his habit of stealing he should be generously rewarded for it. The reward is more than a material gain; it also means heightening his status and self-respect.

Methods of Dealing with Lies. The act of lying is not the chief concern of the case worker. His real concern should be "Why did the person lie?" It is often a healthy thing to ask oneself: "What have I done to cause the offender to lie to me or to be afraid of me?" It seems almost too trite to repeat that the basis for lying, as for other unadjustments, can be traced to other more fundamental and deeper underlying causal factors. Few people lie simply for the sake of lying. At times, no lie is intended. The person may possess only partial knowledge of facts; he may have a tendency to generalize too broadly. His memory might have tricked him or he may have made the wrong mental associations.

If the worker is concerned chiefly with personalities, the products of psychological metabolism, he will be interested in the inconsistency of the account only in so far as it indicates that the offender has or has not fully revealed his attitudes. Professor Lindeman remarks:

Even if the answers are false, they may serve to define the ultimate conclusions. In fact, the psychiatrist who makes inquiries of his subject does not anticipate true replies, but he nevertheless makes use of such responses as he receives. What is in a person's "mind" may or may not be true but it is the sum total of his rationalizations upon which his life has proceeded. If he acts upon the basis of these rationalizations, they are in so far significant in explaining his behaviour.

The interviewer must distinguish between (1) lies as defense mechanisms; (2) pathoformic lies; (3) conventional lies or so-called white lies; (4) lies due to mental conflict; (5) seeming lies which arise in differences in point of view regarding matters; (6) accidental lies, due to tricks of memory, illusions; (7) lies due to a desire to control the situation. Professor Cooley says:

Even telling the truth does not result so much from a need of mental accuracy, though this is strong in some minds, as from a sense of the unfairness of deceiving people of our own sort, and of the shame of being detected in so doing. Consequently the maxim, "Truth for friends and lies for enemies," is very generally followed, not only by savages and children, but, more or less openly, by civilized people. Most persons feel reluctant to tell a lie in so many words, but few have any compunctions in deceiving by manner, and the like, persons toward whom they feel no obligation. "Conscience is born of love" in this as in many matters. A thoughtful observer will easily see that injustice and not untruth is the essence of lying, as popularly conceived.

Aichhorn states that no child is absolutely trustworthy, so we must weigh his statements carefully:

We do not yet know whether he told the truth. The statements of delinquents should always be checked. However, when we catch a child in a lie, we should not shame him. Expressions such as "You lie," "You must tell the truth," should always be avoided. It is much more efficacious to act as if the child had made a mistake. We can say, for example, "Are you sure you meant what you said?", "Now think a minute," or "Take your time; tell me again," etc.

Cyril Burt has given a very comprehensive discussion of the analysis of children's lies and their prevention:

The telling of untruths is a frequent reproach, not only against habitual delinquents, but also against children not otherwise unprincipled. "One of my pupils is an incorrigible story-teller. What am I to do with him?" The appeal is a common one, and the first reply is another question: "What kind of stories does he tell?" Children's falsehoods are of many forms, and the treatment differs with the type. ... Here it is not with moral but with psychological distinctions that we have to do. Classed by their underlying causes, we may recognize at least six or seven varieties, all broadly distinguishable, yet running imperceptibly the one into the other.

1. There is, first, what may be named the playful lie. Tiny children are full of make-believe: "Let's pretend"

is their favourite game, and much of their amusement owes its charm to a passing or a partial self-deception.

2. There is, secondly, the lie of confusion. Children are exceedingly suggestible. They see little disparity between a fact that is real and a fancy that is vivid. What they have genuinely witnessed gets easily jumbled in their minds with what they have simply imagined or what they have merely been told. All such misstatements are to be dealt with for what they really are accidental errors or illusions and not downright untruths....
3. "The lie of vanity." Lies designed to attract self-notice. Such lies may range all the way from the empty but straightforward boasting of the braggart boy, to the subtler and more highly colored romances of the self-centered semi-neurotic, sensation-mongering girl; they merge, at an older stage still, into the baseless complaints of persecution or illness made by the truly hysterical. They express wishes, not perceptions, and are frequently the impulsive utterance of fancies that have long been dwelt upon in daydreams. The most morbid form consists in false self-accusations, in the bogus confession of imaginary misdeeds that have been neither performed nor intended.
4. Graver still are lies where the object is not to extol or magnify one-self, but to belittle, annoy, or even endanger another the lie of malevolence and revenge. Where a serious charge is falsely laid, the outcome may be tragical. Sometimes the persons so traduced are the very ones who have been nearest and dearest to the child. Sometimes, too, the statement—not infrequently an accusation of a sexual assault seems so foreign to the thoughts of a healthy child and the childish denouncer herself seems so guileless, plausible, and innocent, that credence is given at once without inquiry. As a rule,

after careful exploration, some analogous experience in the past, hidden or half forgotten, can generally be brought to light, and may be shown to have provided a basis for the calumny, though the doings or sayings recollected have been fastened, for private and malignant motives, upon a person entirely guiltless.

5. In most of the foregoing examples, harmless and heinous alike, the child is often self-deceived as well as deceiving. In the excusive or exculpatory lie, the child is acutely conscious of deception. The purpose is usually plain.

   There is something done or something left undone for which the dissembler is anticipating blame. Such lies, in the main, are not constructive fictions but negative disavowals or denials. Most thieves lie to cover up their wrongdoings, and nearly every offender will perjure himself over the offenses which with him are most habitual or for which he has been constantly condemned. But even among the honest and obedient, there are few who have not upon occasion proffered a false explanation for being late, for forgetting an errand, or for breaking a cherished vase.

6. In the more hardened and unprincipled, the positive line is exploited no longer as a fear-stricken excuse, but as an audacious pretext—no longer to shirk punishment, for what is past, but to gain profit or pleasure in the near future. Cheating at games and at lessons is the commonest and perhaps the least objectionable form of what may be termed the selfish lie. Where the lie is deliberately manufactured as an instrument to some further offense, the practice becomes more reprehensible. "Mother says will you please lend her a penny for the gas meter," is a favourite ruse for fraudulently obtaining a coin. The begging tales of the young delinquent are, as we have

noted, at times most elaborately woven, and the wiles of the juvenile swindler are often miracles of ingenuity. One curious feature, making it harder than ever to detect the lie and to visit justice upon the liar, is to be found in a result well recognized, namely, that the habitual imposter may lose all sense that he is simulating and grow to believe implicitly in the truth of his inventions. Frequently he is himself his own most perfect dupe.

7. Lies of loyalty and convention are not uncommon among older children. In the elementary school the spirit of a sportsmanlike comradeship which prevents one child betraying another to an elder is not so general as in the public school, and everywhere it seems rarer among girls than among boys and older youths. To keep up a joint or completed lie is much easier for male conspirators than for female. To girlish lips it is the lie courteous rather than the lie of allegiance that comes with greatest readiness.

Conventions differ greatly in different social classes, and just as the poorer classes are sometimes shocked by what seem to them the shams and hypocrisies of their betters, so the so-called better classes regard as indefensible untruths and shameless falsehoods what are no more than traditional tactics tactics quite justifiable in the eyes of the humble diplomats themselves, when they feel themselves confronted by an inquisitive stranger from an alien social sphere.

Lying, then, takes countless shapes and has a thousand different motives. It may be employed to compensate for almost any form of intellectual weakness. It may be inspired by almost any emotion by fear more than any other, but also by greed, anger, self-display, submissiveness, and even by mistaken loyalty and affection.

1. Differential Treatment. In dealing with a particular lie uttered by a particular child, the first step is to ascertain whether that lie is a single isolated lapse or one of a numerous series; if the latter, it becomes important to inquire what type of lies he generally tells and what may be their animating motive. One lie does not make a liar. All children tell occasional untruths, and many have fits and periods of dissembling. The sense of systematic truthfulness comes late.

Different forms of falsehood call for very different remedies. As a rule, what has to be attacked is not the lying, but some deeper trouble in the background, and this may vary from child to child. To treat the lie as a simple, self-subsistent mode of perversity, to scold and castigate the liar each time he is found out, will seldom purge him of his tricks; it will only teach him a sharper cunning for the future. Accordingly, the basis of every lie must be explored before the lie itself is dealt with.

2. Avoid Provocative Occasions. Both the incipient and the habitual liar must be protected from situations setting too great a tax on their intelligence and candor. A regular thief who has been as regularly punished for his thefts should never be questioned as the sole source of information and thus presented with a gratuitous chance to tell yet another untruth. So far as possible, all lies must be immediately detected; the first exculpatory falsehood that a child happens to palm off with success is often the starting point of a long series of deceptions, each cooler and more calculated than the last. Never let the child see you are uncertain whether he is speaking the truth or not. Rather throw the uncertainty to him; let the blusterer feel puzzled whether you may not be laughing at him in your heart for a bluff so silly and transparent. Equip yourself beforehand with conclusive evidence; never challenge him on the strength of pure suspicion, trusting, from a downcast head, a stammer or a blush, a shifting eye, or a brazen stare, to detect his consciousness of guilt. Should you, indeed, be doubtful allow him the doubt's benefit, accepting what he says with punctilious civility, just as you would accept the statements of an equal. Treat the deceiver just as though he were trustworthy and you may shame him out of his deceit. Grant him, therefore, the fullest credit for every particle of fact his fabrications may contain, with the dictum of the practiced charlatan always in mind.

3. Confession. No punishment should follow a confession. To extort an admission publicly, in the face of the whole class or in front of the injured party, is to make that admission insuperably hard and a shuffle irresistibly easy. As a means of eliciting facts, the practice of urging a clean breast of things should be abandoned.

It is amazing how almost every teacher and parent expect the most hardened little sinners still to tell the truth about their sins—as if a lie were the last and worst offense the child could fall to instead of the easiest and the first. Should a child be bad enough to steal, he is almost certain to be bad enough to equivocate about his theft, when taxed with it outright. And once he has begun to delude you, a barrier is set up and any free and friendly discussion about his general situation becomes all but impossible. In the rare case of a frank or voluntary avowal, the outlook is most hopeful. With the remainder, it should be almost an unbroken rule never to begin with a direct interrogation—"Did you or did you not take that sixpence?" For thus asking the child to own to his undisclosed misdeeds, there is but one justification; it might be put to the culprit in such terms as these, though it is better expressed by an attitude than by an argument; "You and I have been friends hitherto. We can remain friends no longer if you are conscious of misleading me and I am conscious of mistrusting you. Let us each be unreserved and open, so that we may start afresh on the same happy basis as before. I am asking you to tell the truth, not because I am too lazy or too stupid to get decisive proof myself, much less I am asking you to bear witness against yourself that I may then reproach and punish you. My only motive is that I may understand you better. Friends have no secrets from each other not even shameful ones. And if everybody lied to everybody else, society would be impossible and all intimacy poisoned." At times in seeking a confidence it is wise to disarm a possible dread beforehand by saying, plainly and explicitly: "You need not answer if you do not wish ..."

The utmost discretion must be used as to when to expect an acknowledgement of guilt. Demand it too soon, and the agitated conscience, all eager to disown the misdeed even to itself, may be hustled into a lie it never for one moment meant to tell. Defer it too long, and the child may feel that, after all, the blame has not been brought home to him, and in reply to some more hasty questioner, he may have committed himself to a denial already and may not think it too late to retract.

4. The Encouragement of Confidence. With young children truthfulness is at first no more than loyalty to persons, a return of gratitude to those who are sympathetic and kind to their mothers, to their favourite teachers, to their closest companions and friends. Children, like savages, feel that frankness and candor are precious gifts, pledges of affection, to be bestowed upon near and understanding comrades, and that a stranger, or an elder, or a representative of authority, is a sort of impersonal or potential enemy, an alien and a spy, with no title to the free exchange of confidence, an inquisitor whose entrapping questions are rightly countered with an equal craft.

Should any form of rebuke or punishment seem necessary the best measure is not to stigmatize the child to his face as a liar, nor yet to thrash him there and then, much less to expatiate on how lie has pained you: it is rather to cur or cold-shoulder him (as you might any adult acquaintance whom you found dishonourable) until of his own accord he resolves to prove himself worthier of your trust and credence.

5. Literary Instruction. With the young fabulist who is telling himself or others extravagant romances because his own life is so limited and dull, the best course is to enlarge and enrich his range of actual experiences. Let him learn that truth may be more thrilling and more entrancing, as well as stranger, than fiction. Travel, school journeys, visits to places of interest, will give him authentic matter to relate. With older children the over-active imagination may be given its needful grist through good fiction, good poetry and good romance.

6. Scientific Instruction. Crude homilies on the sinfulness of lying are of small avail, and to cite the fate of Ananias may create more harm than holiness. The child should be led to understand what a baffling thing it is to formulate the precise and literal truth. The task of the truth teller is two-fold, first to know, and then to express. Each is a science in itself.

To the youthful mind, an ounce of scientific instruction and of linguistic practice is far more helpful and wholesome than any quantity of high-flown narrative or of trite and tedious moralizing.

7. The Avoidance of Pious Figments. Finally, if you wish the child to tell no lies to you, have a scrupulous care to tell no fables to the child. Myths about Father Christmas, the all-seeing Eye, the origin of babies, and the riddle of the sex, should never be offered as facts to the young and sensitive inquirer. The strongest shock may ensue when the child finds out that those whom he thought impeccable have told him tales about the most solemn of mysteries, and it is no more than a natural reaction should he start fabricating lies and legends of his own.

8. Pathological Lying. Both Healy and Burt maintain that pathological liars are rare. Pathological lying, says Healy, is falsification entirely disproportionate to any discernible end in view, engaged in by a person who, at the time of observation, cannot definitely be declared insane, feeble-minded, or epileptic. Such lying rarely, if ever, centers about a single event; although exhibited in very occasional cases for a short time, it manifests itself most frequently by far over a period of years, or even a life time. It represents a trait rather than an episode.

At times workers will spend considerable time in checking and verifying information, or in attempts to change a person's attitude, in having him follow a particular course of action only to discover that they have been deceived at each step. While persistent and pathological liars are comparatively rare, they present perplexing problems, which, if undetected, will cause much concern and loss of time.

There is little that the general worker can do with pathological liars. They are subjects for psychiatrists and psychologists. However, he must be able to recognize the pathological liar and not waste time nor delay getting the patient into competent medical hands.

9. Redefinition of the Social Situation. The cases of Milton M. and Dora J. are illustrations of successful treatment through rather striking redefinition of the social situation and vision of the workers handling the cases.

10. Case Study of Milton M. Petition filed in behalf of Milton, fourteen years of age, arrested in company with another boy his own age. They admitted they had pulled a fire-alarm box at a given address on a certain date. These boys also admitted breaking the glass in three other fire boxes in that vicinity recently. The petition stated also that the Fire Department reported numerous false alarms coming in from that particular locality. The filing was made under Sub-division 13, of the Juvenile Court Law of California and charged specifically Malicious Mischief. The boys were held in custody in Juvenile Hall.

Probation Officer's first call on Milton at Juvenile Hall found him readily admitting participation in this mischievous habit, telling of such activities covering a large area over a long period of time in the section of the city in which he lived. He even boasted of being the leader of a gang that specialized in false alarms.

11. Family Cooperation. Milton is an American-born Italian boy; his parents had been born in Italy. A call on them found them ready and willing to cooperate in any manner of probation. The parents believed that it was more than a year previous when their younger children had first come to them with the story of Milton's breaking the glass in a fire box. They stated they had questioned him from time to time but the boy had always denied any wrongdoing.

The Juvenile Hall Clinic next reported that a physical examination showed the boy well developed, nutrition poor, twelve pounds underweight, jerking movements of muscles, tonsils large, especially left, pus in posterior nasopharynx, adhesions of foreskin to gland, puberty pro, marked course tremor of finger; Wasserman negative. The psychological examination showed physical age of 14:6, mental age of 11:6, giving an I.Q. of 79, dull normal or borderline; just misses twelve-year vocabulary (Italian spoken at home); poor in linguistic (verbal) type of test; successful in arithmetic induction and reasoning (fourteen-year level); quiet, rather indifferent effort, gives up quickly with a shrug of shoulders. The recommendation from the Clinic was for a tonsillectomy and intensive feeding.

12. School Report. Showed the boy to have a good attendance and by an Otis primary intelligence test given a year previous, the boy had received an I.Q. of 77; his marks for all twelve subjects he was studying at school were all twos and threes with the exception of spelling, in which he received a four; his behaviour was reported as quick-tempered, sulky, inclined to "pass the buck"; was frequently reported for quarreling, impertinence, and failure to do his work; gives up easily when task is rather difficult. The school reported the parents as being cooperative.

13. Process of Treatment. Milton was released from Juvenile Hall and taken home to await the hearing in court.

At this time the father stated the boy practiced masturbation and that probably this was the cause for his trouble, and the mother added that Milton was a bed-wetter and she thought this might be the cause of his trouble. Just as probation officer was leaving the house a policeman came to the door to ask if he might come in and talk to Milton. There had been reports of two more false fire alarms having been turned in on the night previous in that district but Milton had been in Juvenile Hall.

In court Milton's story was heard, and the boy was duly admonished. He was declared a ward of the court and was instructed as to just what would be expected of him in the future. It was further ordered that arrangements be made for an operation for tonsillectomy and circumcision. Those physical adjustments were made in due time but on account of the boy's great fear of doctors the final winning of Milton over to having the operations performed would make a story in itself.

Now started the period of supervision. In nine days Milton had pulled another box. He denied his guilt to the police but later admitted to the probation officer that it had been he. This particular box had been pulled at 10:30 P.M., the streets had been slippery from a rainy afternoon although the night was clear and I remembered having read a newspaper account of how a serious accident had been narrowly averted between a fire truck and a privately owned machine. It took three days to get the boy to admit his guilt, so on the evening of the third day Milton and myself were at the fire station for a confidential chat with the captain. Almost an hour was spent in telling the boy of the hazards of sending the fire department on "wild goose chases," of the many dangers to the traveling public when the big machines rolled out on a rainy night; the cost to the city for these extra runs; the wear and tear on the nervous systems of the firemen, getting up and dressing two and three times and sometimes more, a night, for no good reason at all. The boy had been very favorably impressed with this friendly chat. Two days later he had written in school what he remembered about the talk He seemed to have remembered all the high points of the visit. One week later, however, Milton was caught by an alert policeman pulling another box while three of his companions looked on.

Again Milton was told what persistent antisocial conduct could lead to. Then it was proposed to him to become a fireman himself. Milton seemed to be interested in becoming a fireman, but was wondering how he was to become one, and when. Part of the next day was spent in telling the plan to the parents and getting their full cooperation. It was decided that the boy actually thought enough of his home so that the contemplated action would not cause him to run away. So, with everything ready, three nights later the cure began. The probation officer called at the home at 11:00 P.M. The father went with him to the boy's bed; he looked very comfortable and snug and in two minutes time he was out of bed and being hurried to a greater speed at dressing. Once outside he at last came to life and asked where we were going. "To a fire," was the casual answer, but when we got there it appeared the alarm had been false.

This period lasted for five and one-half weeks; an average of two calls a week were made. On four occasions two calls were made in one evening; on one particular good night we got in three calls. When more than one call was made in an evening, just enough time was given the boy to get nicely snuggled back under the warm covers between the first and second call. It might be said that extreme caution was always used not to expose the boy to any dangerous draft or otherwise harm his health. The boy never had to be forced out of the house after he was once up and dressed.

At the end of two weeks it was hoped that Milton might ask for a truce. However, he lasted the five and one-half weeks; the last night of the probation officer's call, Milton had established his sleeping quarters under the bed rather than upon the top under the covers. When he was under the bed he came out on his knees and with considerable emotion fervently begged to be discharged from the fire department; he would never molest another fire-alarm box, and he added that he would see to it personally that none of his gang ever did either. He further promised he would study at school; that he would obey at home and stay in nights.

These promises were all voluntary on Milton's part. It was then he announced with thanks and offered to me as an inducement to cease the treatment the fact that the many trips up at night had caused him to overcome the habit of bed-wetting.

Milton was taken at his word and evidently he meant what he said. At the end of the year his case was dismissed. He made good in much less than that time. He had likewise helped several others to make good. There has never been any further trouble with false fire alarms in that neighbourhood.

A probation officer must have not only considerable imagination and power to win the parents' cooperation, but he must also be deeply in love with his job to undertake a series of nocturnal visitations to the home of a boy and wild-goose chases to reputed fires.

The Case of Dora J., eighteen years of age, senior in high school, has run away from home, secured work as mother's helper in a near-by town, enrolled in the local high school and refuses not only to see her mother and to return home, but to have her mother visit her.

Dora was legally adopted as a small child by Mrs. J., once a well-to-do woman. Dora knows of her adoption but says that she "has no feelings on the matter," but "is violently opposed to her mother because she would not let the girl out of her sight, insisted on sleeping with the girl in the same bed, interfered with all of her interests and activities." The girl accuses the mother of "cruelty to one husband who was driven away from home, and to another who was driven to his grave"; of making a "mess of her business affairs," and of ruining "her life as well as Dora's." She repeated that her mother was cruel, unethical, un-Christian.

The tensions and conflicts between the daughter, who had little opportunity to participate in normal situations, and an overanxious mother are intense and of long standing. Even in her new environment the girl was "unable to forget the treatment at the hands of that neurotic, un-Christian like woman," and continued to be moody, hard to deal with, and at times even desperate when her mother tried to communicate with her. An interview with the mother substantiated all of the statements Dora made regarding her and convinced of the impossibility of any rapid or drastic changes in her.

Dora's health broke down, unable to stand the strain of the conflict and unaccustomed housework. It was necessary to remove her to a rest home, but she applied for relief rather than to accept any help from her mother. Relief was given pending investigation, and considerable attention was given to the medical aspects of the case.

The girl was hard to manage at the rest home because of her morbidity, threats to commit suicide, irregularity of eating. She changed rest homes every few weeks, which created additional irritations and seriously undermined her morale.

It is obvious that in order to work out any permanent plan for Dora a great deal more information must be secured regarding the adoptive parents, the real parents, Dora herself, her health, her relations with other people, and a host of other things. However, the immediate problem facing us calls for some immediate treatment to prevent complete demoralization and physical breakdown.

Dora found life too hard; her antagonism to the mother was at least partially justified, but the girl could not divorce herself from her past and could not create a different social environment even though she was separated from her mother. It was obvious that little could be expected of the older woman which the younger one would recognize as love for her own sake. It is necessary then to arouse, if not genuine affection, tolerance and Christian charity in the girl. A picture was painted of the mother's state of mind and emotions and of what was expected of an ideal daughter under such difficult circumstances.

Since Dora had rather well-formed conceptions of ethics and Christian principles, repeated appeals were made to her to aid her mother, who was unfortunate enough to be left all alone and unable to change her ways because of advancing age and undermined health. Dora's tendencies to self-pity were turned into constructive outgoing energy toward another human being, and the attention on self was converted into a relationship demanding sacrifice and charity. It was not planned for Dora to return home but in order to remove the mental conflict the girl had to acquire a different definition of the whole situation.

❑❑❑

6

Theories and Behavioural Approaches for Social Work

Introduction

Much of the work on learning theory early in this century which provided the theoretical basis for the behavioural approach seems in retrospect a dangerous abridgement of how people learn behaviours. Early attempts at treatment were cold and detached: a paper from the 1940s entitled 'Operant conditioning of a vegetative human organism' captures the harsh language behaviourists routinely employed. The token economy programmes of the 1950s and 1960s cast psychiatric nurses as behavioural engineers; crude implementation of reward and punishment schemes often had to do more with control over a resident population than individual treatment. Further, the pronounced antagonism from some behaviourists toward homosexuality revealed a rigid attitude toward sexual identity.

But that is not the whole picture. In the last ten years a more pragmatic behavioural approach has begun to emerge, one more sensitive to user choice and partnership. Learning theory has continued to evolve; it now takes account of mind and language as important shapers of behaviour and is more frequently found integrated with systems and interactional theory.

There are four broad characteristics of the behavioural approach. First, behaviour is viewed as functional for the individual, including behaviour which is excessive, challenging or poorly adapted to the social environment. The approach therefore rejects a disease model in which behaviour is seen as a symptom of a deeper disturbance. Second, it concentrates on specific and observable behaviour of the present rather than looking for psychological roots in the past. Third, intervention is aimed at change and must provide opportunities to learn other behaviours. Undesirable behaviours are part of a continuum; they are learned and therefore can be unlearned. Fourth, the approach is held accountable through a strong commitment to evaluating the effectiveness of specific techniques. This accountability introduces a dynamic factor into the behavioural approach which aspires to improved effectiveness.

Learning theory, which underpins the behavioural approach, is a set of assumptions about how people learn behaviour. From the outset in the United States in the early part of this century it employed a language that tried to imitate the natural sciences with words like stimulus, response, conditioning, extinction. Much of this language, developed in relation to laboratory work with animals, is still employed by behaviourists. But while the original terminology has remained it now embraces a wider, more complex range of phenomena and thus is easily misunderstood. Stimulus, for instance, can refer among other things to an event, a sound, words, a sensory experience, verbal rules, another person's behaviour.

The early learning theorists invariably began their work with animals from which they discovered their central premise: a rat's pleasure in finding food, or in escaping from confinement, would teach it to repeat the behaviour that achieved that end. Conversely, it would learn to avoid behaviour that brought about unpleasant consequences.

Learning theorists endeavoured to transfer such insights to the human world. The American J.B. Watson was among the most zealous. He saw all human behaviour entirely in terms of conditioned experiences:

Give me a dozen healthy infants, well-formed, and my own specified world to bring them up in and I'll guarantee to take any one at random and train him to become any type of specialist I might select doctor, lawyer, artist regardless of his talents, penchants, abilities, vocations, and race of his ancestors.

Watson popularized a version of classical conditioning which the Russian psychologist Pavlov discovered in relation to animals: he succeeded in inducing a phobia of rats in 18-month-old 'little Albert' by repeatedly putting a rat in the boy's playpen and simultaneously banging a four foot long steel bar behind the boy's head with a hammer.

His doctrine radically downgraded the importance of both the mind and the emotions in shaping behaviour. Although he was criticized at the time by more flexible, indeed interesting behaviourists such as E.C. Tolman, for 'muscle twitchism', Watson exerted an enormous influence. He wrote a best seller on rearing children, and left his mark on, among others, Bertrand Russell and Aldous Huxley in *Brave New World*. Eventually he left his university post in the 1920s to join a New York advertising firm for $70,000, then a fabulous sum of money.

The notion of pairing stimuli, however, did in time provide one of the major techniques of behavioural psychotherapy called systematic desensitization whereby the therapist takes a person suffering from anxiety or phobia through a relaxation routine at the same time as imagining or being exposed in actuality to the anxiety provoking source.

B.F. Skinner's influence has been more substantial than any other theorist. From the 1930s to the 1960s his version of behaviourism dominated the field. Skinner was interested in voluntary behaviour. From his many experiments with pigeons he reached the conclusion that most behaviour is developed and modified by its consequences. He called this 'operant' behaviour because it operates on the environment. Consequences that cause behaviours to increase he called 'reinforcers' and those that cause behaviours to decrease 'punishers'. By studying animal behaviour in relation to these twin forces he believed he had discovered a universal law of 'operant conditioning'.

His insight that the consequences of particular behaviours guide a person's future behaviour was profound and pervasive. Several key concepts developed from this thinking. 'Negative reinforcement' refers to a process in which the removal of an unpleasant stimulus (i.e. a thing, activity, other person's behaviour) will increase the probability that the behaviour which brought about that removal will be repeated. Skinner also thought that if a response is reinforced every time it occurs, the behaviour will quickly revert when that reinforcement stops. On the other hand, behaviour inconsistently or 'partially' reinforced is more likely to persist a principle of which gamblers are all too aware.

By the 1960s, however, psychologists were beginning to acknowledge that learning behaviour was a more complex process than simply through the reinforcing or punishing of specific behaviours. What was obvious to common sense gradually became apparent to learning theorists, although by no means all: the power of the mind in shaping behaviour could no longer be ignored.

The acquisition of language was one area where there was considerable dispute. Behaviourists like Skinner seemed to be saying that language was learned as other physical behaviours through a process of cumulative reinforcement. Anti-behaviourists, such as the linguist Noam Chomsky, pointed out that life was not long enough for the process to happen in this way.

In the 1970s learning theorists split into different orientations and are now fragmented into largely irreconcilable camps. Alongside unreconstructed Skinnerians are cognitive behaviourists such as Meichenbaum who saw behaviour shaped by thoughts, images, internal verbal statements and self-instructions. Social learning theorists, such as Albert Bandura, emphasized that learning behaviour is a social act, acquired through modelling, imitation and observation.

The history of learning theory, then, is one of coming to terms with its own early rigidities. The nature of reinforcement changed from being a factor which essentially elicits and strengthens a behaviour in an automatic way, to one which serves principally as an informant in deciding a course of action. Self-reinforcement and notions of self-efficacy, achievement and symbolic satisfactions were finally acknowledged as important factors in individual behaviour. Bandura wrote, 'Humans do not simply respond to stimuli: they interpret them.'

By the 1980s the time of universal psychological theories such as Skinner's, accounting for all behaviour, thought and emotion, was probably over. Psychologists were increasingly looking at the mind as consisting of a large number of independent systems which operate in parallel, with each specifically keyed to a certain kind of information and governing certain kind of behaviours and competences. The most convincing work in learning theory now is found in the form of behavioural mini-theories which aim to account for specific sets of problems but do not claim universal status. Gerald Patterson's work, elegantly interweaving social learning, systems and interactional theories, is one example of a pragmatic but carefully measured attempt to explain the familial conditions in which aggression in young boys is shaped over time.

Despite the limitations of learning theory a behavioural social work practice has developed over the last twenty-five years with a number of distinctive elements to it. A behavioural *assessment* begins with an exploration of problems. It is important to resist the temptation to identify obvious deficits in behaviour of particular individuals as the source of problems. Increasingly the approach recognizes that users, parents or other family members and advocates have the primary interest in defining problems. Assessment is not a question of professional analysis but ultimately one of values, prioritizing those the resolution of which will contribute most to improving a person's quality of life.

Once a problem has been prioritized it is imperative to generate possible solutions, and if particular behaviours are acknowledged by clients, cares or family members as requiring change in order to resolve a designated problem, some element of a behavioural intervention may be indicated. This phase of the assessment is not complete until a target behaviour is specified: what it is, who is doing it, the conditions under which the person is expected to perform that behaviour, and whether it is to be increased or decreased.

It is critical to establish a *baseline* the rate at which the specific behaviour occurs before intervention. Different methods are used for taking such measurements: self-reports, the observation of those living with or working with the client, or by direct observation by the practitioner. Measuring a behaviour requires defining that behaviour accurately, deciding who will do the observing and ensuring that person has the skills to observe and record accurately. The more minute the selected behaviour, for example eye contact between an autistic child and an adult, the more complex the job of measuring becomes.

Whatever the means the measurement should be quantified. Usually the results are expressed in graph form with the number of occurrences of the target behaviour plotted on the vertical axis and the time span (usually the number of days or hours) of observation plotted along the horizontal axis. Of course measurement continues after a programme has begun; the whole point of establishing a baseline is to measure any subsequent progress in either diminishing or increasing a particular behaviour.

The final element of a behavioural assessment is *functional analysis* which attempts to discover the purpose that a particular behaviour serves for an individual. A person may engage in two behaviours that seem very different for example, self-injury and aggression but analysis may show that they serve a similar purpose. The individual employs the problematic behaviour in order to meet certain needs or desires. Although viewed as challenging, self-injurious or anti-social by other persons, the fact that it is used by the individual at a high rate suggests that it is a reasonably effective strategy in that environment. Functional analysis looks to answer the question why or how a behaviour makes sense to the individual and how its purpose may be achieved by an alternative behaviour.

The purpose of functional analysis is to track those factors which shape a particular behaviour. Behaviourists often refer to an 'A-B-C' analysis: noting the *antecedents,* that is the events or circumstances which preceded the behaviour which may act as triggers; the intensity and duration of the *behaviour* itself; and the *consequences* of that behaviour. The standard way of recording this information is through an 'ABC' chart which simply logs the information under each heading in parallel columns. In practice the observer's recording begins when the selected behaviour is observed. Then careful note is made of all consequences of that behaviour with a view to isolating those consequences that act as reinforcers. The last step is to recall what was happening when the person engaged in the selected behaviour, for example the actions of a care or family member, the setting of a task, the entrance of another person into the room, or a sensory stimulation.

Since behavioural assessment can be rigorous and time consuming, pragmatic judgements have to be made regarding duration, complexity and choice of personnel. Take as an example the assessment of a 4-year-old child who has been referred for behaviour problems. It typically begins with an interview with the parents to establish what behaviours the child is showing and how these are a problem. This is done in as descriptive a way as possible avoiding unclear phrases, such as 'hyperactive' or 'he misbehaves', which are inferential and open to varied, even conflicting interpretation. Some of the possible determinants of the behaviour would be looked at in conjunction with the parents such as the type and extent of parental involvement with the child and their attitude to giving reward and punishment.

As part of the process of problem definition and establishing a baseline of target behaviours parents would complete a rating scale which quantifies both the intensity of behaviours and the degree of distress these cause. One of the most common is the Eyberg Child Behaviour Inventory which asks the parent to record how often the child displays a number of specific problem behaviours, such as refusing to follow a command until threatened with punishment, on a scale from 1 (never) to 7 (always). It also asks which of these behaviours are a problem for the parent.

Some direct observation by the practitioner of the parents playing with the child over a period of between 30 and 60 minutes may also be required. This could involve three components: parents letting the child take the lead in play activity, parents asking the child to play with something else, and parents asking the child to put the toys away. Of particular interest is the parents' use of warning, the kind of commands issued, the use of threats and sanctions for non-compliance and rewards for compliance.

A behavioural assessment of a person with severe learning difficulties would be very different. Greater emphasis may be placed on functional analysis to determine what purpose a particular behaviour has for the individual and whether there are alternative behaviours or skills that could achieve the same end more effectively. Family members, members of staff and others who have frequent contact with the individual may have ideas as to what the specific behaviour achieves and these need to be explored. Some form of trial and error with the setting may be required to discover what the behaviour is actually trying to signal.

For example, after 15 minutes of work at a particular task a man begins yelling and throwing materials on the floor and then runs away. This may be because he has tired of the task and lost self-control, or because the task is too difficult, or because he dislikes someone he is working with. Assessment often highlights a reciprocity between problem behaviours and more effective behaviours; once the function of a behaviour is established a programme which provides an alternative way of achieving the same objective may be builtup.

Behavioural *intervention* seeks to modify selected behaviours or to teach new behaviours using techniques based on learning theory.

The simplest way to increase particular behaviours, according to operant procedures, is to reinforce the person engaging in that behaviour. A reinforcer can be something tangible, such as toys, trips, preferred activities, preferred foods, or intangible such as attention, praise, a hug, personal satisfaction, increased effectiveness.

A reinforcer may be particular to the individual and not at all resemble the stereotypical 'reward'. For instance, behaviours performed at a higher rate can be used to reinforce those performed at a lower rate on the assumption that a frequently performed behaviour is sufficiently attractive to the individual to act as a reinforcer. By definition a reinforcer is whatever increases the likelihood that the behaviour which it follows will be performed again. Most behavioural interventions are built on the systematic use of reinforcers to increase desired behaviours and the occasional use of low-level punishers such as time out. In behavioural language this is called 'contingency management'.

If reinforcing desirable behaviours is the cornerstone of behaviour modification it is also the source of the controversy that has raged over the approach since its inception. There is increasing sensitivity within the field that reinforcers should represent typical and natural consequences that are generally available in the individual's environment and that they must be appropriate in terms of age, gender and culture. Understanding what constitutes an appropriate reinforcer, one that is considered worth working for by the individual concerned, requires careful analysis in its own right. Any reinforcement should be made immediately after the selected behaviour, consistently applied and given with conviction. From this basic operant procedure a number of other techniques follow.

The concept of *shaping* means reinforcing approximate attempts at performing a selected behaviour, and subsequently reinforcing those efforts which more closely conform to the final desired behaviour. *Chaining* means reinforcing completion of parts of a more complex behaviour such as a skill, task or activity, until the entire chain of components are linked together in a continuous behaviour. Forward chaining begins with the first component, linking further training to its successful completion. Backward chaining begins with the final component first and works backwards towards the beginning of the sequence. It is generally regarded as more effective because it uses the consequence of completion as a reinforcement in its own right.

Other techniques flow from social learning theory and are less concerned with manipulating the environment around the individual than teaching specified skills that bring at least partial mastery of that environment. The principal technique is *modelling:* a person who has already mastered a particular skill demonstrates it for another who wishes to learn the same response. The sequence can be as complex or as simple as required.

Modelling combined with chaining is commonly used to master a broad range of self-help and social skills, from basic tasks such as purchasing items in a shop, to handling more complex social situations such as interviews. A successful programme depends on breaking the skill into component parts through *task analysis*, and providing rehearsal and feedback to the person as each component is tried. The objective is a form of stimulus control where the completion of one component acts as a cue to begin the next component.

In practice interventions take on very different constructions. As an example of the slow and painstaking work often involved, Hemsley and Carr have outlined a programme for a young boy with learning difficulties who is hyperkinetic and unable to sit still for even a few minutes. It is impossible to teach him any constructive activities such as doing puzzles, to sit for meals, or to learn toilet training. His speech is non-existent. The first stage is to set an appropriate behavioural goal, one that is both realistic and which those in daily contact with the boy primarily teachers and parents can agree on. They agree on a goal that is modest but attainable: to have the boy sit still for one minute and listen to instructions. Upon this other behaviour can be built. Reinforcers are chosen that are attractive enough to override the boy's continuous motion. The boy is then taught sitting. In a room free of other distractions he is asked to sit down and then held and seated on the chair. Immediately he is praised and given a crisp and a cuddle. The process continues in short sessions of no more than ten minutes with some ten to twenty attempts at the task, each reinforced. After a week it is clear that the boy probably does not understand the meaning of 'sit down' but nevertheless does it in expectation of a reward.

Working with the parents of children who have behavioural problems such as excessive tantrums, acts of aggression, a high rate of non-compliance with parental commands requires a different type of intervention, broadly called parent management training, which in essence helps parents to apply the basic principles of learning theory to the management of their own children.

The programmes, though varied, tend to follow a common sequence. The parents are introduced at the beginning to the elements of the behavioural approach itself and in particular the power of negative reinforcement to generate and escalate unwanted behaviours. The so-called 'negative reinforcement trap' clarifies how it is that the parent-child interaction can have very different short-and long-term outcomes; it has, in effect, a double pay-off. For example a parent asks the child to put its toys away. The child refuses and the parent tells the child off in angry tones. The child begins to whine or cry. The parent stops the telling off and the child stops crying. Both have behaved in such a way as to maximize short-term gains the scolding and the crying stop. Both behaviours have been negatively reinforced in the sense that each was able to terminate unpleasant ('aversive') events. But the room remains untidy and the child has learned how to avoid the task although next time may have to escalate the behaviour.

Subsequent sessions aim to teach specific skills based on learning principles. One of the most important is making commands work. Parental commands are only effective if parents learn how to follow through after issuing them. A taught sequence of steps helps make this happen: compliance should be rewarded immediately (within seconds) with a positive response from the adult, such as praise or approval. If the child has not complied the command should be repeated. Arguing, protesting, whining, crying are all evasive behaviours and should be ignored. Parents also learn not to make too many or difficult commands; after all, on average, all children avoid one command out of three.

Parent training sessions also look at learning to ignore unwanted behaviour and the careful use of 'time out' which, in behavioural terms, means 'time out from positive reinforcement'. This often misunderstood concept should last no more than three to five minutes during which time the child should be placed in a neutral space within view.

Considerable use is made of 'homework': parents apply the techniques and report back at the following session. The training does, therefore, make considerable demands on the participants and a certain percentage do drop out. A number of manuals, detailed programmes and at least one extensive set of trigger videotapes for use in a group format provide key tools for participants and practitioners.

In working with adults with severe learning difficulties the objective of intervention may be to reduce or extinguish challenging or 'excess' behaviours, euphemisms denoting anything from socially inappropriate behaviour, such as taking off clothes in public places, to acts of self-injurious behaviour or aggression. A programme is built either around removing identified reinforcements which the unwanted behaviour is obtaining or by reinforcing another behaviour which is incompatible with the unwanted behaviour and in time will replace it. This latter process is known as the differential reinforcement of other behaviour (DRO). For example, a DRO programme to deal with hand biting might involve providing something the person likes, say a pat on the shoulder or a short conversation, for every two minutes in which no biting occurred.

It makes little sense to diminish certain unwanted behaviours without building up social skills. For teaching a specific activity or skill to enhance personal effectiveness in the community the programme is very different moving from basic to increasingly complex simulations as greater attention is paid to the different types of cues that an individual can expect to encounter. Albin outline four broad steps in developing such a programme:

1. Define the instructional environment in terms of the variations in conditions that the person will encounter.
2. Define the range of relevant stimulus and response variation—when teaching activities in natural settings there is often a range of stimuli or cues that point to appropriate responses; this variation

in what to expect as well as the range of appropriate behaviours in response both have to be taught.

3. Select examples for teaching including those that sample the full range of responses as well as what not to do.
4. Sequence teaching examples determine the order in which examples are to be taught.

For example, a person undertaking a purchase at a fast food restaurant would encounter a number of stimuli: a door with other people entering or leaving, a counter, assistants taking orders, people waiting in a queue, an assistant asking for the order, the position of the till. Each requires a possible range of response: how to move up in the queue, when to give an order, where to pay and how much. Teaching combines simulation in settings where the cues will approximate those found in the natural setting as closely as possible and natural settings. Staff undertaking such teaching need a variety of skills task analysis, pacing the instruction in sessions, recognizing the help levels required such as the degree of guidance and prompting, and the capacity to deliver appropriate feedback and reinforcements.

Evaluating the usefulness of the behavioural approach for social work raises a number of points.

First, despite the misplaced enthusiasm of some proponents the approach does not offer a universal social work method. What suits the clinician does not necessarily suit the social worker. The exclusive focus on behaviour makes the approach difficult to adapt to the general run of social work tasks which are dominated by care management, protective functions and the pressure to ration support services. While the specific skills are well within the grasp of social workers the approach does demand considerable time and consistency of purpose and is therefore more adapted to specialist social work settings, including residential environments, where some access to, or collaboration with, a clinical psychologist is available.

Second, for all that the approach acknowledges that behaviour is functional to a given person in a given environment, it sheds no light on how behaviour can be constructed, and distorted, by pressures which arise from structural and cultural forces. An explicitly anti-discriminatory practice is difficult within the behaviouralist perspective alone since ultimately it relies on broad and often unspecified notions of norms for behaviour which are taken uncritically from the dominant culture. A number of writers have underscored how important it is for any social work approach to recognize that individuals who are confronted by a dominant set of cultural norms because of their race, culture, or ethnicity are forced to adapt to two very different, often conflicting, cultures at the same time their own and that of the dominant culture. What appears to be 'maladaptive' or 'dysfunctional' from a behaviouralist point of view can be the consequence of the struggle to create family systems that can survive the impact of a hostile external environment.

Third, the behavioural approach has a legacy of professional paternalism which was a result of the techniques spreading rapidly in the 1960s without any concern for the values and attitudes of those who acquired them. Nowhere is this more evident than in work with adults with learning difficulties where the contest between behaviouralists on the one hand, and advocates and groups of users supporting normalization goals on the other, has been extremely heated. There are some signs that behaviouralists are willing to admit to past insensitivities, with some further signs that any intervention should directly augment a person's functioning in the community.

There are considerable strengths, however, to be placed alongside these limitations. The approach aims to produce observable, measurable results. Moreover, the techniques it uses to achieve these results are clear and easily understood. In the coming contract culture where social work increasingly will be called upon to explain more precisely what it is doing and how it is doing it, these two assets will make the approach more, not less, attractive. The precision in describing problems in terms of antecedents-behaviour-consequences serves as a useful corrective to a professional culture which has for too long relied on inferential and woolly terminology.

The approach does suggest specific responses to specific, carefully assessed problems. There is no reason *per se* why it should remain the preserve of the clinician and not the social worker. Indeed as a street-level professional the social worker may be ideally placed to add the perspectives of partnership and user choice. Working with parents and children with behavioural problems provides a good example of behavioural work at its most effective: a proven format, based on partnership and joined to clear techniques. But if social workers are to take up their place in this, or in any other behavioural work, it requires detailed, specialist knowledge and practitioner and agency commitment of a kind now only infrequently found.

❑❑❑

7

Social Work in India

Introduction

The development of professional social work education in India can be viewed in terms of three stages. The first stage is a period of relatively indigenous inception of professional social work education in India in the pre independence period. The second stage is the period after independence, when professional social work education in India took shape under American influence. The third phase is a reaction to the inadequacies of the emerged curative model of social work education in India, when suggestions for reforming social work education have been mooted. Thus, in this chapter, we shall discuss the development of professional social work education in India, in three sections in terms of these three stages.

Professional Social Work Education in India in the Preindependence Period (1936-47)

Clifford Manshardt, an American missionary, a graduate in theology from the University of Chicago, went to India in

1925 through the American Marathi Mission, a Protestant Christian organization. This organization decided to undertake social work in slums and, with that objective, founded the Nagpada Neighbourhood House in Bombay in 1926, headed by Manshardt. While working in the industrial metropolis of Bombay, the highly industrialized commercial capital of India, Manshardt felt the need of trained personnel for social work. Thus, when opportunity arose with financing from the Sir Dorabji Tata Trust, Manshardt founded the Sir Dorabji Tata Graduate School of Social Work in Bombay in 1936. This was the beginning of professional social work education in India. Thus, professional social work in India has been initiated through a combination of the religious impulse of charity and the modern scientific orientation of Tata, a pioneer in the field of industry in India.

To illustrate the nature of social work education in India in the preindependence period, in this section we make the following points. Clifford Manshardt, the American missionary who played an important role in the shaping of social work education in India at its inception, while narrating his first social work experience among the industrial workers in Chicago, observed, "It did not take long to realize that welfare work is not a substitute for social action which aims at creating working conditions which are conducive to human welfare, and that social legislation and its enforcement are at times the most basic form of social work.". This observation suggests that probably this American initiator of social work education in India was not part of the American influence, which, as has been argued, resulted in adequate emphasis on social action, and curative social work practice in India.

Manshardt observed that at the inception, the social work training programme in India was based on experience. In fact Manshardt's establishment of the first school resulted from his felt need for trained social workers during his ten years of social work experience in Bombay. Manshardt further stated that when the social work training programme was introduced in India, every attempt was made to make it relevant to India. Moreover, in deciding about the subjects to be taught in this programme, a combination of American as well as British social work education was attempted.

Finally, the inception of social work education in India was influenced by an American idea which has been articulated by Gore and Gore as follows:

> The idea that social work requires training was not particularly American; but that the variety of jobs that go under the name of social work have a certain common content, that they call for study ranging beyond the learning of specific skills through apprenticeship and that a minimum basis of general education up to the graduate level is necessary for professional preparation, was an idea nurtured largely in the United States. The choice of post-graduate education for social work was purely due to the fact that the founder of the first school of social work was an American.

After the initiation of social work education in India, the Sir Dorabji Tata Graduate School of Social Work, renamed Tata Institute of Social Sciences in 1944, remained the only school for professional social work education for ten years, from 1936 to 1946. Other schools of professional social work education came into being only after independence in 1947.

Shaping of Social Work Education in India after Independence

After independence, the second school of social work was established at Delhi in 1947-48. This was a significant step because it was the first school to be established as a part of a university and thus contributed to the academic recognition of social work education in India. The school was organized at postgraduate level. In 1950 another school was established, as a part of University of Boroda. This school was not only a part of the university but constituted an independent faculty. Subsequently, several other schools came into being, including the social work school in Chennai and Lucknow in 1954 and another institution in Mumbai in 1955. By 1975, when the Second Review Committee for Social Work Education appointed by the University Grants Commission undertook a survey, there were thirty-four institutions of social work education in the country. Geographical distribution of these institutions is very uneven. Thus, while Maharashtra had eight institutions and Tamil Nadu six, states in the extreme north and northeast had none. Generally, these projects include community centres, family agency, foster care, adoption and school social work. They are used by the institutions for demonstration, experimentation, field training and research.

Under American influence, social work education in India is generally offered at the university level. The trend is to provide the first education in social work at the master's level and then go beyond it to MPhil and PhD level. As a result a majority of these institutions are urban based. Most are affiliated to state universities.

In the period following independence, an attempt was made to develop professional social work in India through promoting American sponsored study tours for Indian social workers and appointing American trained social workers on the faculties of schools of social work in India. One important scheme in this regard was the US government's Technical Co-operation Mission and Council of Social Work Education Exchange Programmeme. Under this programme, during 1957-62, American social work educators worked as consultants or conducted faculty development programmes in the Indian schools of social work. In exchange, faculty members for Indian schools of social work went for study to the schools of social work in the United States. A corollary was the extensive use of American books and journals in schools of social work.

Social work education in India was a generic course in the pre independence period. The introduction of specialization in social work emerged in the post independence period, primarily under American influence and partly as a result of felt need. An examination of the process of introduction of specialization at the Tata Institute of Social Sciences, the pioneer of social work education in India, suggests that when a specialization was introduced at the Tata Institute, either it was designed and developed by an American social work educator at the initial stage and handed over to an Indian social work educator trained in the United States, or an Indian social work educator was sent to the United States to take training in a particular specialization in India. This resulted in the correspondence of social work curriculum at the Tata Institute with American social work education. What is more important, the Tata Institute, as the forerunner of social work education in India, was closely followed by other schools in designing their curriculum. Thus, American influence of social work education in India become widespread.

However, there are some viewpoints which to an extent counter the preceding argument. For instance, Kulkarni argues that professional social work in India has a very distinct model of its own, in spite of adopting and adapting a lot from other countries. Further it should be noted that some developments in social work education in India were a departure from American social work. Besides, from time to time some changes to the existing pattern of social work education in India have been suggested. Whatever small changes have been generated, in terms of those suggestions, they, in general, are not in the tradition of Americanization of social work; rather they are to the contrary. However, the fact remains that, in spite of these departures from American social work, dominance of American influence on social work education in India persists.

It should be noted here that this American influence in the shaping of social work education in India is not a unique development. It has been pointed out that social education in the developing countries in general has been influenced by the American model of social work. For instance, comparing social work education in five developing countries, Bringham noted that these countries which were predominantly rural had adopted an American urban model of social work education.

Here, it is important to review the shaping of social work education in India under American influence. Indian social work educators have reflected on it on several occasions. Some of these observations are presented here to highlight their core content.

Gore observe that as social work education in the United States leaned heavily on curative social work mainly through casework, the American influence made social work education in India more concerned with method and techniques of work. It deemphasized the needs of social and economic development, promotion of preventative services and social action the prime need of the country in the post independence era.

Pathak observes that it "led to the curtailment of the social science content, inadequate emphasis on social action, alienation of a group of trained social workers from the *sarvodaya* social workers and neglect of social reform."

In pointing out the inappropriateness of the American model for India and other South Asian societies, Nagpaul observes that American history and culture are influenced by ideologies such as capitalism, social Darwinism, the Portestant ethic and individualism. These ideologies emphasize the individual's responsibility in shaping his or her own welfare; public responsibility arises only when the individual grossly fails to benefit from the existing social system. However, during the Great Depression of 1919, these ideologies had a setback and there was a reorientation of social work strategies which led to widening its scope. But, this reorientation of the American model retained the general framework of psychological orientation and casework principles. The American model of social work with the characteristics cited is unfit for India and other developing societies whose problems and developmental needs are substantially different from those of a developed capitalist society. A similar point has also been made by some others.

Finally, one consequence of the shaping of social work education in an irrelevant manner is that it limited the employability of social workers and consequently affected the development of the profession in India.

It should be pointed out here that it is not that social work education has been shaped inappropriately under American influence in India only. It has been argued that social work education in developing countries in general has thus been shaped inappropriately because the American model does not suit the situation of the developing countries. It is argued that social work education should take shape in the societal context. Thus, Humphreys and Dineman have pointed out that even within the United States, the definition of social work has evolved as society's need for and definitions of professions have changed in response to changing social conditions and values.

Further, one gets the impression that American social work is concerned only with the curative function. It should be noted that social work in America has been influenced by curative as well as preventive, "residual" as well as "institutional" ideas of social welfare. However, the fact remains, as is obvious in the assertion of the Indian social work educators, that American social work has remained primarily oriented to a curative model and it is mainly this curative part of American social work which has influenced social work education in India. This has made it irrelevant to the prime need of Indian society. However, this conclusion does not imply that there was no positive contribution of American influence on social work education in India. Pathak and Gore, for instance, have also pointed out the benefits of American sponsoring of social work education in India.

Suggestions for Reforming Social Work Education in India

We have seen how social work education in India has been shaped by close contact with American social work education. We have also documented the observations of social work educators on that influence. It is evident that there is a widespread feeling among social work educators that the influence of the curative and micro based school of American social work has made social work education irrelevant to the needs of Indian society. Thus, it is not surprising that social work educators gave several suggestions for reforming social work education. For instance, as a result of American influence, social work education in India is mainly developed at the postgraduate level. It has been suggested that social work training should be provided at various levels and there should be a ladder programme of social work education. The need for training paraprofessionals has been emphasized. The urban bias of social work education has been deplored and the need for rural social work emphasized. However, apart from these reforms, the prominent suggestions for remodeling social work education in India have been in terms of a social development orientation of social work and promotional social work.

Social Development Orientation of Social Work

The most prominent viewpoint regarding the remodeling of social work education is that it should take on a social developmental orientation. Time and again, it has been argued that social work education in India requires a social development orientation. However, this concern has been characterized by the fact that the meaning of social development orientation remained vague. Thus, Gore cautioned, "I am afraid that unless we can think through clearly what social development means and what role social workers can play in bringing out such development, we only use the word as part of a rhetoric, without stating pragmatic implication for social work."

One discovers that exactly that is happening. Though the need for social developmental orientation in social work has been voiced on several occasions, the type of change that will be required in social work curriculum to equip social workers to perform a social developmental role or the steps that will be required to make social work development oriented has rarely been outlined.

One such rare exercise was undertaken by Sugata Dasgupta in an article where he provided an outline for a social development model of social work education. In this article Dasgupta argued that the nature of social work in India, in fact in all the less developed countries, should be different from that of the developed industrial countries. In a developed country, the concern of social work is helping the marginal section of "deviant" individuals or groups adjust to the society, whereas in a less developed country the main concern should be to bring about changes in society that will mitigate the problems of the disadvantaged.

Having made this point, Dasgupta did not suggest any change in the major components of what he calls "the classical model of social work education," consisting of (1) classroom instruction, (2) fieldwork, (3) supervisory conferences, and (4) research, though he does suggest modifications in the substantive content. We briefly present Dasgupta's suggestions in this regard.

Dasgupta suggested that the subjects to be taught under social development model of social work education needed to be grouped under three broad categories. The first will include those subjects which help understanding of the society and of the individual in the broader context of their being the creatures of this planet and the products of history. Second, social work should teach subjects which concentrate on the change process and on the whats and whys of this change, as well as the how-tos of it. This will be the course on method. Third, social work should deal with planning, decentralization, technology, irrigation, family planning and a substantial reorientation of the traditional fields of practice. This will require a reorganization of theories which would involve inclusion of courses on cultural history, methods of change, social philosophy, political sociology, environmental sciences, and others. This curriculum will train change agents and should lean heavily on "case studies" that depict the process of change.

Gore has expressed his disagreement with Dasgupta's suggestions on at least two occasions, once in the journal that published Dasgupta's article and in an expression of his view on social development orientation in social work. Gore is of the opinion that social workers should address themselves to a limited area of social development:

The distinguishing characteristic of social work lies not in its social know-how or even in its skills in interpersonal relations, but in its concern for those in need of help the deprived, the unprivileged, the unadjusted and the handicapped. Our interest in social policy is in terms of preventing this suffering and promoting rehabilitation.

Gore further adds:

The wider field of social development in all its aspects can at best be added...as tertiary area adjacent to the area of professional concern to social workers. In this perspective, social work practice may be said to have three types of foci and settings: (1) the core area of "welfare" services directly oriented to "handicapped" sections of the population: (2) the secondary area of social service in which social work skills can be practiced either fully as in medical social work, school social work and personnel social work or peripherally as in the planning and administration of these services for "handicapped" segments of the population; and (3) the tertiary area of general social planning where social workers have to call upon their resources as social scientists more than on their professional skills as social workers.

Gore feels that to attain social development orientation, a restructuring of social work curricula is needed:

The undergraduate programme should be developed to equip the students primarily to take the responsibilities of preventive and generalized care services. The postgraduate programme should be strengthened in the areas of social sciences and social policy and should primarily equip a person for clinical and guidance type of work with individuals, some type of group work, the whole sphere of community work, welfare planning and administration. The programme beyond Master's degree level should aim at equipping a person for social developmental tasks in the areas of social welfare and in the allied fields of social service and for teaching and research.

Thus, we have observed that there is a viewpoint which holds that social work education in India should take social development orientation and it is felt that the said orientation can be achieved within the existing frame of social work education with some modifications in its course content.

Promotional Social Work

"Activists" or "action groups" have gained prominence in India particularly since the 1970s. Their emergence as a model of social work has had a systematic expression in a project undertaken by Ramachandran at the Tata Institute of Social Science, Bombay. This project enumerated views of social work alumni of that institute on developing plans and programmes for meeting the future needs of social work training. Analyzing the views expressed by this group, graduating between 1956 and 1981, Ramachandran concludes that there exists a "Great Divide" in the perspective of social work training. There are two positions on the question of the nature of the relationship between social work and social change. The models of social work we have discussed so far belong to one side of this divide. According to Ramachandran, these models of social work are committed to retaining the existing form of training system and institution, subject only to some redistribution of teaching courses and loads, and consequently, some modification in the content of the existing training programme. They are "in favor of *perpetuating the system*, i.e., that professional social work must continue to be concerned with responding to social change and on such of its fallout on society as have been the traditional concern of professional social workers in India" (emphasis in the original). Ramachandran calls this position curative social work.

The other side of this divide, which Ramachandran calls promotional social work, is strongly of the view that "the role of professional social work is to actively participate in *reforming the system*, a stance reflecting the belief that the role of professional social work should be to initiate such social changes as are desirable for one and beneficial to society especially, to its marginalized sections".

Thus, Ramachandran proposes that there should be two major streams of social work training curative social work and promotional social work. One may, however, keep moving from one stream of activity to the other, and preferably training for both the streams should be offered in the same institution for social work education.

What is new in Ramachandran's suggestion is this stream of promotional social work. Ramachandran outlines the content of the promotional social work training programme:

This will address itself more pointedly to promoting equality, social justice, and working for human rights. The emphasis in training will be more on analyzing and understanding the oppressive structure in which society lives, the inequality structures old and new the macro dimension of social problems, exploitation, social conflicts and non-party interactions. Problem focused discussion, people's participation, theory and strategies for change, social movement, politicization, critical analysis of various facilities offered by different agencies and understanding of distortions in Indian developmental models are other areas of emphasis in promotional social work.

Field work would involve greater exposure to projects which reflect the developmental situations, with direct experiences in different settings. Though the base of this work may he in a formal setting, it is not unforeseen that the trainees may be placed in such specific situations as may provide the necessary learning experiences for promotional work non-structural settings or crises situations. There would be a greater degree of freedom given to teachers and students to experiment. Hence, there would be more flexible interaction between theory and practice, and by implication, a less rigid time-table of work.

The key component of this model is *social reform action*. According to Ramachandran social reform action involves awakening of the "marginalized to their condition, so that they can be helped to grow out of it through their own collective sense not necessarily through a political party formation, but perhaps, through people's own movements."

Thus, we observe that there is a school of thought which proposes such changes that cannot be accomplished within the existing frame of social work curriculum. Thus, a separate stream of social work training has been proposed. The purpose of the proposed stream of social work training will be to prepare persons for social reform action.

To conclude, in India a relatively indigenous beginning of social work education was made in the pre independence period. After independence, professional social work education in India has been shaped by American influence. Reflecting the need of that country, social work curriculum in America is predominantly curative. Being shaped under the influence of this curative model of American social work, social work education in India has become predominantly curative. However, as the social work needs of a developing country like India are quite different from those of America, the predominantly curative social work model, developed under American influence, misfit Indian society. Thus, social work educators in India have expressed their dissatisfaction with the predominantly curative social work curriculum in India and have suggested remodelling social work education in India in terms of social development orientation and social action orientation. Both these models of social work have been widely debated and they have prompted some changes in the social work curriculum in India. However, it is still predominantly curative and the social work profession in India remains a shortcoming of the inadequate emphasis on broader developmental issues.

❑❑❑

8

Social Work for Disable People

Introduction

A review of the literature suggests that social work has left much of the understanding of the learning disabled and interventions to assist this population to our colleagues in such allied professions as education, psychology, and the health field. Yet we need to pay attention! The prevalence of learning disabilities among all ages is wide and represents possibly the most common disorder of children seen in mental health settings. These clients are referred to social agencies or are seeking help with a wide range of behavioural problems affecting their social interactions and their ability to effectively carry out certain, expected developmental tasks. We need to understand the possible etiologies of their problems if we are to effectively develop strategies to address their needs.

Defining and Explaining Learning Disabilities

It was not until the 1960s that the concept of *learning disabilities*, a term originated by an educator, Samuel Kirk, became known to professionals and the general public. During this same period, Clements introduced into the psychiatric literature a syndrome he called *minimal brain dysfunction*, and these two terms were used interchangeably. Johnson and Myklebust broadened this definition to refer to children "as having a psychoneurological learning disability, meaning that behaviour has been disturbed as a result of a dysfunction of the brain and that the problem is one of altered processes, not of a generalized incapacity to learn". To understand the development of these concepts, one needs to trace two sometimes parallel and interrelated areas of study: *how people learn and what determines behaviour.* In accepting the meaning and implication of these terminologies, people began to reexamine some of their earlier beliefs.

Our thinking about childhood development in the first half of this century was dominated by the introduction of psychoanalytic thought. Clinicians viewed problems in children as originating in the experiences or unresolved conflicts of early childhood, and parents, especially the mother, were viewed as critical influences. For example, difficulties in learning, as well as behavioural problems, were widely thought to be the result of some underlying emotional problem.

The professional literature prior to the 1960s was replete with descriptions of learning and behavioural problems of children that did not fit into existing classifications and were not responsive to the usual interventions based on such classifications. In the 1930s and 1940s, a few pioneers were exploring other avenues of explanation and began to produce research and new hypotheses based on clinical observations of patients with neurological disorders. Increasingly, evidence was provided about the relationship between brain processes and various cognitive or behavioural disorders. In 1937, Samuel Orton, a neuro pathologist, became interested in the relationship between cerebral dominance and language disabilities and developed a theory about how differences in specific aspects of brain functioning affected a child's capacity to read. Several years later, Kurt Goldstein's research revealed that people with brain injuries exhibited certain disordered behaviours, such as distractibility, which persisted even after healing.

Strauss and Lehtinen's classic work, *Psychopathology and Education of the Brain-Injured Child*, marked the beginning of learning disabilities as a field of study. In their work, Strauss and Lehtinen carried out close observations of children with similar patterns of behaviour, who had been categorized with such diagnoses as mentally retarded or emotionally disturbed. They theorized that these behaviour and learning problems were the result of brain injury and were not emotionally based or caused by psychogenic factors. Their definition of the brain-injured child included the following:

The brain injured child is the child who before, during, or after birth has received an injury to or suffered an infection to the brain. As a result of such organic impairment, defects of the neuromotor system may be present or absent; however, such a child may show disturbances in perception, thinking and emotional behaviour, either separately or in combination.

Similarities in certain behaviour manifestations between children with brain damage and a large group of children with problems of behaviour and learning led to the concept of *minimal brain dysfunction*. This latter group did not give evidence of "hard" neurological impairments, such as motor weakness, but rather of "soft" signs, such as clumsiness. Compelling evidence for the existence of minimal brain dysfunction can be shown by the similarity between children with these symptoms and those with organic brain disorders, and in the response of this population to medication.

There have been changes in the nomenclature, and more important, in the definitions and working hypotheses in the field of learning disabilities since the advent of

Strauss and Lehtinen's book. During this process, social workers have had to incorporate new knowledge, question old beliefs, and look at the effects of new educational, physiological, and therapeutic interventions on identified populations.

Certainly, the discovery of psychotropic medications in the 1950s, and their impact on mental illness, led to a resurgence of interest in the brain and its effect on behaviour. Internal processes or the external environment could no longer be seen as the sole factor in the etiology of behaviour. This discovery played a major role in dispelling long-held myths. Social workers now realized that behavioural symptoms can be, at least in great part, organically based.

Perhaps the first, and among the best-known, examples was the discovery that autism is a behavioural disorder based on some dysfunction in the brain, and not the result of a psychological disturbance. Similarly, over the years, the symptom of hyperkinesis/hyperactivity has been demonstrated to be neuro biologically based.

In the 1960s, Thomas, Chess, and Birch introduced the concept that temperament was an inborn trait. In their pioneer research, they showed how a child's temperament affected family relationships. Their findings were very influential in demonstrating the reciprocity between nature and nurture. Additional findings about the impact of inborn traits, referred to as temperament, on human development were subsequently identified by Thomas and Chess and Kagan.

In the 1980s a whole new body of research was developed through long-term studies of twins and adopted children that validate that the core or determinants of many behaviours and personality traits are genetically determined. These include social potency, e.g., shyness and extroversion; stress reactions, e.g., vulnerability; and aggression and control. Our common understanding that physical attributes and intellectual potential are affected by heredity was enlarged to include many personality characteristics.

Now our understanding of learning has been expanded and refined to reflect that all areas of learning development and dysfunction are affected by complicated, yet subtle, brain processes. Findings demonstrate the impact of genetics and brain function on a great range of behaviours, formerly considered to be solely based on psychological, cultural, or environmental influences. Such understandings have a profound impact on how we define the disorders and syndromes of learning and behaviour, and the options for intervening effectively.

The definitions of learning disabilities have been affected over the years by newly emerging information and by differences of professional orientation and opinion. Following Kirk's original definition of the term learning disabilities, the National Advisory Committee on Handicapped Children formulated the following definition in 1967:

Children with special learning disabilities exhibit a disorder in one or more of the basic psychological processes involved in understanding or using spoken or written languages. These may be manifested in disorders of listening, thinking, talking, reading, writing, spelling, or arithmetic. They do not include learning problems which are due primarily to visual, hearing, or motor handicaps, to mental retardation, emotional disturbance, or to environmental disadvantage.

This definition was widely quoted and became the basis for landmark legislation that resulted in the establishment of educational programmes for handicapped children and the training of professionals in this arena of service, called PL 94–142. This law provided a systematic methodology for the identification, assessment, and education of children with handicaps and was followed in later years by important amendments. The significance of this legislation has been considerable. Yet the definition quickly created certain theoretical and service delivery problems. The National Joint Committee on Learning Disabilities was joined by others in its position that the federal definition did not convey the heterogeneity of learning disorders, it incorrectly limited the application of the definition to children, and it did not clearly state the etiology of learning disabilities, but rather made a listing of terms.

The vast changes in this field can be seen if one compares the proposed federal definition for the term learning disabilities. It refers to: "a heterogeneous group of disorders, presumed to be due to central nervous system dysfunction and manifested by significant difficulties in the acquisition and use of listening, speaking, reading, or mathematical abilities, or of social skills" (Interagency Committee on Learning Disabilities. This definition is particularly significant because it acknowledges that many individuals classified as learning disabled have significant difficulties in establishing and maintaining satisfying peer and adult relationships.

The cause of learning disabilities is not known. There are various hypotheses about its origin, including the probability that in any one person there may well be multiple origins. What we can also surmise is that the cause in one person will probably differ from the cause in another, which may explain why this syndrome has many variations.

Beginning with the assumption that understanding the etiology of a problem will assist in the selection of appropriate interventions, the practitioner may need to establish the probability of a specific etiology or to rule out, at least, those that are unlikely. More than forty different causative factors of learning disabilities have been reported in the literature of the last three decades. The following paragraphs include the major etiologies.

At some time, a learning disabled person may have experienced some *brain damage.* Such injuries may have occurred during gestation, the period of prenatal development, the birth process, or the early years of life. Such injuries may have been caused by disease, by exposure to lead or other toxic substances, by trauma, or by ingestion of drugs or medication by the mother, or by anesthesia. Depending on the location, extent of damage, and time period in the life cycle, an individual may suffer severe damage or a minimal form of subtle brain dysfunction.

Maturational lag, which is defined as some delay in the development of the central nervous system, is another possible cause. Another common explanation relates to some *biochemical or physiological dysfunction.* This hypothesis suggests there may be some deficiency or altered homeostasis in metabolic functioning of the body. For instance, some allergic conditions are associated with specific behavioural manifestations. An example of this problem can be found in Feingold's work in which an *allergic reaction* to food additives can result in specific learning or behavioural problems.

As already indicated, *genetic transmission* is commonly identified as a probable etiology, although in some families with such histories, it is not a determinant. Genetic factors may be important predictors for people with certain types of learning problems. Twin and foster child rearing studies further support a genetic etiology. In as many as 40 per cent of learning disabled children, family histories of learning disabilities were discerned. Reports also show that children of low birth weight are at risk for learning problems as are those with seizure disorders.

Another factor that compounds developmental outcomes has to do with premature birth, which has been associated with various developmental or behavioural problems, including learning disabilities. There is a school of thought that certain *dysfunctions of the eye,* especially in its ability to effectively gather visual information, can lead to dyslexia and are correctable by special eye exercises. Other examples of possible causes include, *low birth weight, environmental pollutants, radiation exposure of the mother or child, cortical dysfunction,* etc.

The clinical picture of the person with learning disabilities is not homogeneous. Though each person's functioning reflects a different combination of characteristics, they all fall into the same, broad unitary syndrome. *Learning disabilities can affect cognitive, social, emotional, and physical development and functioning.* Some general characteristics commonly include: an uneven growth pattern, which results in areas of maturational lag; average or above average intelligence; and discrepancies between achievement and potential. This syndrome can affect a person's capacity to meet academic and life tasks.

Demographic Patterns

It is complicated to determine the number of persons affected by learning disabilities from the demographic data used to describe such persons. Prevalence varies, in great part, by the definition used. Criteria for inclusionary and exclusionary measures have changed over the years and differ further depending on the perspective or source used. School-based reports are most easily obtainable, yet these exclude youngsters who are learning disabled but whose major deficits may not be in the academic sphere, and, of course, these reports exclude adults. The U.S. Department of Education reported in 1987 that almost 5 per cent of all school-aged children received special education services. Other studies reflected higher findings among youth, ranging from 10 to 15 per cent. The National Institutes of Health reports that 15 per cent of the total population has some type of learning disability ("Facts about. Prevalence was slightly higher among *socio economically disadvantaged* populations, and at least twice as common in *males than in females.* In 1992, males with specific learning disabilities represented 7 per cent of public school enrollment, while females with this disability accounted for only 3 per cent. The population of people diagnosed with a learning disability has grown markedly, about threefold, between 1976 and 1993. Studies to date are not adequate, largely because of the problems in achieving a consensus about definition, which are further influenced by political factors such as when funds are sought to address the needs of this population.

Societal Context

The advent of federal legislation for people with handicaps, and in particular the learning disabled, was associated with two major phenomena. In the 1960s, America learned about equal rights for minorities, and legislation for racial and ethnic minorities paved the way to consideration of the needs of other minority groups. But for people with learning disabilities to be perceived as a group with special needs, they had to be so identified. As already indicated, the labelling of this population and the growing understanding of the ways in which people with learning disabilities were disadvantaged, especially in the educational system, enabled legislators and professionals to articulate the special needs of this population. Lobbying efforts seemed especially effective, because children from middle-class families composed a sizable portion of this group. Their parents were effective in initiating efforts for legal recognition and resources.

Two profoundly important pieçes of federal legislation have supported the rights and need for services for the learning disabled. In 1973, Congress passed Section 504 of the Rehabilitation Act, prohibiting discrimination on the basis of physical or mental handicap in any federally assisted programme or activity. Its intent was to effect fundamental changes in the attitudes of institutions and individuals toward handicapped persons. People with a diagnosis of specific learning disabilities fell into the federal definition, if their impairment(s) were severe enough to limit one or more major life functions. This legislation provided assurances that no handicapped child would be excluded from a public education because of a disability, that these children would be educated with non handicapped students to the extent possible, and that their parents or guardians could object to evaluation or placement decisions. In addition to supporting the rights of children in the educational system, it also mandated that postsecondary institutions could not discriminate against its applicants or students because of a handicap. The law further stipulated that employers could not refuse to hire or promote solely because of a worker's disability and that health and welfare services must provide equal access to services to persons with disabilities.

Then, in November of 1975, Congress adopted PL 94–142, the Education for All Handicapped Children Act, and it became effective in October 1977. The spirit of this law was to assure handicapped children a free and appropriate education, and it set forth procedures to ensure that all parts of the law were implemented. The legislation introduced important concepts, including a mandate that children be educated in the least restrictive environment; that they be provided with individual educational plans (IEPs); that decisions on evaluation and placement be made by a committee composed of representative educators, professionals from related disciplines, and parents; and that due process provisions allow parents to challenge the school system's decisions or inaction. Subsequent amendments, namely the Education of Handicapped Act of 1986, extended services to handicapped infants and preschool children (National Center for Clinical Infants Programme. The Individuals with Disabilities Act (IDEA) of 1990, reauthorized the federal law passed in 1975. The Americans with Disabilities Act (ADA) of 1990 is a civil rights law protecting people with disabilities from discrimination in such areas as employment and public accommodations.

The opportunities generated by these acts are extraordinary, but the funds to support such options are often extremely high for local and state governments to support. The federal government's good intentions far exceeded its fiscal generosity. For example, one finds local communities, large cities, and small villages torn between serving the needs of its children, some of whom are severely handicapped by physical disabilities, by retardation, by autism, etc., and at the same time, trying to keep local taxes from spiraling further. Taxpayers' pleas compete with the pleas of desperate parents. Committees on Special Education are mandated to make sound educational decisions in behalf of children, yet anyone observing such a group in action will become aware that fiscal concerns loom large in the background. Similarly, many communities cannot keep pace with the growing needs of its handicapped population.

Other issues were raised about the mandate of this legislation. The notion of the *least restrictive environment* implied that moving toward mainstreaming was the preferred option, especially for children with learning disabilities. Clearly, the requirement enabled many formerly forgotten or "hidden" children to return to neighbourhood schools to learn and socialize with peers; yet for others, it was not the panacea. Assigned to regular classes meant that many would not have the opportunity for more individually designed learning and were singled out by classmates as being "stupid." Others could not keep up socially, lacking the skills or self-confidence. Placing children in regular classes with resource room supports or in self-contained, special education classrooms is only a beginning. Again, unprepared or overburdened staff, with limited resources, have not been able to carry out the goals set for each child.

Special education is a contentious issue in many state governments. Some experts contend that children have been diagnosed as learning disabled when their teachers wanted to rid themselves of disruptive students. In New York State, the special education programme was criticized for placing a disproportionate number of black and Latino students into separate classrooms.

Persons with learning disabilities often have an invisible handicap. Their problems are less blatantly observable than those of a person with mental retardation or pervasive developmental disabilities. The very definition that a learning disabled person must have average or above-average intelligence may further camouflage specific limitations. It is not difficult in our society to find those who feel that learning problems are precipitated by unmotivated or lazy students or serve as a symptom of some psychological "block." They are unsympathetic to people identified as learning disabled, feeling if only they tried harder, or were not obtaining secondary gain, they could overcome whatever cognitive or behavioural problem they possess. The situation is even more difficult for adults with learning disabilities, because learning disabilities were originally deemed to be a problem for children that they would eventually outgrow. The research amply demonstrates that the characteristics of learning disabled youngsters persist into adulthood and that learning disabilities often exist, some in changing form, throughout the life span. Legislation and accompanying funding have largely been geared toward youth. While some laws provide for vocational education for adults with learning disabilities, their other needs, such as for support in independent living and training, receive less attention. Finally, professional training and funding reflect society's primary concern with academic and employment issues. Society does not seem to understand the primacy of the area of social needs of the learning disabled and the ways in which such deficits have an impact on total life functioning. This lack of understanding takes its toll on all levels, from the kind of expectations we have for the learning disabled to the kinds of services and resources we make available to them.

Vulnerabilities and Risk Factors

Having a learning disability "is, in itself a risk factor; however, there are wide variations in the emotional and social adaptation of individuals with learning disabilities". Risk factors, may be internal, namely a function of neurologically based features that influence behaviour, or risk factors may be external, influenced by peer, family, or societal values, expectations and interactions.

Studies have revealed different outcomes regarding the relationship between individuals with learning disabilities and emotional problems, specifically depression and anxiety. Some studies report that individuals with learning disabilities score higher compared with their counterparts without disabilities, whereas other studies report less than half of persons with learning disabilities present clinical symptoms. The greater risk is associated for those with a lack of social relationships or with poor social relationships.

The incidence of learning disabilities in *delinquent populations* is considerably higher than in the general population. Estimates of prevalence range from 26 per cent to 73 per cent. According to a study by the Learning Disability/Juvenile Delinquency Project at Fordham University, individuals with learning disabilities are 22 per cent more likely to be adjudicated delinquent than those without such disabilities. Several hypotheses attempt to explain the link between learning disabilities and delinquency, such as vulnerability to peer group pressure and school failure. Current investigators postulate that ineffective problem solving skills increase the risk for delinquency in learning disabled youth. Certainly, people with problems of impulsivity who lack social judgement skills would have an increased propensity for engaging in antisocial behaviours.

Students with learning disabilities are more likely to become *school dropouts*, and those who do drop out of school or whose academic achievements are low are at greater risk vocationally and socially. School and employment policies or practices that are not responsive to the needs of this population contribute to feelings of failure, alienation, and disengagement. Academic and social problems persist into adulthood. One of the common characteristics of adults with learning disabilities is a prolonged dependence on families, which emerges from difficulties in finding employment, in developing independent living skills, and in maintaining social relationships. Denial of this disability further affects the individual's capacity to cope, and adults who are in denial are less likely to develop strategies for vocational or academic success.

Karacostos and Fisher found that higher proportions of adolescents with learning disabilities than those without learning disabilities were classified as *chemically dependent*, although there is limited research pertaining to rates of substance abuse prevalence in this population. Factors that may put adolescents at higher risk for substance abuse are behavioural problems, peer rejection, and school failure experiences. The Office of the Inspector General reported that learning disabilities and substance abuse are the most common impediments to the employment of clients on public assistance.

Having a family member with learning disabilities often places greater stress on families. Some of these families report greater chaos, disorganization, or conflict. Parents experience high levels of anxiety when they have a child with special needs, especially when there are limited family or community resources. Moreover, family responses to the member with learning disabilities, such as unrealistic expectations, lack of acceptance, impatience, etc., increase risk factors.

Disorders of *learning and attention* commonly co-occur. A high proportion of individuals with learning disabilities have problems with attention, especially hyperactivity. It has been estimated that 30 to 50 per cent of children who have been diagnosed with learning disabilities meet criteria for attention-deficit/hyperactivity disorder. The features of this disorder, such as impulsivity and hyperactivity, are additive risks that place a person with learning disabilities in greater jeopardy.

Resiliencies and Protective Factors

A significant proportion of people with learning disabilities have positive outcomes in various areas of functioning and experience overall life satisfaction. Protective factors may come from the individual's other level of skills or talents, his or her temperament, or in the responsiveness of the environment to the individual.

Resilience may be viewed as protective factors that act on risk conditions to reduce the impact of the risk factors. Factors contributing to resilience may lie in the individual or in the environment and are often created by the interaction between the two. Certain *personal characteristics,* such as strong verbal skills, athletic ability, and the completion of different milestones in education, serve as protective factors and are often predictors of positive adult outcomes. Major protective factors for depression and anxiety are self-esteem and self-awareness, which contribute to a sense of well-being and competence.

Gerber and Reiff cite the importance of self-understanding in enabling people with learning disabilities to make appropriate accommodations and to utilize compensatory mechanisms. Self-understanding also generates self-confidence, the ability to strategize in stressful situations, and the capacity to take action that helps people feel in control.

"Reframing" is a strategy used by successful adults with learning disabilities. It refers to "reinterpreting the learning disability in a more positive or productive manner," which includes recognizing the disability, accepting it, understanding its meaning and implications, and taking action appropriate to that situation.

Another protective factor is the family's ability to handle stress along with the availability of *external resources*. Additional supports for resiliency are related to the degree to which a family accepts and develops realistic expectations for the member with learning disabilities and has the knowledge and flexibility to address their needs.

Schools and the workplace that make accommodations, provide supportive environments, and develop arenas for the learning and application of skills are critical protective factors that lead individuals with learning disabilities to make successful adaptations. The capacity to ensure responsive social environments for learning disabled people with behavioural or social problems is far more complicated and elusive.

Programmes and Social Work Contributions

Social workers have not been in the forefront in identifying or addressing the needs of this population. Over the past four decades, educators have played a prominent role in advocating for and developing services to meet academic needs. Public schools offer an array of options for children with learning disabilities, though there is a significant gap between actual need and available services. Private schools have also been established, which broaden options for parents with economic means to make their own choices for their children and for overburdened school districts to provide support to children referred to private resources. Libraries for teachers abound with literature on theories and specialized techniques for teaching these youngsters. Educators are even in the vanguard of the learning disability movement in now devising and offering social skills training programmes.

Psychiatrists and neurologists have carried out extensive and important research in this field, as well as offering both assessment and intervention services, including medication. The community has often turned to psychologists to administer testing to children and adults, to make learning and psychological assessments and to determine the nature and extent of learning and behavioural deficits and strengths. Both psychiatrists and psychologists have been major providers of therapeutic services and also work alongside other disciplines, such as speech therapists, in serving this population's needs.

Social workers in child guidance clinics, mental health and family agencies, and school systems are receiving sizable numbers of referrals and working with people of all ages who have learning disabilities. Similarly, child welfare and criminal justice settings serve youth or adults who struggle with many problems including learning disabilities. Clients with this diagnosis come to social agencies primarily because their social, behavioural problems have led to difficulty in some aspect of their life functioning. Parents may also seek help with a range of reactions to their learning disabled child, for assistance in acting in their child's behalf, or for help in dealing with child development or management issues. In these agencies and community institutions, social workers are offering multi method interventions ranging from evaluation to consultation to counseling to advocacy.

In response to clients' needs and requests, various other programmes are available. Beyond academic programmes, there are special camps or recreational and social programmes for learning disabled youth and young adults. Such settings feature structured programmes in which youth with learning disabilities who have social or motoric deficits may function with needed supports and in less competitive environments conducive to growth. Parents of learning disabled children may wish to join educationally oriented or mutual aid groups to enhance their understanding of their child's difficulties, to obtain new child rearing skills, or to gain the support of others in similar situations. Many parents or learning disabled adults have also made active use of information and referral centres.

Middle-class parents have been effective in spearheading movements for their children. They have joined together in local and national associations to lobby for legislation, funds, and services. They are active presenters at professional conferences and join boards and school committees to enlighten the community and to advocate for resources. In lower socioeconomic communities, progress is slower, probably because parents besieged with so many life problems generally have not mobilized themselves in such organized efforts. Yet the numbers of learning disabled are great and their needs are naggingly persistent. There are never enough services, and as professionals, we are still somewhat neophytes in fully developing our technology for helping the learning disabled.

Assessment and Interventions

To obtain a total and accurate picture, carrying out an assessment of a person with learning disabilities often involves contributions from other disciplines, including neurologists, psychiatrists, speech and occupational therapists, psychologists, and remedial specialists. Each discipline, if relevant, will administer its own set of tests to illuminate areas of strength and the nature of the problem. A social worker can make an overall assessment, which, among other things, usually includes history taking. One important aspect involves documentation of exactly how the person's functioning deviates from what is normally expected, with emphasis on information about language, motor, cognitive, and social development, including delays in reaching developmental milestones, and inconsistencies in performance. Questions to determine possible etiologies would include exploration into such areas as genetic factors, nutritional and allergy problems, mixed dominance, and prenatal, birth, and medical history.

Evaluations would include interviewing the person, family, and significant collateral contacts, such as a teacher or recreation counselor. Observations may be carried out in the office, home, and/or school. It would be particularly important to see the person in his or her social environment and to understand and assess the impact of the supports or stress factors, chaos or structure, cultural norms, performance expectations, and degree of acceptance or rejection in the environment on the person's functioning. If the client is a child or adolescent, it is also important for the social worker to understand the meaning of the disability for the parent and siblings, the family environment, pressures, and resources. In making an assessment, a professional needs to inquire into the following areas of functioning where evidence of deficits or delays may exist.

An early sign of learning disabilities may emerge in the area of *language development.* A disorder exists when there is a qualitative difference in some aspect of language behaviours from expected normal development, based on a child's chronological age. Language disorders encompass many different kinds of disruptions in the content, form, and use of language. Sometimes children do not express themselves well conceptually because they may lack the verbal acuity or because they think in more concrete terms. Children also may not express themselves well grammatically and cannot, for example, produce full sentences or utilize the correct parts of speech. Sometimes a child will speak in an immature manner.

Thus, a frequent signal of learning disabilities is a delay in language development, e.g., children who begin to speak at the age of 3 years or later. Children may also experience difficulty in articulation and do not produce sounds correctly.

This can be the result of a motoric problem in which the mouth, tongue, and lips do not function well together in producing certain sounds. Language provides a person with a means to communicate and to socially interact with others, so that significant deficiencies can have a impact on a child's social development. If the disorder is readily apparent, it can also be a form of acute, public embarrassment.

Problems in *motor coordination* may be another early sign in the learning disability syndrome. While some learning disabled children have histories of reaching early milestones in motor development and possess strong athletic skills, many more have histories of awkwardness or clumsiness. Children may have difficulties with gross motor coordination, such as running or hopping; with small motor dexterity, such as cutting with scissors, tying shoelaces, or with handwriting; or in both areas. Others have problems with balance. All these deviations usually show up as "soft" neurological signs, rather than as "hard" classical neurological symptoms.

Visual perception plays an important part in learning. Problems in visual perception may take one or more of the following forms. Some people have difficulty with spatial relations, which refers to how objects are viewed together in space and of how one organizes oneself in space. For example, a person might have trouble reading or doing arithmetic because of how they view letters or numbers and their relationship to space, or they might have difficulty discriminating left from right, or they might feel disoriented or dizzy when placed in a more open environment. People may have difficulty with depth perception, in which distance is misjudged, so that a person may miss a step in climbing stairs, or bump into things or fall down while trying to sit. Visual discrimination problems often occur when people reverse letters (e.g., *d* and *b*) or words (e.g., *saw* and *was*) or see symbols in reverse, as in mirror reading. They may copy incorrectly, become confused with visual directions, or experience visual motor problems, as in trying to track and catch a ball. Visual perception problems often lead to difficulties in reading, due, in this situation, to some limitation in the ability to decode correctly.

Some people's problems occur more in the area of *auditory perception*. There is no problem with hearing acuity, but people may have difficulty distinguishing subtle differences in sound, in distinguishing significant sounds to pay attention to, or in integrating different phonic sounds. Other possible difficulties occur when a person experiences auditory lag, so they cannot process quickly what they hear and the speaker must speak more slowly; or a person might have trouble with auditory sequencing, i.e., not being able to remember the order of things given in oral directions.

A particularly serious dysfunction occurs when a person has a *memory disability*, i.e., problems with either integrating, storing, or retrieving information from memory. The two primary forms of memory are short-term and long-term, and the problems may occur in visual or auditory sphere. Short-term memory refers to information that needs to be retained for a short time while a person is using it. In long-term memory, knowledge is retained and is available for retrieval when required. For instance, a person may look up and remember a number long enough to dial it on the telephone; this only requires short-term memory. When a person learns that telephone number and can retrieve it at will many hours or days later, then it has become a part of long term memory. With constant repetition a person usually learns to store things in long term memory. When this process fails, learning is seriously affected and impaired.

A pervasive problem that many people with learning disabilities experience is one of *disorganization*, which takes many forms and affects many areas of daily functioning and learning. People are bombarded constantly with all kinds of sensory stimuli coming from the environment. The learning disabled are often overwhelmed by the stimuli. They cannot easily process, integrate, and act on the stimuli appropriately or effectively.

Two major areas of *behavioural characteristics* coexist with learning disabilities or are viewed as part of the learning disability syndrome: (1) *problems in attention*, and (2) *social immaturity or problems in social competence*. The *Diagnostic and Statistical Manual of Mental Disorders*, 4th edition classifies the first group as attention-deficit/hyperactivity disorder (AD/HD). *Hyperactivity* is physiologically based rather than anxiety based, meaning that evidence of hyperactivity can be traced to early childhood. Frequently, though not always, children with this disorder were very active since birth, frequently in motion, often colicky, and not always easy to cuddle. Their movements can be described as jittery, their cries as piercing, and their meals as fraught with difficulty. Such children leave their parents exhausted, with the house looking very much like a combat zone. Hyperactive people are described as "always on the go" as "if driven by a motor", have difficulty sitting still, fidget excessively, and run around or climb on things excessively. Some children are more appropriately classified as *distractible*, meaning that some external stimuli are affecting their behaviour and they are distracted from attending to the task at hand. To differentiate between these two sets of behaviour, hyperactive persons act as if they are driven internally into motion, whereas distractible persons are excessively disturbed, for example, by the noise of a pencil dropping in the rear of the room while a teacher is speaking in the front. A much less observed symptom that people with learning disabilities sometimes have is the reverse problem, known as *hypoactivity*, where there is a lethargic appearance.

Other people have what is described as *problems with inattention*, for they lack the capacity for sustained attention or have a short attention span. They do not seem to always listen or to finish what they start. Sometimes they are described as daydreaming. Problems with impulsivity, or what is sometimes called *poor impulse control,* is a common manifestation in many people with learning disabilities. Evidence of such behaviours is seen in a person's tendency to act before thinking, to experience difficulty in delaying gratification, and generally to have a low frustration tolerance. Such people will become quickly upset when things or other people fail to react as anticipated or hoped. Impulsive people also may experience problems in disorganization or in staying with one activity for a period of time. Impulsivity often results in unplanned or socially inappropriate responses.

Children with problems in attention, especially hyperactivity, experience difficulty during infancy and in preschool years, but it is during the advent of the school years that the problems are markedly apparent. Virtually every aspect of the child's environment is affected: school, peers, and home. AD/HD is considerably more common in boys. It was initially thought that problems in inattention greatly subside in the early years of adolescence with the change in hormones. However, studies reflect some dissipation of gross motor symptoms but a persistence into adulthood of many of the other attentional problems.

For many years, the definition of *learning disability* did not include the identification of social behaviours or social adjustment. Yet, throughout this period, studies increasingly demonstrated the evidence of various patterns of *social immaturity* endemic to the learning disabled syndrome. Studies further reveal that people with learning disabilities are often poorly accepted or rejected and exhibit significant social skill deficits. Therefore, social skill deficits can be viewed as a primary learning disability. In terms of total life functioning, social ineptitude tends to be far more disabling than most cognitive deficits.

Previously, some characterized the problems observed as secondary problems resulting from children's difficulties and frustration in coping with cognitive and other previously identified deficits. Yet the proposed federal definition, coupled with extensive research, suggests that, indeed, social skill problems are an1 integral part of the learning disability syndrome and are the result of some physiological determinant or delay. This finding fits in with what we are now learning about the effect of genetics and brain function on many behaviours.

Characteristically, socially immature people exhibit difficulty in some of the following areas. They may lack acuity in social perception and tend to misread or ignore the cues of others. They may have problems in exercising social judgments, namely, in how they choose to handle social situations, so that behaviour often appears immature or inappropriate. Such lack of sophistication also results in difficulties in social problem solving. Many experience problems in social interactions, especially with peers on age-appropriate levels. Their desire to make friends is clearly apparent, but their social behaviours are often awkward, lacking in social competence and appropriateness. The picture looks different at different age levels, but almost always it is not what would be expected at a specific age. For instance, in young children, there may be extroversion: excessive hugging and kissing; inviting friends too quickly, such as asking a stranger on the street to visit their home; or joining into games without considering possible rejection and the impact on others. They may blurt out what they think without the expected social prohibitions (e.g., "you look fat" or "your house is messy"). Children with such problems may have inappropriate expectations of others so that the judgements they make may be met with annoyance. For example, if an 8-year-old learning disabled boy is playing with a 3-year-old girl and she takes his ball away, the boy acts as if the 3-year-old were his peer, grabs the ball back, and does not take into account the age difference.

As children grow older, they will learn and integrate various age-appropriate interactions; however, these are offset by frequent lapses into less age-appropriate behaviours. Initiating and sustaining friendships and making mature social judgements will still prove to be a problem. By adolescence, the peer group takes on greater importance, but learning disabled children are often excluded by peers because they lack peer-valued attributes. Thus, the gap for social opportunities for learning and interaction is widened. The behaviours of learning disabled adolescents, and adults as well, is varied and colored by the accumulation of other life experiences. Yet one can factor out certain traits that seem to be characteristic of the learning disabled person. For example, they may miss the point of what is being said, they may overreact, or they may make inappropriate remarks, actions, or poorly timed responses. They may need to be in control, which grows out of their need to organize other people and situations from their own sense of internal disorganization. They may sometimes, incorrectly, project blame. Yet they can be simultaneously and acutely aware of the messages of others toward them, but have difficulty knowing how to effectively respond. They may seem stubborn, or they may need time alone to pull themselves together and to withdraw from bombarding and overwhelming stimuli. For some, poor judgment may result in antisocial acts. The form these behavioural symptoms take is varied, but the common denominator is usually eagerness for interaction, coupled with qualities of social ineptness.

Three other behavioural traits may be seen in many people with learning disabilities. The first is what is called *emotional lability*, meaning strong vulnerability. Excessively labile people may be hurt out of proportion to what one might anticipate and then react with a corresponding degree of pain. It may be as simple as how one responds to a belonging being broken or misplaced, or to losing in a game or to teasing. The second is *perseveration*, meaning a person seems to "get stuck." The learning disabled do not easily pull themselves out of a situation to look at options, or they create a mental set, a script of expectations that may not come to fruition. One common and sad example is the child who gets into a physical fight and cannot stop. Finally, there is the problem of *slower adaptive mechanisms*, meaning that people cannot deal with unexpected changes easily and need more time to integrate changes that are nonroutine or unexpected. A change may be small (e.g., a new textbook); it may be an unanticipated visitor, a trip to a new place, or almost any change in known ritual, plan, structure, or interaction.

It is not uncommon for the learning disabled to experience *secondary emotional problems* that grow out of many years of experiencing frustration and failure and to which they react in many ways. They may develop such symptoms as withdrawal or hypochondria, or they may resort to clowning to divert attention from their problems. In one form or another, most struggle with a poor sense of self-esteem.

Still, people with learning disabilities bring to their lives some very special qualities. They may display a hearty enthusiasm, spontaneity, or adventurousness . Particularly impressive is the courage, resilience, and persistence they may ultimately apply, over and over again, to facing difficult life tasks. One is often captivated by the uniqueness of their personalities and their ability to draw on their resources.

In working with this population, recommended interventions are dictated by the implications of an assessment for learning disabilities. For some children, where difficulties are predominantly cognitive, academic remediation will undoubtedly be very important. Specific suggestions should be made, including the kind of individual or class structure needed and the specific remediation techniques suggested to help a person to learn required skills or to find appropriate compensatory measures. Such options abound; the following is a simple example. A child with problems in handwriting may learn to write more effectively if he can learn to draw in sand or finger paint, may copy over dots more readily than trying to copy from a picture, or may need wide lines rather than open space as a guide.

Speech therapists have been effective in helping children with a range of language problems, and early intervention, especially, reaps important success. In the field of medicine, the use of medication has had a profound impact in alleviating such symptoms as hyperactivity. Although the use of medication, especially on children, has been controversial, medication that has been carefully monitored to reduce possible side effects has achieved significant results. Research findings indicate that 60 to 90 per cent of hyperactive children can focus their attention better and can reframe from physically and mentally responding to diversions when taking stimulant mediations . Hence, there is a decrease in motor activity and an increase in attention span. These medications do not affect specific learning deficits but modify the child's activity level, so that the child becomes more available to learning. Wender argued that substituting psychotherapy for medication could be viewed as malpractice, a harmful withholding of needed treatment from a child. He suggested that psychological help is popular, but as pragmatists, the question is not what is popular, but what works.

Social workers may assume various roles in working with learning disabled clients and their families. They may serve as coordinators, helping the client or family to locate appropriate resources for evaluation and future planning and to think through decisions and needed actions. Social workers often function in the role of consultants, providing information and suggestions, usually to parents, about learning disabilities and ways in which they can understand and be helpful to their child. Clients with learning disabilities and their families are often referred to or seek help from social workers for counseling, because of some interpersonal, developmental, and/or environmental problems. Finally, social workers serve as advocates or mediators and help to empower clients to act in their own behalf or in support of a family member.

Having a learning disability often means experiencing some difficulties throughout the life span. Therefore, help may be obtained to cope with tasks at different points in the life cycle, during crises as well as for longer periods of time. If one traces the path a learning disabled person takes, it is not uncommon to see him or her moving in and out of different kinds of helping relationships.

The first encounter is usually when problems are initially identified. Parents often become aware during the infant, toddler, or certainly the latency years that their child's development is different from that of the child's peers. By the time the parents seek help, they already suspect that something is wrong. They may even imagine that the problem is worse than it is. On another level, parents go through different stages as they assimilate their observations and try to cope with emerging anxieties. Parents may begin by denying the problem, trying to minimize what they observe or are told. This stage may be followed by anger, as parents ask "why me?" These emotions are coupled with feelings of helplessness or frustration. If this anger is directed inward, they become depressed, and for some there is attendant guilt. They worry about something they may have inadvertently done that created the problem. If the anger is directed outward, the parents may begin to blame others, including their child. Parents then move into a time of grieving, as they slowly give up their hopes and dreams for a certain "kind of child." During this period, they are especially vulnerable to panaceas. From this point, they gradually begin to move toward greater acceptance, and in many cases, they begin to take needed actions.

Unlike parental grieving at the birth of a child with a visible handicap, such as a physical deformity, the process of mourning for a child with a marginal and less observable handicap is prolonged. The parents' reactions are staggered and not clear-cut, as they may move from panic to anger to grief, in any given situation or period of time. How parents react has implications for professional intervention.

The period of denial has many ramifications. For many parents, denial may serve an important function, as they need time to prepare to accept the painful reality and its implications. Therefore, professionals who provide evaluative interpretations may need to give parents several weeks to assimilate what they have heard before they meet with them again to plan. Still, during the time of denial, a child is often left vulnerable. The child knows something is wrong, that she or he is different, but feels "if my parents can't accept me for who I am, how will others. I must hide my problems."

Parents need guidance and support through the lengthy grieving process as well as in separating when they are irrationally angry from when their rightful expectations are not being met by other professionals. How often one hears of the frustrations of perceptive parents who have brought their concerns about their child to a pediatrician, only to be told they are being impatient and overanxious. Parents need to be relieved of their guilt. Raising a learning disabled child will have an effect on the family. Parents need to know they did not cause the problem, for if they feel so, they will then feel they can "cure" the problem. Social workers can be most helpful when they recognize the legitimate pain that raising a child with problems may cause, as well as the sadness parents must experience as their child struggles to cope.

Raising a child who has special problems means parents often need assistance in specifying expectations and learning effective techniques for helping their child gain mastery in their environment. For example, parents need to learn how to break-down everyday tasks for a child who is less adept and easily overwhelmed. Learning how to put on a pullover sweater can be demonstrated to a child step by step, as can learning to brush one's teeth, or learning how to order and buy an item in a store. For those who cannot master certain tasks, alternatives need to be considered. Zippers and buckles are more easily handled than buttons and laces. Youth who adapt to new or unanticipated situations more slowly need anticipatory guidance and more time. A child who is going on a class trip needs help in thinking about what to expect and how to handle any problems, for instance, what to do if she or he gets lost. Parents tend to end up in power struggles when children insist unrealistically that an event will happen a certain way. Rather than argue, parents are more effective when they say, "That's what you wish, but that is not what may happen."

People with problems in social competence need parental assistance at many levels. They lack natural ease in relationships, and efforts at engaging and sustaining contacts can be awkward and therefore laboured. When children are young, parents can take the initiative in structuring social opportunities for their child. They can play a more active role in helping their child to connect appropriately and to engage in successful play. As their child grows older, role modeling, direct advice, and active problem solving help people learn needed social skills. Since people with learning disabilities are often taken advantage of or rejected, without provocation, they need help in dealing with peer reaction. Efforts to strengthen social skills take on special relevance in view of a recent study showing that learning disabled youth have demonstrated their capability of improving social-perceptual skills, so that by late adolescence they are closing the maturational gap.

Children with problems in attention may need medication. In addition, providing structured and predictable environments, setting clear boundaries, and minimizing distractions will lend important sources of support to these children. Parents need to learn how to effectively handle disciplinary issues and to evade futile power struggles and attacks on their child. For example, impulsivity in children can best be addressed by helping them develop awareness and then creating an extra moment between impulse and action, which provides youngsters with time to stop and think so they can alter their response.

Adolescents with learning disabilities do not achieve autonomy at the same rate as their peers, and therefore have a prolonged and wider dependence on adults. They also are more vulnerable to stress and experience greater anxiety as they confront difficult tasks. The dilemma for parents and educators is to find the appropriate balance between providing needed help and offering increasing supports toward achieving independence.

People with learning disabilities face certain common tasks with which they often need help. It is the social worker who can, and indeed should, address these needs with them. By the time children develop a sense of awareness about themselves in relation to peers or siblings, they may well realize that in certain subtle ways they are different from others. It may be apparent in the difficulties they experience in mastering academic expectations (e.g., reading); in the way they behave (e.g., hyperactivity); or in the way they are perceived socially by their peers or family (e.g., ignored). The child begins to worry and thinks, "Why me? What's wrong anyway? What can be done? Will I fail? Why don't I have friends?" Those are the kinds of questions a professional or parent needs to help children with, clarifying that what they are having trouble with (e.g., sitting still or writing poorly) is not their fault and helping them specify strengths and weaknesses, and to avert gross negative generalizations (e.g., "I am dumb"). Learning disabled youth are often teased by their peers, and they need specific ideas on how to respond. For example, people make fun of them because they may attend a different school or class, or they may taunt them because they perform poorly in athletics. Expecting a youngster to ignore these comments is not realistic; rather, they need to learn to respond with straightforward answers, such as, "I know I am not good at sports."

The therapeutic context for work with people with learning disabilities should have both structure and predictability. They need a sense of organization; for some, open-ended sessions will evoke greater anxiety and loss of control. It is often necessary to depart from traditional psychotherapeutic strictures, for with the learning disabled, the worker takes on a more active role. This population responds best to a strong, positive working alliance, one in which the worker moves patiently and very supportively with the client while interceding to develop receptivity in the environment.

By adolescence, problems may intensify and family, teachers, and peers may be less patient. Adolescents may be angry about the demands made on them that they cannot meet. Those who lack social or communication skills feel deepened inadequacy and loneliness because they are not part of the teenage group. Adolescents who have poor impulse control and lack social judgment may be exploited by peers and become easy targets for involvement in antisocial acts. Parents and other adults have become worn out, are less tolerant, and express such feelings as, "It's time to shape up already. ... Aren't you ever going to grow up?" Thus, the cycle of conflict already present in this phase of life may greatly intensify.

Adults with learning disabilities have been a less visible and identified population. As noted earlier, it was originally assumed that people outgrew these problems by the time they reached adulthood. We now know that this outcome is not necessarily valid. We see adults discovering, for the first time, that they are learning disabled. We also see learning disabled adults struggling in the job market, being discriminated against because of their handicaps or losing employment because they do not adapt well to more sophisticated workplace demands.

People with learning disabilities are born into a wide range of families, some functioning more or less effectively than others. Having a learning disability cannot be attributed to a problem within the family, but rather families may need help in coping with their reactions to existing difficulties and stress. A social worker may need to reinforce and support a family's efforts to improve behavioural management, to enhance avenues of communication, to help define realistic expectations of each other, and to tolerate periods of ambiguity and frustration in the context of long-term progress. Marital stress may be precipitated by the birth of a learning disabled child. Parents may find themselves not able to draw strength from their relationship; rather, they may be divided by their own fears, their anger, their disappointments, and their impotence. Differences in decision making while raising a disabled child may similarly result in additional marital discord. Last, families carry extra emotional and physical burdens in living with a learning disabled member and will need assistance in locating and using resources for support within the community.

It is often helpful to focus on and offer service to the siblings of learning disabled children and to understand their reactions. Some siblings experience guilt because they function more effectively than their learning disabled sibling, especially if the sibling without the disability is younger. More frequently, however, brothers or sisters experience acute embarrassment in having to explain to their own peers their sibling's differences in behaviour or achievement. They may bear the brunt of teasing. Some siblings long for a "real" brother or sister with whom they could share more, one who would more closely reflect their own feelings and experiences. Finally, siblings resent what they may experience as a double standard in their families when there are two levels of expectations, one for the learning disabled child and another for the sibling . These siblings will need help in sorting through their own reactions, opening up communication within the family, and, finally, developing strategies to deal with their peers' reactions.

A person's disability touches every family member. As a problem throughout the life cycle, we are only beginning to learn about how emerging issues will affect family members as the learning disabled person carries out his or her respective roles as child, spouse, and then, perhaps, parent.

The kinds of problems for which the learning disabled and their families seek help from social workers may occur at various points in their lifetime. The tasks that they face, often coupled with and unresponsive environment, may produce situations that warrant crisis intervention, short-term consultation, or longer-term counselling. The following case was selected because it provides the opportunity to learn about a child with learning disabilities and her parents who obtained needed services intermittently over the period of a decade and a half.

This is a story of Cindy , her brothers Barry and David (ages 21 and 23), and her parents, Edward and Lucy Stone. This is a middle-class, Unitarian family who live in southern Connecticut. Mr. Stone is a journalist and a devoted and caring father. Ms. Stone is an early childhood educator, who works part-time, and is deeply invested in the well-being of her children. Their sons are both bright, competent, and highly engaging young men who have fared very well in both their academic and social lives.

Ms. Stone's first two pregnancies were normal. She was 35 years old and pregnant with Cindy when she developed a serious respiratory infection for which she took antibiotic drugs. She remained healthy for the remainder of her pregnancy, and Cindy was born, at full term, by forceps delivery. Cindy appeared to be a healthy, quiet, content infant whose sole problem, at that time, was some colic she experienced for several months after the introduction of whole milk into her diet. Ms. Stone became concerned about Cindy's physical development when Cindy reached 9 months and still had difficulty sitting without support. Ms. Stone's worries remained dormant until she began to realize that Cindy continued to reach other physical developmental milestones at a slower pace than most of her peers. Ms. Stone's efforts to bring her questions to the pediatrician were met by reassuring statements that "some children develop more slowly than others, but Cindy would soon catch up."

Ms. Stone tried to engage her husband in listening to and acknowledging her fears that Cindy was not developing normally, but he offered reasons for any differences and cited areas in which she performed at the norm. Feeling alone in her growing anxiety, even panicked by the gloomy picture she fantasized and foresaw for her child, Ms. Stone became depressed. She was obsessed with thoughts about Cindy, impatient with the ambiguity of not knowing what was wrong, and distraught with her own impotence. She went to a local mental health clinic for help. The social worker played an instrumental role in alleviating the symptoms of depression but was not able, understandably, to offer Ms. Stone the assurances she repeatedly sought that her child would eventually achieve the capacity for normal functioning. The social worker offered to meet with Mr. and Ms. Stone jointly. She gently helped Mr. Stone to hear his wife's concerns and to move past his own denial.

Cindy began to walk at about 18 months and Mr. and Ms. Stone went through a period of relief and renewed hope. However, after several months, it became apparent that Cindy's receptive speech was limited, and she understood less than children her age who were already speaking words, if not sentences. Although a seemingly self-contented child, Cindy often played in an isolated fashion away from her peers. Family and friends began to notice and comment on Cindy's lack of ability to speak. Again Mr. and Ms. Stone became alarmed and concerned and contacted a pediatric neurologist for an evaluation. The physician pointed out uneven areas of development, ruled out retardation or autism, hypothesized what was then called "minimal brain dysfunction" and recommended speech therapy to address Cindy's delayed language development.

Cindy attended a local speech therapy clinic and made rapid strides in gaining language. Some difficulties in articulation persisted because of problems in the proper placement of her tongue in mouth coordination.

Cindy entered nursery school at the age of 4, and delays in certain areas of emotional and social development became readily apparent. The noise level and active environment of preschoolers were overwhelming to Cindy, who sometimes sought refuge by herself or under a blanket. Other times, she tried to engage with her classmates, but her judgments on how to enter play and her ongoing social interaction skills were inept. She was easily upset with changes in routines and her excessive vulnerability led to outbursts of crying, if someone, for example, sat in her chair by mistake.

During this time, her parents sought professional guidance in order to understand Cindy's behaviour, to learn needed new parenting skills, and to make future educational plans. For many months, they met monthly with the social worker and provided her with examples of Cindy's behaviour. She helped create a framework for understanding Cindy and frequently pointed to areas of strength and effective efforts Cindy was making to cope with a sometimes overwhelming or rejecting environment. Through these interventions, the social worker helped to alleviate some parental anxiety, offered new perspectives on Cindy's functioning and progress, and helped the Stones to learn to influence Cindy's school experience. One poignant example occurred when Ms. Stone described a recent meeting with the nursery school teacher. This teacher was critical of Cindy, saying she had entered the room of an adjoining class to play and that many of the children began to yell and ridicule Cindy. The envisaged pain of this scene caused Ms. Stone to suddenly dissolve in tears. The social worker softly asked Ms. Stone, "What did you say when the teacher told you this story?" Ms. Stone replied, "I said nothing. I felt she was telling me how my daughter misbehaved." The social worker commented, "But this was a 4-year-old not acting in malice. You should have said to the teacher 'and what did you do'?" This important lesson that parents don't have to accept someone else's definition of a problem, and that parents have the right to expect that their child be appropriately represented and protected, became a model that the Stones used over and over again in their negotiations with the programmes in which Cindy was enrolled.

Cindy entered kindergarten in a small school when she was almost 6, so she could have an extra year of developmental time. Although she lacked competence in both social interaction and motor agility (especially graphomotor skills), her cognitive abilities were within the norm, and she was even precocious in reading. This was surprising because an aunt and cousin had histories of dyslexia. Cindy's behaviour was seen as immature, rather than deviant, and she was not well organized. Still, Cindy was an appealing youngster, had a quick sense of humor, and related well to adults. Her perceptiveness coupled with her unusual resilience and persistence served as important strengths in facing daily problems. Throughout her latency age years, she progressed in most areas, especially in speech and academic work. Her continuing difficulty in social functioning remained a source of frustration to her and of concern and sadness to her family.

As Cindy entered adolescence, she appeared dissatisfied, if not somewhat depressed, by the disparity between her aspirations and what she could actually expect for herself. Her parents tried to locate a counseling group for learning disabled children, where she might obtain professional help in acquiring skills and feedback in this social context, but they were not successful. So they returned to a social worker to seek additional help for themselves and now also for Cindy. Mr. and Ms. Stone moved to a deeper level in sharing their worries, especially whether Cindy could move toward greater independence in functioning. They also were helped to reflect on how their frustrations were inadvertently being communicated to Cindy, and how they might try to respond positively to her new efforts to communicate and interact.

Cindy was immediately receptive to the social worker's active, interested style and the kind of support, patience, and acceptance she experienced in their work together. Cindy has been meeting weekly with the social worker for the past two years. They have explored many themes, including Cindy's feelings of being different, and her search for who she was, as she straddled two worlds, one of normally developing children and the other of the learning disabled. By the age of 14, Cindy developed some secondary problems attendant to her differences in development. Primary among them was her lack of self-esteem, which increasingly affected her expectations for herself and her communications with others. It became so marked that she sometimes walked with her head down to avert any possible peer rejection. Nevertheless, Cindy made slow, but consistently positive strides. The use of a dual educational and therapeutic focus on coping skills as she faced interactional tasks in her family, school, and social arena gave her new confidence and mastery. She also gained self-awareness, so she could "catch herself" when acting in dysfunctional ways, such as "I guess I am nervous about getting a new coat, because I am so used to the old one." She can better anticipate problems and plan accordingly, e.g., finding ways to organize her school assignments. She also learned to move from initial rigidity to greater flexibility in handling everyday situations.

Finally, Cindy has been helped to handle the multiple demands of high school. At this time, Cindy was able to taper off contacts with the social worker and assume some greater responsibility for autonomous functioning and to advocate for her own needs. It is anticipated that Cindy may need to return for help when she prepares to move toward her college entrance year.

Summary

Several salient issues emerge. The first is that the learning disability syndrome is extremely common. This term serves as an umbrella category covering certain dysfunctions in cognitive, language, physical, and/or behavioural functioning. Initially, this syndrome was seen as affecting only children, but it is now a documented problem that persists, sometimes in changing form, into adolescence and adulthood. In this relatively young, and still growing field, there is ambiguity and lack of agreement about the definition and etiology of learning disabilities. Recent research attests to the effectiveness of a range of new interventive techniques and particularly highlights the usefulness of medication, counseling, psychoeducational techniques, and environmental supports. Certainly early identification, assessment, planning, and intervention have reaped important gains in ameliorating the effects of this dysfunction and its attendant secondary problems.

The challenge for social workers lies ahead. We have inadvertently played a major role in working with people with learning disabilities, because this population abounds in our social agencies and institutions. Yet we have not been in the forefront of service but have sometimes relied on old and improper diagnostic categories and models of psychotherapeutic interventions that have not been necessarily helpful. In other instances, we have focused on addressing the secondary rather than the primary problem.

Our expertise in work with individuals, families, and groups and in helping clients with their problems in the context of their environments certainly bodes well for the responsibility of our assuming increasing leadership in services to the learning disabled. Within our own range of social work settings, we have the unique opportunity to reach out, to innovate a practice technology, and, in collabouration with other disciplines, to offer much needed help to this population. We also need to join with other professionals in developing programmes, influencing legislators, and educating the public about what life is like and how to support people with learning disabilities in our society.

❑❑❑

9

Social Work for Unemployed and Youth People

Introduction

Some are specific to particular attempts to provide programmematic assistance. Others are more profound and relate to both the biases as well as the limitations of the policymaking process in this country when it addresses issues of justice and equity. This chapter will stress these latter aspects.

One component of a framework for explaining the existence and perseverance of contemporary poverty and homelessness comes from understanding the theory of housing production and employment in our regulated market economy and the Marxist critique. Housing production is reviewed because of its central importance to the question of available shelter options. Employment is reviewed because access to shelter is regulated by income in market economies.

To suggest that there is a debate between Marxists on the one hand and defenders of regulated market economies on the other is somewhat artificial. It must be stressed that utilizing this concise bipolar theoretical alignment is an analytical expedient. Rather, there exist many different schools of thought that fit uneasily into these two paradigms. For instance, Medcalf and Dolbeare, looking at the existing spectrum of American political theory identify eight distinct schools of thought: liberalism, neoliberalism, particularistic reform movements, economic democracy, democratic socialism, neoconservatism, conservatism, and the new right. For the sake of simplicity, all of these, save democratic socialism which has Marxist elements, will be considered variants of the regulated market school of thought. It is also recognized that to consider Marxism as a. unitary category is a simplification since to do so hides the rich diversity of thought in the literature of socialism and communism. Nonetheless, this simplification will aid the analysis of the distinct approaches to housing and employment policy inherent in these two major contending theoretical paradigms. While this is not the place for an extensive analysis of these paradigms, a brief review serves to highlight their relevance to the foregoing discussion. Only those aspects relevant to that discussion and the issue of homelessness will be presented here.

Marxian Primer — The Low Cost Housing Shortage

While housing policy is not a central theme in Marxian analysis, it was the deplorable conditions endured by the inhabitants of British slums in the nineteenth century that helped form the political views of Friedrich Engels. More recently, urbanists both here and abroad have begun to develop a structural Marxist theory that provides a fresh perspective on urban development and its attendant problems. Previously, leftist urban analysts tended to concentrate on what Zukin has called "radical empiricism" whereby urban scholars enumerated the particular problems affecting the poor in our cities. These studies tended to propose new social programmes as solutions, thereby accepting the liberal democratic state as agent of social reform. Structural Marxists view cities and their problems from a different and broader viewpoint. M.P. Smith describes this viewpoint:

For structural Marxists economic logic is the primary determinant of class inequality. The logic of private capital accumulation, as mediated by the state and modified by the social conflict engendered by the accumulation process, are the basic causes of urban development. The "urban" realm is a by-product of economic organization; the political and cultural spheres are only "relatively autonomous from the economic.

There is much ferment among proponents of structuralism; in particular, there is intense debate over the role of groups and individuals in the structuralist paradigm.

All Marxist analysis is based on viewing the free market economy as meeting the interests of the capitalist class by ensuring the subservient position of the working class. Marxists would ascribe the rise of homelessness to the failure of our housing delivery system which is based on a free market ideology. This free housing market serves the class interests of those in power. The bulk of the population functions as passive consumers, a resource to be manipulated to further the profit making ends of the capitalist class. In such markets, expensive new housing is constructed for the affluent and older housing is supposed to become available to the less affluent since it will drop in price as the increasing supply of new housing lessens its desirability. In essence, housing is competed for like any other good and the poor get the aging slums that are left over. In a free housing market, housing is viewed as a commodity to be sold to the highest bidder and the issues of equity or justice are largely ignored. Indeed, housing is viewed as an investment more than as a means of shelter. This has led to severe under occupation of housing, the profusion of second and third homes for affluent families and empty inner city shell properties owned chiefly for speculative reasons. The capitalist system is typified by stark contrasts: huge opulent homes that bear little relation to the housing needs of their rich inhabitants on the one hand and decrepit urban slums and rural shacks that do not meet local housing codes on the other.

Indeed, the provision of housing in a capitalist system provides an excellent example of the system at work since it forces the poor to live in slums surrounded by the most deplorable conditions. These slums will exist so long as their owners can make a profit on the units. They will attempt to cram people in these slums and charge the highest possible rents in order to increase their profits. Landlords will fight any attempts by authorities to regulate their business and are steadfast against the introduction of building codes and rent control laws—a battle that continues to this day in many of our cities. If, during conditions of housing surplus, they no longer can make a profit on a building, they abandon it. Many private units in urban submarkets are lost annually when the cost of repairs to older units cannot be recouped via higher rents or sales prices. In such cases, the units are seen as a bad investment and are abandoned. Frequently, conditions of market disequilibrium occur when a condition of excess housing supply exists simultaneously with a shortage of low cost housing. When there are not enough slums to house the rising numbers of the poor, a phenomenon common to many of our older urban areas today, then the final indignity of homelessness results.

All our older cities have large and mounting inventories of abandoned housing units that all told could easily shelter the nation's homeless. They are not utilized because it is not profitable for the private owners to make them available. Paradoxically, city governments often come to own these abandoned houses due to tax foreclosure, and many find their way into government-financed housing programmes that aim to rehabilitate these units for low income households. The problem is that the rate of publicly supported rehabilitation is greatly exceeded by the rate of continued private abandonment of other units. Not enough public money is appropriated to repair these units at a sufficient rate so as to ensure that all the poor can find safe shelter.

Thus it is the shortage of low income housing due to the reliance on the free market in housing that has occasioned homelessness. In this view, homelessness, particularly in cities saddled with large inventories of abandoned housing, is proof of the failure of many postindustrial societies to adequately protect their citizens from the cruelties of market capitalism. Indeed, Marxists argue that the provision of publicly supported shelters for the homeless should be resisted since it only serves to paper over the fundamental problems of capitalism which should see the light of day and thereby influence public opinion. They think opinion should be influenced to the point that the public demands that adequate housing become a government provided right rather than a private sector commodity. In the Marxist view, low cost public housing should be provided by the central government so all citizens would be guaranteed access to decent and affordable housing. Private ownership of land and housing would be severely restricted. Housing should be seen as providing shelter rather than as a private financial investment instrument. Such housing could be provided in a number of ways. Public rental housing or subsidized owner-occupied housing could be provided throughout the country in sufficient quantity and at such a price or rent as to ensure the goal of adequate shelter for all. Resale restrictions, for example, could ensure that owners receive a predetermined return on their investment thereby eliminating the windfall profits so characteristic of much of the free market in housing.

A Marxist critique of the free market in housing would also include a strong denunciation of the tendency of large corporations to dominate the agenda for the revitalization of our older cities. Specifically, these corporations usually support a type of revitalization of the central areas that eliminates the existing low cost housing and replaces it with commercial buildings or upper income housing. Central city revitalization often serves to "cream off" more affluent residents from outlying older urban neighbourhoods, destroying their socioeconomic balance. Indeed, studies of central city revitalization show that many of the newcomers to these areas are former residents of urban neighbourhoods and not suburbanites returning to the city. Thus, in these areas owner-occupiers move out and are replaced by lower income renters. Building maintenance slips and the area begins to cycle downwards. At the final stages, renters are evicted from these units as landlords finally walk away. Once again homelessness characterizes the final stage. The losers in this kind of revitalization programme are the central area residents actually displaced as well as those citizens in peripheral urban neighbourhoods. This is because reinvestment in these latter areas is not similarly encouraged; instead, the buildings and general infrastructure are allowed to decline.

The Marxists also link neighbourhood decline to the actions of large banks and corporations. Specifically, it has been shown that many banks withdraw capital from older inner city neighbourhoods at the first sign of economic change, thereby sealing the area's fate. While continuing to take deposits from residents, they often refuse to lend money or grant mortgages. As a result, housing conditions deteriorate as investment falls off. The end of the process for the residents is wholesale housing deterioration and abandonment. Marxists claim this so-called "red lining" is done not for sound economic reasons as is claimed by the banks, but rather so as to be able to create new markets for their services in the future. Viewed from this perspective, older urban areas have been fertile territory for investors, since money is made on all phases of its life cycle: birth, growth, maturity, decline, and eventual rebirth through redevelopment. This pattern of infusion and withdrawal of capital funds ensures that the neighbourhood goes through cycles of boom and bust that typify the capitalist system. The fact that "red lining" leads to the loss of low cost housing and precipitates homelessness is what is important here. The Marxist critique stresses the impotence of the individual and the neighbourhood in the face of the countervailing corporate agenda. This impotence stems from the basic inequities inherent in free market capitalism which treats citizens as depersonalized consumers to be manipulated by entrepreneurs so as to maximize profits.

A particular concern of Marxian analysts is the type of self-serving redevelopment which occurs after older urban neighbourhoods have suffered a period of disinvestment and are then redeveloped to meet the needs of large corporations. They argue that when corporate investors become involved in older neighbourhoods, it is only to further their own interests at the expense of the local community. An example of this occurred in the Poletown section of Detroit, Michigan, where General Motors Corporation leveled large areas of a working-class community in order to build a new car plant. It is a measure of the economic depression gripping these older cities that such a plan garnered political support on the strength of the promised jobs. For Marxists, this type of corporate economic blackmail is the essence of free market capitalism. In fact, there were many dispossessed households without a member employed by General Motors. For these people the plan was a no win situation that could be the first step toward homelessness since affordable replacement housing was in short supply.

Another important aspect of the housing issue for Marxists is the geographical location of low income areas and the poor and homeless populations. In the United States, the inner city has long functioned as the zone for transitional and/or slum housing as well as for the social services that cater to the poor and homeless. The minimal governmental efforts to provide low income housing and remedial social programmes have also been concentrated in the core cities.

This is because the suburbs were established by the corporate elite to function as the preserve of the middle and upper classes and as separate governmental entities, able to enact laws to ensure that low income classes are excluded. Marxists point to the resulting disequilibrium that forces impoverished cities to care for the preponderant share of the nation's poor and needy while the affluent suburbs avoid such responsibility. Thus, corporate interests devised the mechanism that has fostered the creation of the stereotypical black and minority dominated city surrounded by the "white suburban noose".

In actuality, this pattern is always shifting somewhat as some older inner city areas revitalize and become more affluent. Today, some central city districts are the preserve of the affluent young who are eager to sample the cultural enticements of the city. Many will leave when it becomes time to educate their offspring, however, thus ensuring that this urban revitalization will remain limited in impact. More important than this small scale revitalization process is the fact that the suburbs have not allowed the production of any significant amounts of low cost housing to enable them to accommodate their fair share of the poor or minority population. The segregation of the poor and minority groups denies them access to plentiful suburban educational and economic resources that nurture advancement. Such inequality remains a salient product of housing patterns in the United States thereby furthering the interests of the dominant economic class who are content to live in their "suburban foxholes".

A further refinement of this critique has been advanced by Castells who suggests that capitalist development has served to separate the locus of social interaction and human development from that of economic organization and political power. Castells worries that the need to contest the local implications of spatial and employment dislocations engendered by new capitalist modes of production will force local social movements to cut from their agendas more important issues concerning government responsibility for the needs of the working classes. This concept is in many ways an extension of Webber's more positive view of a communications based urban structure.

Marxian Primer on Jobs/Incomes Shortfall

Income generated by meaningful employment is a crucial determinant of one's ability to obtain shelter. A Marxist view of employment is based on an analysis similar to that of housing. Again, labour is viewed as a resource to be used as required by the capitalist class. Thus, by definition unemployment is tolerated since capitalists require a reserve army of cheap labour ready to meet their short-term needs. There will also be periods of greater unemployment when less labour is required due to shifts in market demand or changes in production processes. Of course, job opportunities might be available elsewhere and labour is expected to pack up and go seek them. Each individual is on his own in this search. Constant insecurity prevails as do significant and lasting income disparities. There is no commitment between labourer and capitalist, since that would interfere with the profit motive of the latter. So it is the inherent structural aspects of the system that force the capitalist to adopt this attitude, for to do otherwise would risk being crushed by competitors not so kindly disposed. In addition, racism and the economic precariousness of life for minorities who form a disproportionate share of the lower classes results in a psychological pressure cooker that destroys many minority individuals and their families. It is this dehumanizing aspect of free market capitalism that Marxists find so abhorrent. Labour unions, while initially very helpful in collectivizing the power of the labour movement, are not a sufficient counterforce to capital in today's global economy since there is always the threat that production will be moved elsewhere in order to find a cheap labour market.

Such structural realities force the state and local governments to be active participants in this process by assisting in the internecine competition to attract jobs.

In recent years this country has experienced high rates of unemployment reaching 10% for significant periods of time. This figure is recognized as an undercount since it does not include those discouraged jobseekers who have dropped out of the market. The rate also obscures the fact that certain populations are disproportionately affected. Minorities have significantly higher rates of unemployment, particularly young inner city blacks who often have rates of unemployment approaching 50%. Lack of adequate education is a causative factor as is the loss of traditional entry and middle level manual or blue-collar jobs in many areas caused by the restructuring of the job supply. In some areas, there has been considerable growth in higher paying professional job categories and in the low paying service sector job categories. However, many of these new service sector jobs offer little hope for advancement and do not pay enough to cover reasonable living expenses even when two family members work.

Financial restructuring unrelated to the production process also exerts a toll on labour. Particularly galling is when profitable local operations become pawns in a corporate takeover game in which investors milk the assets of the local operation in order to fuel further corporate takeovers. The end result of such mismanagement can be plant closings and more unemployment. The Marxist alternative is for the people acting through a strong central government to replace the private sector and to make the necessary contract with labour to plan jointly for the wider needs of the economy and labour as a whole. Since competition will no longer exist, the will of the wider community will prevail over the selfish needs of the individual capitalist.

Marxists also criticize the tendency of capitalist societies to foster severe and lasting regional economic inequalities that lead to conditions of local high unemployment. These inequalities result from the manipulation of capital by monopoly interests that seek more favourable returns available in certain geographic areas. Thus, many parts of the country find themselves cut off from lending streams that are available elsewhere. A good example of this tendency is the movement of capital, industry, and jobs to the Sunbelt in the mid-1970s. Economists have long been concerned with the detrimental impact such volatility fosters, such as local inflationary pressures and overdevelopment in the expanding areas and depression and decay in the abandoned regions. Much of the rationale behind such wrenching dislocations is the search for cost advantages by investors, in particular, labour cost savings. That these advantages will inevitably erode, forcing another round of dislocation with all the attendant costs, is irrelevant to the individual decision maker who must abide by the market's imperative to minimize costs and maximize profits in the short-run.

The reaction of President Reagan to the plight of those people adversely affected by these dislocations was that of a classic market supporter. He counseled the "get on your bike" approach that would have the unemployed abandon their homes and community in order to seek employment elsewhere. The resultant negative impact on those who are left behind because they will not or cannot relocate does not count in this calculation, needless to say. The young are the most able to pull up roots and relocate. Those left behind are those older and less skilled individuals who have little likelihood of finding new jobs and now must rely on an increasingly impoverished local community for assistance. The result is local economic depression with increased social deprivation and homelessness. Marxists reject as simplistic the view that these phenomena are not manifestations of free market capitalism but the result of the expansion of knowledge and therefore purely technological in nature.

This brief review of some of the relevant aspects of Marxian analysis is not intended to be exhaustive. Rather, those aspects of Marxist thought relevant to the occurrence of widespread homelessness were included. Much more could be said about the market disequilibrium caused by monopoly capital and the role of local and national elites to name but a few of the important concepts in the rich field of Marxian analysis.

To some extent, the Marxist view of market economies is based on a non regulated model of the classic free market economy. It is probably accurate to assume that none of the original Marxist critics of free market-based societies ever imagined that the capitalist powers in these countries would allow the type of market regulation that was to develop over time. Today, all market-oriented liberal democratic societies have complex market regulations based on the authority of their governments for taxation, commerce, and administration. While these regulations do much to dampen the volatility of free market capitalism and cushion many of its negative socioeconomic effects, few would claim that this regulatory system has been perfected, particularly in the United States. As a result, it is important to review the theoretical aspects of regulated market housing production and employment.

Regulated Market Primer – The Low Cost Housing Shortage

Porter and others who support the free market housing system make their case on more than just aggregate housing output. Specifically, they argue that the so-called filtering process in a free market housing system ensures that both rich and poor will be able to find suitable accommodation. The filtering process is predicated on a stage or cyclical view of housing market dynamics in a free housing market. In such a situation the market caters to the potent demand for the highest priced housing since this will result in the most effective housing production schedule and the highest profits for the industry. The construction of such housing for the wealthy also results in improved housing opportunities for the middle and lower income groups since for every top-priced home built, an extended series of moves (the multiplier effect) is initiated back down through the categories of lower-priced homes. This occurs because the new top-priced homes lessen the effective demand for former top-priced homes by siphoning off some of their potential consumers. In short, the aging process puts former top-priced housing at a competitive disadvantage; they are not as up to date or prestigious as the newest housing. House prices fall, first in the category of homes that were formerly top-priced and eventually rippling down through all housing categories. As a result, many households opt to move up into homes that are now more affordable to them. All of these moves entail a distinct improvement in the families' living conditions.

Supporters of the filtering process point out that as households move up into newer housing, they will also be moving into newer communities. As a result, they will be likely to benefit from improved municipal services and community infrastructure.

According to its supporters, the only real problem inherent in the filtering process is that it is dependent on the health of the economy in general and interest rate fluctuations in particular. Sufficient funds for housing construction and mortgage lending must be available at reasonable rates through primary and secondary financial markets. This liquidity is essential to the maintenance of sufficient demand to maintain housing production and thereby the filtering process. Free market supporters urge that housing policy be centered on the maintenance by the Federal Reserve Bank of a supportive financial environment for housing production.

Empirical tests of the multiplier effect have provided evidence that the filtering process does work to a degree in some situations. In other situations, it does not work in any uniform way and, perversely, it can even hasten the decline of an area. For instance, there is no way to control the geographic aspects of filtering. Filtering may well result in the availability of additional units of housing, but these units may not be in the area of greatest need. Similarly, filtering can be truncated if households in the middle of the process decide to spread out and consume more housing in their initial location. Additionally, rent control and zoning restrictions as well as other factors that have an impact on market operations can adversely affect the filtering process.

Proponents of the regulated market see homelessness as simply the result of mismanaged social welfare and housing policies and not a fundamental flaw in the market-based housing delivery system. Regulated market supporters tend to view the problem of homelessness as one caused more by a shortfall in incomes rather than in a shortage of housing units. They justify this viewpoint by pointing out the sheer number of housing units built since World War II in this country and the concomitant increase in the housing standards enjoyed by the vast majority of the population, standards which are the envy of the world.

At the same time, they would acknowledge the existence of real hardship at the bottom tier of certain urban and rural housing markets: households unable to locate affordable housing and others living in overcrowded conditions in below-standard units. In these cases, they would call for job training and employment programmes. These programmes would help the poor to better themselves by improving access to employment, thereby providing the income necessary to obtain decent housing. In cases where employment is not an option, they would call for government-supported income maintenance programmes. An alternative or combined approach, which is less favored, would be for the government to fund low cost housing programmes which deliver adequate supplies of low cost housing to enable those who are on welfare or otherwise on very low incomes to find adequate housing. Such programmes would be considered crucial components of the so-called safety net that ensures that the poorest in our free market society are looked after by the rest.

Proponents of a regulated market would claim that significant housing problems in our society are largely confined to certain housing submarkets in our older urban areas. Looking at the desolation that characterizes so many of our inner city neighbourhoods, they draw very different conclusions than the Marxists would. To market proponents, the presence of abandoned units in our central cities is proof that the majority of the former inhabitants of these cities have moved up and out to newer and better quality housing in the burgeoning suburban areas. They would cite numerous surveys that show an urban locale is least favored, while a small town or suburban locale is most favored by consumers. They would also mention the postwar decline in the populations of our large cities as further proof of this desire on the part of the public. Their view is that inner city housing is old and obsolete, a legacy of the industrial era "gritty city." It was built in another era for people with vastly different lifestyles than those of today. As a result, most urban row houses or apartments are cramped and inefficient; they were built at a high density with little surrounding public or private open space or parking facilities. Those who can afford to move out, do so at the earliest opportunity which is a positive function of the vast choice in housing available to the public in a free market system.

Market proponents agree that the problem of disposing of the housing units when they have cycled through to the end of their useful economic life is one that is not easily solved. This is because old neighbourhoods do not decline in a uniformly predictable way. Units that are clearly beyond repair sit side by side with units that are well kept. Many units that remain occupied are below standard, however. The fact that some old neighbourhoods have gone through cycles of revitalization and renewal confounds those who predicted the demise of most old inner city residential areas. Nonetheless, market proponents claim that most older inner city areas need to be closed out and their remaining residents relocated to newer areas. This should be done in a timely fashion so as to lessen the pain involved. This policy is based on the "triage" approach since it denies help to those areas that cannot be revitalized and gives it to those that have a realistic chance. They recognize that triage is very unpopular among many housing advocates who support the right of people to remain in their old areas. Unfortunately, given the prevailing economic structure, such a policy ensures that many poor households must suffer substandard accommodation in blighted areas that are continuing to decline. If their building is condemned or the owner cannot make basic repairs, these people could easily join the ranks of the homeless; either way, displacement and redevelopment would be inevitable.

Market proponents claim urban neighbourhood decline is due to technological forces working in the fertile environment of a regulated free market, namely the revolution in transportation, communication technology, and the service economy that has lessened the advantages hitherto enjoyed by the cities. Simply put, the car, the telephone, and more recently, the computer, have all functioned to deemphasize the need for the frequent and easy face-to-face contact which cities facilitated. In a service economy more and more services are not place-oriented but can be produced anywhere. As a result, the city has lost its dominant function as locus for employment and production of goods and services. The weakening of the economic primacy of the city has led to the decline in the quality of its housing stock that no amount of money can forestall. Units in many older sections will age, decay, and be abandoned as they no longer have an economic function. Indeed, to attempt to reverse neighbourhood decline by the inclusion of publicly funded housing rehabilitations is doomed to failure since the value of the resultant rehabilitations will be dragged down by the prevailing depressed market conditions. Instead, public policy should be aimed at ensuring an orderly market-led transition rather than trying to prop up uneconomic housing.

One market-oriented urban theorist ties urban decline

to the aging of cities and their physical infrastructure. Thought to be too highly deterministic by some, the theory holds that as cities age they go through cycles of growth, maturity, and decline ending in abandonment of the commercial and residential structure of the city. While the existence of exceptions to this rule are granted, they are considered to be few and small in impact.

Other market-oriented analysts tie the decline of American cities to the post-World War II governmental policies that set up a massive programme of government-insured, low cost mortgages for veterans that specifically excluded their use in urban areas. This effectively shunted much of the postwar housing growth out to the suburbs and made necessary the costly system of expressways designed to allow these far-flung areas to grow. This anti-urban tilt persisted in all federal spending programmes until the mid-1970s when the Carter administration made a concerted effort to eradicate it, but by that time the damage had been long done.

Other governmental policies and programmes have been blamed for fostering inner city housing decline. Reliance by local governments on the property tax as a source of revenue has been cited as a causal factor in housing decline and abandonment. Much has been written on the often inequitable market distortions occasioned by this method of raising revenue, particularly the negative impact of this tax on older urban neighbourhoods. Some market proponents argue for a shift toward greater use of a uniform, progressive income tax system to generate local revenues as is done in much of Europe. Others suggest greater use of tax rebates and caps for selected populations and areas.

Much attention has also been given to the influence of social tension that resulted from the ebb and flow of population groups, particularly in urban neighbourhoods. For instance, the Chicago school of urban sociology developed theories of "invasion and succession" that focused on the social and economic changes that resulted from the arrival of new ethnic and racial groups in particular neighbourhoods. Urban decline was often identified with so-called "zones of transition" which accommodated a high per centage of such lower-class newcomers to the city. Urban decline was ascribed to the inability of some newly arrived groups to ensure that their properties were maintained or in some instances, to their lack of familiarity with homeownership and its responsibilities. In any case, broadly conceived patterns of socioeconomic housing stratification were linked to urban residential blight and decay due to conditions of unequal access to services.

Market proponents would also argue that homelessness in urban submarkets has been worsened in part because of local opposition to a rational housing policy built on the principle of triage. They feel it is not the free market in housing that has occasioned problems but rather the misguided disruption of market forces by local political interests bent on protecting existing residents at all costs. Some would agree that the homeless situation has been exacerbated by the drastic cutbacks in low cost housing programmes instituted by the Reagan administration and that the solution lies in the restoration of these cuts. These funds would allow the hard-pressed cities to begin to refurbish vacant public housing units, build new scattered site units, and most important, begin to rehabilitate the vast array of abandoned housing units that exist in our older cities. But increasingly, housing experts are insisting on the need to utilize the triage concept in order to redevelop large areas of our older cities along the low density pattern so popular in our suburbs. In this way, they reason, cities will have a chance to compete on more equal terms with the newer suburbs.

Regulated Market Primer—Unemployment

Proponents of the regulated market view unemployment as a regrettable but necessary result of a dynamically changing economy that is moving through periods of growth and transformation due to innovation. These transformations often lead to unemployment which, while painful, cannot and should not be prevented. At the same time, it is the government's responsibility to ensure that these unemployed individuals receive sufficient income to tide them over until they find new employment. It is also the responsibility of the government to support adequate retraining programmes so as to ensure that the unemployed can be rehired in newly emerging fields. In recent years, the U.S. economy has produced a prodigious number of new jobs. The problem has been that they are different from the bulk of existing and now declining job types. This growth and change in job categories is due to the working of a healthy and innovative market-oriented society, adherents would claim. Innovation in a consumer-oriented world market and the need to nurture the entrepreneurial spirit that is its necessary medium is the fundamental *raison d' être* of free market capitalism. Supporters point to the superiority of the capitalist democracies in producing unparalleled prosperity for the majority of their citizens. The system also nurtures the creative spirit in science, medicine, and the arts. The way to maintain these beneficial outcomes is to ensure that the government's role must be limited to that of safety net provider for those who are adversely affected by the market's changing priorities. A central debate in U.S. politics concerns the size and role of the federal government as it goes about fulfilling this role.

Regulated market proponents would agree that postwar development patterns have made it more difficult for the inner city poor to have access to entry level jobs in the suburbs. Most would address this problem by aggressively enforcing fair housing laws so as to ensure access to all housing for people of all racial and ethnic backgrounds. Nonetheless, they would eschew policies that would ensure similar access for the poor who are an economic minority.

Currently, the free market economies have weathered a difficult period of adjustment as they have evolved into postindustrial service economies. In so doing, many jobs of long standing have been lost due to market dislocations. Many careers have been destroyed. Workers have been forced to adapt to the reality that the types of jobs that they held for so long are no longer available. It is true that other jobs have been created but they require new skills, particularly the ability to communicate and calculate effectively. Lost are the blue-collar jobs in the steel mills and manufacturing plants; newly created are the "white coat" jobs in the high technology and service sector. Older workers are hardest hit, but the need to make adaptations also affects the young and minorities.

Related to this problem of employment dislocation are broader questions concerning the high rate of individual failure within our socioeconomic system. Many educators trace such failure to low success rates for students in many of our urban school districts. Such students are often condemned to lead lives on the margins of a society increasingly oriented to high technology. Such individuals often lose their tenuous place in society due to local or national recessions that are so frequent in a free market economy. One cause of this problem is the poor quality of segments of our educational system and its inability to prepare students for a future based on rapid technological change. These changes may require an ability to switch careers several times during one's lifetime. Such career paths would be quite different from the single sector employment expectations of third generation steel, rubber, and mine workers. Responding to the training needs of this dynamic and constantly evolving economy is seen as a major task facing the leaders of market-oriented societies in the future. Failure in this area may lead to mounting numbers of American citizens who are unable to secure and hold jobs that allow them to maintain the kind of lifestyle Americans have enjoyed for so long. Put more starkly, as more Americans become downwardly mobile, more will join those who have bottomed out and are now counted among the homeless in our society. Supporters of a regulated market would attempt to solve such problems with appropriate training programmes and temporary economic support oriented toward reintroducing workers into the free market. They feel that only free enterprise coupled with social and economic support programmes to cushion the impact of rapid dislocations caused by this market can produce innovations necessary to tackle the numerous problems facing society. Naturally, the prospect of such an insecure, strung-out society is odious to Marxists who feel it reflects the complete capitulation of government to the increasingly disruptive demands of capital interests.

While this situation may be seen as a rough description of what prevails in periods of prosperity, it is recognized that free market economies are subject to swings or cycles of expansion and decline. Here again a regulatory approach to the market has evolved. In the market downswing, there is clearly a need for increased governmental intervention to rekindle growth. Likewise in periods of expansion, credit restrictions serve to dampen inflationary pressures. Such macroeconomic regulations based on Keynesian economic theory are now an accepted part of the market system. This regulatory intervention has been the basic guiding philosophy that has fueled our postwar prosperity. Thus, there is a need for a regulated economy responsive to macro-level market cycles as well as micro-level dislocations. All told, these and other regulatory interventions guide and control the performance of the market. The aim is to preserve the ability of the market mechanism to allocate goods and services in an efficient and timely manner while providing a safety cushion for those individuals adversely affected by the dislocations inherent in all dynamic markets.

In most instances, Marxists and market-oriented urbanists ascribe different root causes to the same phenomena. For example, market proponents would agree with Marxists that our disjointed pattern of local governments impoverishes our older urban jurisdictions and thereby contributes to urban housing decline and abandonment. They would agree that this is reprehensible and therefore should be subject to reform. They would cite attempts at regional local government reform in Dade County, Florida and elsewhere. Where Marxists differ is that they argue that such reformist measures are doomed to failure since they inevitably come up against resistance from the same societal forces that produced the problem in the first place.

Many, such as Dahl, specifically reject the arguments of structural Marxists and point to factors such as technology and the division of labour as exerting influence independent of the capitalist mode of production. Bensman has called upon Marxists to prove their assertion that contemporary urbanism is a product of capitalist development. Indeed, there is evidence that some communist societies struggle with urban problems strikingly similar to those of capitalist societies. Bensman states: "General problems of urbanization, industrialism, population density, and the struggles for the control over scarce resources by organized elites, classes, regional groups, and rural and urban dwellers exist in all societies whether capitalist or socialist, developed or undeveloped, colonial or neo-colonial".

This review of the essential differences between Marxists and regulated market system proponents serves to explain some of the profound differences of opinion and approaches that inform the national housing and employment policy debate. Most policy experts, however, accept the need to fashion workable solutions within the context of our regulated market economy. As a result, it is appropriate to take a brief look at the theory of decisionmaking in the American policymaking process because, here too, there are considerable differences of opinion and approach.

American Policymaking Process

The study of government in this country has a long and contentious history that has emerged from the intense debate surrounding representative theories of government. This debate involves attempts to assess the relative importance of conceptual notions concerning the rationality of man, the influence of bureaucracy, and the importance of interest groups, among others. This contentiousness continues to the present day and appears ready to outlast all of us. Briefly, the debate has been dominated by the pluralists, who see a somewhat open policymaking process, and the elitists, who see a very constrained policymaking process.

Pluralists such as Merriam, Truman, and Schumpeter base their position on the need of public officials to periodically respond to the voters if they wish to keep their positions. Pluralists agree that influence is not equally dispersed in our society but maintain that concerned citizens can often have an effect on policy. They see policymaking as being influenced by the extreme diversity of interests that exist in a democratic society, a diversity that forces public officials to engage in politics if they wish to see anything accomplished. Thus policymaking is seen as emerging from a complex process of bargaining, persuasion, rewards, threats, as well as the exercise of leadership authority; bureaucrats, business managers, interest groups, elected and appointed officials, are seen as heavily involved in this process while most citizens are not.

The policymaking process as envisioned by the pluralists is anything but rational. Rather, it is the product of countless incremental adjustments and compromises that are made in response to a particular issue or problem. Arriving at these adjustments and compromises is a difficult task often involving countless meetings with a myriad of individuals and groups all representing different interest. As a result, policymaking is seen as an intensely political process that often defies the best efforts of policy analysts to explain it much less develop predictive models for similar situations.

On the other hand, elitist theorists such as E.E. Schattschneider, Mancur Olsen, William Domhoff, Floyd

Hunter, and Henry Kariel see our society as being dominated by a business elite that effectively controls the policy agenda so that it remains responsive to the needs of private enterprise. This control extends to the political system and is so complete as to enable them to settle some issues out of the public spotlight and leave the inconsequential issues for public contention. This power emanates from the control of employment opportunities by the private business sector. Elitist theorists contend that relatively small groups of business oriented individuals exert this control at both the local and national levels. Proponents of both theories stress the need to test their theories in real world situations. By and large, such tests focus on the exercise of power at the local level and avoid applications to broad issues like the persistence of slums and income disparities.

Much of the foregoing debate involves political scientists and sociologists. A separate but parallel school of thought can be found among students of public policy and administration. By and large, this school of thought focuses on a broader and more conceptual level of debate as it labours to defend the pluralist vision. According to its main proponents, the public policy process can be seen as following one of three basic models. The first is the centralized policymaking approach adhered to by countries with strong, often Marxist-oriented central governments. In such cases, the main claim made in favor of this method is that it affords a rational and comprehensive perspective on the policy process. Such a method assumes that the policymaker possesses a high degree of control over the policymaking process, access to complete information, techniques for choosing between competing courses of action, and a hierarchy of values by which to judge outcomes.

Criticisms of this approach center on the fact that the requirements for the model are unattainable. Critics question the ability of any one policymaking source to operationalize a value hierarchy which could win public acceptance. In addition, Lindblom and others argue that it is simply not possible to absorb and relate the myriad conflicting informational inputs necessary to devise a rational policy.

Going beyond a critical analysis of centralized policymaking, Lindblom has developed a major conceptual alternative known variously as partisan mutual adjustment or disjointed incrementalism. This theory has policy being made by small scale marginal adjustments to current policy. Change is gradual since policy formulation is based on a "testing the waters" approach rather than centrally conceived goals. Thus, Lindblom argues that the proper policymaking process in a democracy is a product of the final compromise of many competing interests in society, a paradigm in keeping with the prevailing pluralistic view of American society.

Critics of this approach to decision making point out that its formulation is based on the participation of partisans or affected parties and that this would ensure that the interests of the most powerful would prevail. Moreover, disjointed incrementalism, which relies on a series of marginal policy adjustments, abrogates any responsibility for charting new policy initiatives; marginal policy adjustments may lead to significant change but it is more likely that they would not. Rein, in particular, criticizes disjointed incrementalism since its stepped decision making process might allow for a series of small scale rational decisions and yet lead to an irrational final outcome. More recently, Lindblom has admitted that large corporations do exert a disproportionate degree of influence, thereby lessening responsiveness to weaker interests. Still, some policy analysts still feel that disjointed incrementalism provides a good description of some aspects of the policymaking process in this country.

Unhappiness with the incrementalist paradigm has led to a number of derivative theories; one of the best known is authored by Etzioni. In it he tries to combine the salient aspects of the rational-comprehensive and the disjointed incremental approaches by positing what he calls "mixed scanning." A mixed scanning policymaking process would be composed of a mix of "fundamental" decisions and incremental decisions. These "fundamental" decisions would represent a limited form of rationalism in that these decisions are made with respect to policy goals but without the depth of detail and specification required by strict rationalism. A rotational principle is also built in so that all policy sectors would eventually come in for a fundamental review.

Mixed scanning represents a compromise that appears to answer some of the criticisms leveled at both existing decision-making paradigms. What it does not do is explain how to operationalize the fundamental review portion of the concept in a country having a governmental system characterized by elite-dominated decentralized decision-making.

To elitist theorists such a mixed scanning approach is utopian; it relies for its success on the very corporate interests that stand in the way of real societal change. As a consequence, any reforms resulting from "fundamental" decisions in such a system would be minimal at best. They may well be right, as evidenced by our continued toleration of the fact that a small but significant proportion of our citizens live in abject poverty and homelessness. Yet, history is replete with examples of the resiliency and adaptability of free market societies which, in other contexts, have been able to solve such problems. Postwar Britain and Scandinavia, among others, have evolved into highly organized welfare states with mixed economies that stress the advantages of combining the best features of centrally planned societies with those based on free markets.

Students of American policymaking are still in search of a definitive paradigm that incorporates all of the various aspects discussed above. In order to prove their respective cases, proponents of a particular approach conduct elabourate tests of their theories based on the examination of actual decisions as well as the investigation of those reputed to exercise power in actual situations. Needless to say, there is continued debate over how best to establish a definitive measure of power in real life situations or whether or not the development of such a test is even possible.

Implications for Policymaking and Analysis

The promulgation of simple policy reform in American society. These blockages are due to a host of factors inherent in both the broader policymaking process as well as specific elements such as the limited competencies of system operators, inadequate resources, conflicting criteria, and the like. The complexities built into the process have been described by Lindblom:

> Instead of reaching solutions that can be judged by standards of rationality, policy making reaches settlements, reconciliations, adjustments, and agreements that one can evaluate only inconclusively by such standards as fairness, acceptability, openness to reconsideration and responsiveness to a variety of interests. Sufficiently flexible, sufficiently open, and sufficiently given to endless reconsideration of policies, it encourages an eternal hopefulness even among the disadvantaged. Few people, consequently, try civil disorder or rebellion.

Lindblom is quick to point out that the blockages are not all systemic:

> Many people do not understand that their fellow citizens are a principal obstacle to their achieving an influence on policy. In recent years many proponents of educational reform, new foreign policies, liberation movements, and other causes on the frontiers of public policy came to a stop, not simply because elites stand in their way but because millions of their equally empowered fellow citizens also do. To move them is a massive and improbable undertaking.

Those policies that are enacted into law are often ineffective due to the fact that they are the compromised product of the incredibly complex policymaking process with which all policymakers must deal. A few policies such as Social Security stand apart and can be characterized as successful due to their relative simplicity and clarity. However, it should be remembered that Social Security was a product of the focused energies marshaled by a strong leader in the context of a business crisis. It also had the advantage of being a universal entitlement as distinct from potential programmes for the poor and homeless.

The Marxists may well be right; liberal free market democracies may not be capable of adequately providing for their poor and needy due to the inherent social and economic contradictions of the free market and the extension of these contradictions into the policymaking process. Yet there are examples elsewhere of well regulated market societies such as Sweden that have ensured a more even distribution of wealth while preserving democratic institutions and private property interests. Why has it been so difficult for us to do the same? Why have our social and economic policies resulted in the continuing toleration of significant poverty and homelessness?

❑❑❑

10

Assimilation of Social Work Services

Introduction

It has examined agency and institutional provision for case finding and for treatment with attention to all the intervening processes. Assumed throughout and described to a limited extent is the integration of the separate efforts in a context of community accountability. This notion requires further definition and the mechanisms for its implementation are yet to be specified. First, let us recall the problems here addressed. Efforts to deal with children in trouble are not nearly effective enough; exploration soon reveals that the resources committed to the effort are inadequate in quantity and in quality. As one seeks potent remedies, it is necessary to go beyond the question of the adequacy of individual programmes, the sufficiency of resources in a given category, or even the qualifications of a given staff. Clearly, there are also problems relevant to the system of community services as a *system*. The following overlapping generalizations are central:

(*a*) Cases are found, but opportunities are lost. "Services rendered" are too often considered as "needs met." Case finding may be followed by the minimum of service prescribed by an agency's function; by unskilled service or a failure to follow up consistently based on a limited concept of agency responsibility; by the dropping of cases because of resource lacks.

(*b*) Far too much agency service and action is not based on adequate case appraisal or diagnosis.

(*c*) Agencies often "drift" into case dispositions or make plans for services which are known to hold little promise of effectiveness. Conflicting philosophies and objectives operate at the level of case disposition, and punitive impluses often outweigh treatment strategy. Knowledge is in some instances limited; in others adequate staff is not available to make plans anchored in available knowledge. Resources may be in short supply.

(*d*) Agencies are often in competition with one another for treatment resources; staff members within an agency are often in competition. Referrals are often made by "shopping," not through wise apportionment of available resources.

(*e*) Agency service efforts in the individual case are not adequately integrated. Far too often agencies work with portions of families and segments of individual problems, and their efforts are unrelated except in the most superficial sense. Cases are "lost" in the gaps between agencies and services which do not "mesh." The complexity of many of the case problems, their family and community ramifications, is such that only the systematically interrelated efforts of the appropriate agencies will make an impact.

(*f*) The sum total of agency prerogatives and rights and their implementation are such as to leave major gaps in the community pattern of services.

(*g*) The deep and basic deficiency in the total community

programme, viewed as a whole, is in responsibility and accountability.

Of necessity, our efforts to specify the elements of a total community approach and to suggest philosophy and method which might be appropriate are general. A given community must translate guidelines, principles, and a large number of action proposals into priorities, specifics, next steps. Moreover, a given community requires mechanisms and structure for constant evaluation of its achievements and for review of policies and strategy in the light of changing problems, changing knowledge, and experience. Therefore, it becomes necessary, in the final phase of this present undertaking, to discuss community provision for planning, coordination, evaluation, and research.

Available experience suggests that the provision must be on several levels. First, there is the problem of ensuring the integration of services for the individual case in the context of the philosophy of accountability already discussed. Then there is the coordination and planning relevant to the neighbourhood or the city subdivision. Finally, there is the provision for community-wide planning and coordination and the relationship of community-wide provision to the neighbourhood structure, on the one hand, and to city and state structures on the other.

Context of the Problem

The sociologist would define much of what is here under discussion as a problem in bureaucracy. In a complex, industrial society, and particularly in its urban areas, the nature of population concentrations, the wide ramifications of needs, the multiplicity of skills required and services offered all lead social welfare programmes to that inevitable formal organization (technically, "bureaucracy") which is characteristic of most organizations in the modern world. Wilensky and Lebeaux have reminded us that "red tape, buck passing, inaction, inflexibility," which are ways in which the layman would characterize many of the service problems, are actually pathological manifestations of some of the most basic and valuable features of modern formal organization. In their attempts to achieve efficiency, reliability, continuity, precision, and fairness, organizations are inevitably and increasingly characterized by *specialization* (within agencies and as between agencies); *hierarchy* (the distinction between workers and supervisors is especially important for present purposes); an emphasis on *rules* (activities are routinized where possible and all relationships are formalized); *assignment of roles to specialists* on the basis of assumed technical qualifications; and official designation of areas of jurisdiction for the several roles.

These are necessary features of social organization in our age, but they were unknown in the days of mutual self-help in simple, agricultural communities, nor were they in evidence in many of the social welfare programmes which developed earlier in the history of the industrial revolution, when religious and humanitarian impulses, and not technical training or scientific knowledge, were the basis for action, and when specialization was almost unnecessary and unknown. Even today, there is far less bureaucratization in rural areas or in some of the smaller religious charities which have not professionalized and which have limited themselves to small subpopulations. Those who would solve the problems created by the pathologies of bureaucracy by harking back to the "good old days" ignore the facts of modern life, however. While some islands of simple and informal organization may continue to exist in social welfare, the matter of size alone size of client groups, size of agencies, size of staff demands formal organization for the bulk of public and voluntary provision. Solutions are needed for the problems which seem inevitably to arise, but it is fantasy to assume that social welfare alone, of all areas in modern life, will avoid this normal development.

Many specific problems already identified as present in individual programmes dealing with children in trouble or in the total pattern of services are recognizable as manifestations of broader problems described by observers of social welfare bureaucracy. To the client, of course, they often appear as "obstacles and impediments."

Thus, the pattern of social work supervision may decrease the caseworker's initiative and independence just where it is most needed. Moreover, stress on eligibility and intake rules may keep services from people on irrelevant technicalities, or discourage those who are poorly motivated or not socially equipped to deal with the requirements. A high degree of specialization may lead to formulation of job requirements which eliminate most of those available for the jobs—and leave programmes unstaffed. Or it may narrow the service given to that range sanctioned by the specialty, despite the needs of the case or the abilities and inclinations of the practitioner. Specialization, too, may leave gaps in service, may leave some client groups or social groups or geographic groups unserved, or may segment the client. Specialization of some kinds ("delinquents") also adds to stigmatization of some clients. A given service tends to define in quite specific ways how a client should behave (the reciprocal of the professional's role); people who do not fit into the mold may be dismissed as too poorly motivated to benefit from the service. Considerable assignments of resources are made to keep records and to provide formal devices (conferences, etc.) for communication between personnel within agencies; the investment represents a serious problem since it decreases the time available for direct work with clients; moreover, the communication routines and records often become ends in themselves, while the organizational machinery serves to decrease the sense of urgency in serving people. The greatest hazard, in brief, derives from the tendency to envisage the organization and its preservation as ends in themselves while the original objectives of service and help may become lost.

Some of these problems are obviously outside of the scope of the present work. Some are alluded to in connection with developments on the forefront of practice which address themselves to the correction of professional concepts and methods obviously unequal to some of the tasks posed. Another group of problems would be faced directly if there could be adequate provision for evaluation, planning, coordination, service integration, and case accountability.

The generalization of these problems both for social welfare as a whole and for all large-scale organizations serves an additional purpose, however. The analysis suggests that just as many of the defects of current programmes are best understood as consequences of what might be called the ever-threatening psychopathology of bureaucracies, so must a substantial part of the solution be sought through organizational measures. This discussion addresses itself, therefore, to *organized means* for ensuring accountability and service integration.

On first impulse, one might be tempted to eschew more organization as both costly and likely to create its own complications, and instead to seek solutions through an appeal to professional ethics. This has a measure of validity. The true professions have codes of service which stress concern for the client. A major tenet in the social work ethic, for example, involves a stress on the identification and meeting of client needs. Social workers are much preoccupied with improving services, upgrading their skills, adding to their knowledge, breaking through unnecessary "red tape." Identification with the professional association and its ethics often supersedes the limited perspective of the local agency.

On the other hand, professionalization, not unlike formal organization, does encourage specialization; formalization of relationship; control of spontaneous emotional responses to people's problems; and emphasis on roles, qualifications, techniques, and procedures. Thus, while all that is possible should be done by educators and professional associations to solve some of the problems described through an emphasis on professional ethics and codes of service, organized solutions must be sought simultaneously.

Accountability and Service Integration

The agencies here in focus are instruments of public policy and social control. Their staff members are employed to achieve objectives defined in statutes, charters, and statements of purpose. The evidence is abundant and disturbing to the effect that where the objectives sought are not achieved, and this is quite often the case, the costs are high in destruction, waste, misery, and tragedy. In this context, the probation officer, medical social worker, social investigator for the welfare department, teacher or any of the others who might be mentioned—may not be regarded as individual practitioners whose actions and practices affect only themselves. They represent agencies carrying well-defined community responsibility and must, each of them, come to appreciate that failure to exercise that responsibility has serious community consequences. The term "responsibility" thus may describe community allocation of function to a given agency or service and agency allocation of role to a specific practitioner as well as the acceptance of such allocation by agency or individual practitioner.

It is helpful to consider devices for protecting or following the implementation of that responsibility with particular reference to the individual case. The concept of *accountability devices and instruments* may be useful in this regard. Put in slightly different phrasing: The case accountability device is a system or method designed to implement community responsibility by ensuring the continuity of work with the individual case until a point is reached at which community policy calls for case closing. (Implied, of course, is some assurance that the agency which maintains the contacts meets professional standards; this is a function of a variety of departments and of the planning machinery, perhaps, but is a burden too huge for any accountability system.)

An accountability system, by definition, must involve both some infringement on agency prerogatives and some increased invasion of an individual's privacy and of the confidential status of material about him known to social welfare agencies and others. Therefore, one would not wish a case accountability system so comprehensive that it would apply to all those who make use of social welfare, health, and educational services (i.e., most people). A "police state" atmosphere would not advance our objectives. Rather, there is need to define when and how a community should follow closely the service to members of the "high hazard" group in "clear and present danger" and how their rights are to be protected in the process. There is far less of a problem in the inclusion of those already subject to authoritative action because of their delinquency, neglect, or unlawful behaviour as determined through court adjudication.

An acceptance of the accountability notion and the recognition that a major source of service failure is the fragmentation of services, fragmentation of clients, and loss of clients in the gaps between programmes lead one to the view that *service integration* must be planned simultaneously with the creation of devices for case accountability.

It is helpful to differentiate between coordination in relation to the programmes, policies, objectives, and plans of agencies, on the one hand, and coordination of the work *on the individual case*, on the other. The latter process, best identified as integration of services, involves ways of ensuring the meshing of resources and services for the individual client. It also includes concern for the consistency of approach and policies of various agencies or parts of agencies as experienced by the person for whom the service is designed.

Coordination devices, invented in the nineteenth century and introduced widely by the charity organization movement, had the potential for case accountability and the integration of services, but they were addressed to the problems of another era. Thus, the social service exchange long served the primary function of detecting those who sought and obtained relief in more than one agency. This problem has ended with the growth of public welfare. The social service exchange still makes it possible for an agency to know the names of other agencies which have had contact with a family; however, registration is selective and some communities have abolished the exchange because they did not consider it helpful or because the ethics of registration without permission seemed questionable. In addition, the volume of work, the inability to separate good leads from poor ones on a social service exchange slip, and uneven levels of staffing have limited the extent to which the exchange is regarded as useful. In some instances case summaries are requested; this may lead to some meshing of efforts. In even fewer instances, records are read or an exchange slip leads to telephone conferences or to actual full-dress interagency conferences. These may foster considerable integration of effort but generally are seen as timeconsuming and costly. It is doubtful that the exchange will ever become a potent service integration instrument unless it becomes more selective or is tied somehow to a system of case accountability.

The first charity organization societies of the 1880s were actually created in order to attain service integration (they did not, of course, use the phrase) where there seemed to be chaos. They soon discovered that the need for adequate relief and qualified service was greater than the demand for service integration, and they became today's family service societies. Several decades later, their heritage was seen in the community council movement, but here the major emphasis was on coordination on the level of agencies, not individual cases. Nonetheless, from time to time councils have sought to encourage case integration by promoting interagency understanding and communication, facilitating case conferences between two agencies working on a case, and conducting the kinds of workshops and institutes which lead to mutual clarification of function and greater readiness to work together. Most recently some councils have experimented with the new form of case conference described below or have initiated valuable projects.

The agency "merger" movement has also been in a sense a step toward case integration although actually a variety of motives are involved. Family agencies and children's agencies tended to join together after World War II. It was clear that efforts to maintain a family may be made more consistently and with greater skill before child placement begins; a protective unit requires close ties to a child placement service; etc. Attendance bureaus have joined with guidance and psychology programmes to form more complete pupil personnel departments. Children's and family courts have been joined in one structure. There have even been a few instances in which child guidance clinics have become associated with in-patient treatment facilities.

Obviously the merger has important potential in case integration. The judge sitting in the children's case should have the family court record on the family. Without too much effort the psychologist should be able to review the experience of the attendance officer, and so on. Mergers appear to have achieved the desired effect where they were real, rather than mere paper actions, where staffs in the several components were on equivalent levels of status and skill, and where the programmes were not so large as to demand formal integrating devices within the agency. The merger has obvious limits, however: one cannot achieve case integration in a large urban area by putting all the agencies under one organizational title and administration.

The case conference. While the older and earlier devices have not been adequate in their original forms, they have inspired recent developments which are encouraging. Central to these developments is a *new form of multiagency case conference* which serves both as an accountability device and an instrument for case integration. Cases are carefully selected for presentation because they represent "multiproblem" situations, a number of agencies are involved, and adequate progress has not been made. Agencies are represented by personnel on a supervisory and/or administrative level (augmented, perhaps, by the worker directly responsible for the ease).

This form of case conference involves a sharing of information and evaluations, culminating in a new case diagnosis or evaluation, as well as in an action plan mutually arrived at. Professional confidentiality of material revealed in the conferences is ensured through agreement. Particularly crucial is the agreement generally made as to which agency is to "take the lead" with the family and how the others are to support the effort (case integration). Furthermore, a "reporting back" date is set for review of progress and the making of further plans (case accountability). Once the case thus comes into the center of community attention, it is not so readily "lost."

From time to time this kind of practice has grown up in a community without much publicity or reporting, but it has had special attention in a number of communities in recent years as a way of dealing with families considered particularly difficult. Thus, to illustrate rather than to enumerate all developments, the Montclair Council of Social Agencies organized a case conference committee several years ago, one of several such in New Jersey, and emphasized "reporting back"; it stated that positive results could be documented. The Roxbury Family Project, working for several years in a Boston neighbourhood, developed a similar plan. Oakland County, Michigan, is said to find a case conference "very effective."

The St. Paul, Minnesota, Family Centered Project promoted service integration through a continuous "workshop" for the special staff members assigned part-time by the agencies for purposes of the project. Because the project was a demonstration and research endeavor and staff were in a sense "loaned," if only part-time, it did not change the basic community pattern. The service integration emerged, in this instance, as a by-product of a joint study effort directed at the problem of designing treatment methods effective with so-called multi problem families. A *Casework Notebook* produced by the project defines the case conference as "the best device we have for joint planning." This project stressed that case conference effectiveness depends on the caseworker and his immediate supervisor; while policy agreements may be reached on the administrative level, or in interagency councils, service integration requires at least one meeting of those who will work together on the case.

A more limited device which is described as very effective is the case review committee in the Philadelphia schools. Top administrators of special services (medical services, pupil personnel and counseling, special education, etc.) are joined by experts where needed to confer on the most seriously disturbed and potentially dangerous young people in school. While the conference may decide on school exclusions or may initiate commitment, school transfers and special programmes are also possible. Unlike some of the other case committees, the Philadelphia plan is not tied to ongoing treatment decisions and does not involve reporting back to review progress and make new plans.

Los Angeles reports that during 1958-59 there were 49 case coordinating committees associated with local community coordinating councils. During the one year, the committees considered 314 new cases and 476 ongoing cases, approximately hall involving a focus on children under 14. In a current Madison, Wisconsin, project a "case conference demonstration" is being used for general coordination and planning purposes and to create a climate for use of such conferences as part of normal service.

In England, most local authorities (93 per cent) have some kind of coordinating machinery and half use the case conference device—mainly in the instance of work with children. There is emphasis on neglectful families. Younghusband's definition and advice is applicable on this side of the Atlantic as well:

> A case conference provides a setting for a limited number of workers directly involved in the case under consideration to assess the need, work out a plan of concerted action, and carry it out in cooperation with each other and with the person or family under discussion. It should be attended only by officers [involved] in the case under discussion, one of whom should take the chair.

She comments further that "the main problem is not so much multiplicity of visiting as multiplicity of independent and uncoordinated visiting."

Case conferences have been used in New York City in a number of special projects. In 1957 the Welfare Department pioneered with what became known as the Borough Committees of the Mayor's Interdepartmental Committee for Multi-Problem Families. Administrative or supervisory personnel from public departments (Education, Buildings, Health, Hospitals, Police, Welfare, two courts, Housing, Mental Health Board, Youth Board) met monthly in each borough both to promote interdepartmental coordination in general and to ensure integration of services in the eases at hand. They constituted a permanent committee. All of the departments listed could refer eases. A conference sought to develop a plan of action for the particular case, to devise ways of cutting "red tape" and modifying directives where it seemed essential for the case being reviewed or for similar eases, and to designate the agency which would assume primary responsibility for service. Monthly reports of progress were required as a means of ensuring continued service integration as well as accountability. The total volume was small since only one case was discussed per meeting, but the effect on services and policies was said to be broader. While the plan was given up in the light of subsequent developments, its strength seemed to be primarily in the area of policy and programme coordination. Unlike the practitioner case conference, the administrator and executive conference identifies action to be taken in definition of roles, filling of service gaps, and untangling of "red tape." It is not an efficient way to deal with many cases individually since the direct-service practitioner must follow through with the eases.

In 1958, taking account of expressed concern at the fragmentation of services as well as the gaps between agency services and the frequency with which cases are "lost," the Youth Board developed an experiment in one of its Referral Units. Under the plan, a highly resistive, multi problem family was selected for review and the project staff convened a meeting of an appropriate *ad hoc* committee which included representatives of all agencies, public or voluntary, currently or previously in contact with the family (usually four to ten in number). Prior to the meeting, the project staff prepared and circulated an up-to-date case summary. The Youth Board case conferences sought to attract the staff members directly concerned with the case, even though administrators were also welcomed.

At the meeting proper, the representative from each of the agencies reviewed his agency's experience with the family and the total group then explored the situation, pooled evaluative judgments, and developed a plan and reasonable goals with the family. Although the initial picture of a case as it emerged in a conference was often discouraging, the "pooled" thinking tended to discover positive factors and to suggest possible "leverage." One agency was eventually requested to assume the lead in work with the family and to integrate the services of the others. Follow-up reporting was scheduled for a date three months after the meeting. So gratifying was the experience during the first year that the Youth Board determined to assign similar activity to all of its Referral Units. Preparatory meetings with all interested agencies met enthusiastic responses.

While the Youth Board experience with the case conference is substantially encouraging, organizational aspects have not been solved. A small community might achieve service integration and accountability through a "coffee-time" conference. Large cities need to staff many cases. What volume is possible? How are cases to be selected? Given considerable volume, what administrative devices are needed to implement accountability?

As will be seen, the unclear status of the Referral Units in recent years and their staffing difficulties have precluded the development of large-scale case conference machinery. In addition, the limited development of New York's "multiproblem' register has precluded its use for case selection. Yet the Youth Board conference experience suggests that it would not be at all unreasonable to expect a coordinating agency in a large city to use its machinery to organize and staff a network of case conference groups along the lines of the Youth Board pattern. Twenty-five or thirty such groups would be required for New York City, and they would staff two or three new cases each week and hear reports on eases previously staffed. This would bring about two or three thousand new cases into the accountability network a year—a reasonable total if the conferences are reserved for situations involving child neglect or delinquency, for cases with ramifications in a variety of agencies, for cases of considerable family disorganization and evidence that routine handling will not do.

Since the case conferences would generally not involve the same practitioners at each meeting, this kind of plan would not impose too heavy a burden on any staff member. It would depend in New York City on using Referral Unit staff resources or comparable staff to select the cases, prepare the conferences, and follow through. Other cities would need proportionately fewer conference groups. Organization of conferences on the basis of a neighbourhood or city subdivision would seem desirable. Oakland, California, has setup a conference group for each of five high school districts and finds that both service integration and programme coordination are possible. The Roxbury Family Project, which investigated the matter, stressed that coordinators and resource personnel involved in case conference procedures make their optimum contributions if they are "neutral," that is, if they do not have a direct service function.

Registers. The problems of case selection and administrative controis for this kind of machinery remain. A small community does not find it difficult to develop an accountability card index which is an integral part of a case conference system. It comes into play at the point of case finding. There must be some work done in advance to arrive at mutual agreement as to cases to be added to the register and scheduled for conference. (Among the possibilities, to illustrate: all cases of alleged neglect, all cases in which a child is temporarily separated from his parents, all adjudicated delinquency cases under certain types of circumstances, public welfare cases with certain interagency ramifications.) Following conferences and mutual planning, a simple process of notation of "return dates" would be adequate and would provide for the preparation of follow-up conferences at appropriate times.

The large-city roster is a more complex matter. Thus, despite frequent announcements of intent, the New York City Youth Board has not been able to use its roster for accountability purposes or for any other ongoing administrative operation even though some research use has been possible. Part of the problem is that of criteria for listing: cases have been placed on the roster on the basis of intrafamilial relationship patterns and parental attitudes, the outgrowth of Youth Board interest in the Glueck prediction work. However, the core accountability notion would be better served and the roster kept within manageable limits if a committee of experienced practitioners were to formulate criteria relative to problems, behaviour, and, most important, the community agencies' experiences with the family.

Having solved the problem of criteria, the large city will have to use an electronic system to keep its roster usable and flexible. Cases could easily be coded by "conference group" (i.e., neighbourhood), basic characteristics, agency ramifications. An electronic system could help select cases for conferences in the terms of predetermined priorities, while agencies themselves could add cases to the agenda in the light of their experience. The register could also provide, at appropriate times, suitable rosters of cases to be followed up, rosters of unreported cases, rosters of cases closed by an agency while core problems remained, and so on. Its costs, while important, would be small when weighed against current futile, uncoordinated, and pro longed services. Economies might eventually emerge if the social service exchange were properly to curtail its own activities in the light of the existence of the register. The community might, in fact, choose to place the register under social service exchange auspices and to merge it with the exchange. This is a matter of administration and financing, rather than a substantive issue.

The point is raised as to whether the use of a register does not abuse the client's confidence or stigmatize him. In some cases there is no question at all about the community's right to use a register as an instrument of intervention, since there has been either an adjudication which places the family or child under court supervision or protection or because the service is an outgrowth of a statutory charge to work with relief recipients (public welfare cases) or to help enforce the compulsory education law (many school-referred cases). Where the community's rights are not clear, discussion of the social service exchange and/or register should, under any circumstances, be a normal part of agency intake. The client accepts or rejects the register when he uses the service (or the decision may be deferred for reasons relevant to the case). Where the client cannot move voluntarily and children are endangered, the community may need to exercise its police power, which includes registration as part of the protective investigation process.

In fact, one may say of accountability devices generally what has been said of the register: if one limits cases listed to those which need to be in the forefront of community concern because of hazard, "clear and present danger," and complexity of interrelated problems, most cases will in fact present a legitimate basis for the partial invasion of privacy which is involved. Where such basis does not exist technically and the client rejects voluntary service, the protective services machinery may be called into action. If there is no legal basis for protective action and the client does not wish the service, his privacy should be safeguarded, despite the convictions of some professional workers that there are hazards involved—at least unless the predictions are validated by identifiable and justiciable "acting out."

"Intensive" workers. Accountability devices and service integration measures should ideally affect the practice of all agency staff members. A number of special studies and projects also have suggested the possibility of a degree of specialization with some families found to require particular and concentrated attention. Agencies often have several staff members particularly suited for intensive, rehabilitative work on the basis of understanding, experience, and skill. Why not reduce their caseloads, increase their prerogatives, and stress the integration of their work with other agencies? Recommendations for this work in a British study of *The Neglected Child* are also supported by American experience:

(*a*) Caseloads should be small, consisting of not more than twentyfive families for each worker. With a larger number than this, the families that are passing through a crisis of some kind cannot be given sufficiently close attention unless other cases are neglected.

(*b*) One worker should have responsibility for the whole family and for helping it in all its difficulties. Specialist workers will often have to be called in to deal with particular problems, such as poor physical or mental health. But one worker, from whatever service, must have full responsibility for the family, and others should visit only when necessary and only after first consulting with the worker in charge.

(*c*) Help of this comprehensive kind must be available to a family as soon as its problems grow too complex to be dealt with by the functional services.

(*d*) Those offering this help must be allowed to work in the same district for long enough to become well-known and trusted by the families they visit.

(*e*) There must be close coordination of all services, based on fairly frequent discussions beth between those directing the services and (more important) between those actually visiting the same families. It matters little whether this is achieved through formal committees, over a cup of tea in the town hall canteen, or in other ways.

(*f*) When the immediate crisis is over and families once more begin to lead a fairly normal life, it must be possible for someone to keep in touch with them for long enough to prevent a relapse.

(*g*) People of the right character and experience should be chosen to undertake this personal service, and they should be encouraged to work in an independent and experimental manner and to develop new methods. This is the most important condition of all.

Perhaps, after a family comes into focus, the first attempts might be on the basis of careful integration between agencies. For it is not the multiplicity of visits per se but uncoordinated work which is so undesirable.

If this produced no improvement, one of these specially chosen workers would take full responsibility for the family after discussion between all the services concerned. Other visitors would not abandon the family altogether but would henceforth visit as little as possible and take no action without first consulting the person in charge. Which service would be chosen to assume responsibility for any given family would depend on which worker appeared to be in the best position to help. In most cases there would be several visitors already calling on the family; by discussion between them it could be decided who was likely to exert the most influence (owing to personality, function, pressure of work, or any other reason). That person would be put in charge and asked to report progress at intervals to other organizations interested in the case.

In this way, most of the conditions necessary for effective personal service would be achieved without radical change. Families would merely find that one worker, whom they already knew and trusted more than others, was giving them more attention and was taking responsibility for matters upon which they had previously received calls from many people. Every organization would make its contribution. The distribution of casework would be decided not by theoretical arguments about the value of the different services, but by practical demonstration of their success in individual cases. No service would be condemned to limit itself henceforth to a narrow range of duties; each would be encouraged to think in terms of the whole family, and to gain a wider understanding of family problems. Good workers need no longer waste years of their time in dealing with the symptoms of trouble; they would be given a chance to tackle its underlying causes.

Several British health and social services have, in fact, assigned "intensive" workers. The St. Paul project, which defined its special staff members as "general family practitioners," sought coordination of treatment (what we have called service integration) by assigning them responsibility for working with families "to bridge them over to a more productive use of community resources"; developing better interagency collabouration in behalf of families; using their observations in order to contribute to community planning and social action.

In the St. Paul project, in New York's Neighbourhood Services Centre, and in many special units for multiproblem families throughout the United States, the case is transferred to a special unit and then assigned to an "intensive" worker who carries a variety of the ramifications. We have yet to experiment systematically with intensive workers who remain within their agencies and are unassigned to special projects—but whose job assignments permit the special intensive work on a selective basis. The California Youth Authority is launching intensive community treatment of delinquents along these lines.

Accountability and agency prerogatives. A community cannot develop service integration and keep families in focus via accountability machinery unless there is some surrender of agency prerogatives. Individual agencies alone cannot make final determinations about cases to list—or about when eases may be dropped. A conference should be able to decide who takes the lead, even if there is not unanimity. Community reports must be free to compare agencies on their "sticking" and "holding power."

All of this can be made possible by democratically conducted community planning and coordination machinery with local, neighbourhood subdivisions in large cities. The agencies involved are either public services or voluntary programmes supported by community chests or individual, tax-deductible contributions. In either instance it is legitimate to expect that an agency will cooperate with the community network, making its views known, participating in decisions, and supporting plans which are made. The *social* services are not the domain of individual entrepreneurs; those which act as such are hardly responsible in the sense in which the term is here employed.

In fact, once an agency accepts the philosophy here outlined, it will find its own ways of going even beyond the registers, conferences, and intensive units described. For example, a school system may develop a cumulative record system (or cumulative records plus confidential guidance files) to ensure continuity of service to a child from term to term, once his difficulties have identified him as requiring special help. The register must be in competent hands lest a child be stigmatized and forced into an unchangeable mold. The child health station offers similar opportunities to public health nurses and medical social workers.

Or, to illustrate further, a housing authority social service programme might assign staff or obtain the help of public or voluntary casework services to maintain close contact with that "small hard core" of public housing tenants who require support and help lest their inadequacies produce new problems and lead to even further family disorganization. The Neighbourhood Improvement Programme of New Haven, Connecticut, places a casework unit which concentrates on multiproblem families within a public housing project. Within the unit are recreational and community organization personnel as well, offering a rounded programme to casework clients and to the project as a whole.

Neighbourhood Base

Staff members from a variety of agencies, responsible for cases in a given neighbourhood, must eventually find ways to mesh their efforts. Any case integration system must therefore be brought down to the neighbourhood level in some fashion. And this is just as well, since intensive knowledge of a locality is usually a prerequisite to successful service. This suggests the hypothesis that it may be useful to tie accountability and service integration provision to some kind of structure of neighbourhood organization.

The Chicago Area Project, the model for many others, has had more than twenty-five years of experience and reports positive results. Its programme in the neighbourhood tends to lead to recreation provision, general community self-improvement endeavours, direct work with gangs—but not to service integration or accountability. On the other hand, the South Central Youth Project, in a blighted Minneapolis area, arrived at the agency case conference structure and assignment of one responsible worker per case as its major working method, but concluded in its report that "more community forces should be involved."

Given agreement to explore local organization in relation to service integration and accountability, several structural approaches would seem to be relevant. Any of these would require innovation and change, since much local organization in the youth field is concerned only with the provision of leisure-time and recreational resources. A proposal that there be some local ties to central planning and coordination bodies would win agreement in the abstract, but there would remain the need to define the realistic parameters of local initiative in fields in which decisions are made on city-wide or county bases. The question of the best possible relationships between social agencies, volunteer service groups, citizen self-help activities, and local planning bodies would still remain.

A search does not yield ready answers. Many patterns are obviously being considered, however, as urban areas seek to fill a vacuum created by the breakup of neighbourhoods and the changes in urban political machines which in one sense provided for a degree of accountability of a sort. Many of the larger urban areas are, in fact, in transition in their patterns of neighbourhood organization, as they take account of urban renewal, the problem of racial integration, and population mobility. Some special neighbourhood organizations, created in order to deal with delinquency, are carrying out broad local improvements on the assumption that grass roots activity of this kind decreases antisocial orientations in the total community, creates needed services, and offers sound role models for youth.

This is, then, an area for tentative exploration and testing despite its urgency and substantive importance. The remainder of this section is devoted to brief mention of a variety of interesting developments. All aspects of local organization not immediately relevant are bypassed.

Oakland's "associated agencies." Oakland, California, in a plan under way since 1957, has created a coordination-service integration structure on a local basis by dividing the city into five high school districts. The executive of the programme is based in the city manager's office and is called the "juvenile control coordinator." Costs are shared by the Board of Education and the City Council. Policies are made by an executive committee consisting of the executives of the agencies involved (schools, recreation, police, probation, Youth Authority, welfare, health). Each agency is represented on a coordinating committee, which is city-wide, and on the local district units. There is thus provision for joint planning, programme coordination, and local case integration.

The heart of the programme is the twice-monthly local district meetings which serve to ensure service integration and reporting back and to initiate new policies and provision needed to deal with emerging problems. All reports are positive. The effectiveness with which the agencies deal with local "emergencies" such as gang fights, as well as with individual cases, is impressive.

Coordinating councils. At one time the delinquency field was especially concerned with promoting the local coordinating council, a device for periodic meetings of local agencies or responsible local citizens concerned with delinquents. The movement's main development has been on the West Coast. Councils have lay and professional participation, generally combining both, and include a range of organizations, from law enforcement bodies to civic groups, schools, churches, and social agencies. They sometimes develop surveys or initiate activity to provide new resources. At other times they serve as informal centers for service integration. They are considered more effective in small communities and do not seem to meet an urban area's need for formally organized service integration and accountability involving large caseloads. Particularly lacking is a specification of roles appropriate to laymen and roles which should involve professional staff in order to protect confidentiality and ensure qualified help.

The New York City police-inspired precinct Youth Councils are like similar councils elsewhere. Theoretically, each police precinct has a council, but approximately one quarter are active. Local professionals, civic leaders, church leaders, and merchants join together to support PAL fund raising and to devise programmes to meet special needs. The council is a means to organize some activity and occasional coordination, but is not structured either for accountability or integration. On occasion, it may have a vital, energetic programme. The police are currently assigning professional staff to revitalize the councils but there is no city-wide policy guidance in relation to many areas in which other public and voluntary agencies also have youth councils and neighbourhood organizations.

Washington, D.C., has given a larger task to its more than twenty boards setup in natural neighbourhood areas, under the leadership of the Commissioner's Youth Council.

Prevention, coordination, and some case integration tasks are undertaken by each local group.

New Jersey has juvenile conference committees in almost forty areas, having created them after a 1953 directive from its Supreme Court to local juvenile courts. A Monmouth County plan, was the model. Committee members are court appointed; the committees are designed to encourage the locality to come to grips with delinquency, particularly in the early stages. According to a recent report, thousands of citizens have actually served on committees. As New Jersey has sought to strengthen all of its services to youth in trouble it has had to look at the conference committees and to recognize that they have sought to carry out case evaluation, treatment planning, and case supervision, often in open committee, without diagnostic understanding or appreciation of what the experience could mean to participants, and without adequately qualified personnel. On the other hand, the committees have led to some effective screening and informal handling of cases which might otherwise have gone to court. They have channeled much constructive citizen interest in community services. As needed probation services and court intake structures expand adequately in New Jersey and as community social agencies offer alternative forms of informal help, it would seem likely that the direct case handling by conference committees would end and that these would become juvenile court advisory committees and local citizen committees concerned with planning. By their nature, they cannot adequately undertake service integration, which should be a function of an operating staff. The generalization applies to similar activities in many states.

The Baltimore area projects represent an intermediate type of development. They are, in effect, local community centers setup under the Welfare Department. The local community supplies all the needs of the project, but the Welfare Department adds clinical staff and a coordinator who encourages local organization to deal with local problems.

Precinct youth councils, juvenile conference committees, parentyouth aid committees, and their thousands of equivalents throughout the country are excellent recruitment grounds and orientation centres for "big brothers" and "big sisters" who may supplement professional helping services in valuable ways and who may act in lieu of such services for children referred through professionally qualified channels.

LENA. The Lower East Side Neighbourhoods Association in New York City (LENA) is an elabourate and unusually imaginative effort in an area with a population of over 200,000. It was created in 1955, at a time of rapid neighbourhood change, in response to local violence. It now joins together in a vigorous, effective, and in some ways unique organization five local neighbourhood councils (four of which it initiated), community members, professional members, and 90 community organizations, from banks and trade unions to settlements and churches. Much of the work is carried on in divisions which have their parallels in the local councils: housing, health, education, youth, community arts, intergroup relations. Work is carried on in such a way as both to raise the tone and quality of community life and to deal with dangerous deviance. For example, the community arts programme seeks through a summer concert programme, dramatics, and a variety of offerings in the arts, plus a local "talent hunt," to enrich daily experience and to create pride in neighbourhood—thus striking at one of the roots of its problem. Energetic self-help efforts are directed at problems and gaps in health, education, housing. Systematic work is done to increase contacts between diverse ethnic and social groups and to improve relationships.

There is much concentration on the youth. Neighbours, settlements, churches, schools, public departments are heavily committed to a two-pronged approach which includes a rich recreation and sports programme (teams, leagues, competition, instruction, trips outside the area) and youth services. The neighbourhood councils have their youth councils with similar emphasis and all give priority to grass roots volunteer-neighbour involvement and to youth participation and initiative. At the same time, a tightly coordinated network of area teams, consisting of professionals in local agencies, representatives of public departments, and neighbours, keeps its fingers on the pulse of youth gangs, meets immediately on call, and intervenes rapidly at the first signs of tension. Where constructive programmes are possible, they are initiated; mediation is often undertaken; however, if danger threatens, the forces of the law are called into action at once.

Although more systematic testing of effectiveness is planned under the Mobilization for Youth project, being developed in a section of the LENA area, participants are convinced that the programme has had considerable impact. Intergroup relations have been improved in the area, public services and housing have been brought more into harmony with need, closely coordinated agency programmes-particularly social-athletic and social services—have ensured more complete coverage and have served many who were previously unreached. Particularly dramatic have been the successes in recent summers in heading off threatening gang violence and bringing together previously unfriendly groups.

While this description does not do full justice to LENA, it may serve as a backdrop for noting the extent to which an enthusiastic local self-help effort may both increase agency coordination on a neighbourhood basis and approximate a system of accountability. As the result of the explorations and plans of local councils and LENA divisions, and as a natural by-product of the experiences which professionals and board members have in serving together in these activities, the public-voluntary coordination has been much enhanced. Public services in particular have often found new ways to adapt to local priorities and needs. At the same time, it has become routine, to take another illustration, for local settlements so to schedule their social and athletic programmes as to provide the best possible neighbourhood coverage for the entire week. Joint activities are common.

This total atmosphere, plus the activity of the area teams, increases the sense of accountability which is so important. Sometimes it is provided formally, as when LENA's Youth Service director helped meet a school suspension crisis by assuming responsibility for a group of 120 youngsters designated by the school officials as requiring concentrated attention. Local social service, medical, psychiatric, and educational help was rallied. At the same time, the district's best teachers cooperated in a Foster Teacher Plan to give special attention to a group of children with intense emotional difficulties.

Informal accountability and service integration develops particularly through the work of the area teams which keep attuned to the pulse of the youth gang situation and plan how to act in relation to specific individuals and gangs. This informal but intensive follow through is most impressive when contrasted with the anonymity and "crisis service" of the typical area. In a sense it becomes an urban neighbourhood re-creation of the small town primary group relationships on which social control is based. Youth perceive that significant adults (parents, neighbours, church, social agency, police) know and care about what they do and will intervene if unlawful action is threatened. Unfortunately, not every urban area has the continuity and concentration of agencies and churches of the LENA area nor is it possible always to create such primary group controls.

Whatever the success of local organization (and it should have enthusiastic support), it will be necessary to ensure full coverage and to take account of intracity mobility through the establishment of some combination of formally organized case conference committees, "intensive" workers, and accountability registers or rosters.

Perhaps there is a systematic way to relate these to a local neighbourhood organization without violating confidentiality. A neighbourhood service center may offer some possibilities.

Neighbourhood service center. Early in its history, the New York City Youth Board experimented with a neighbourhood "Department Store of Services," housing one of its Referral Units and also representatives of such public services as welfare, health, housing, employment, etc. The objective was facility in reaching the client, increased availability to him, and ease in referral by the Referral Unit, rather than service integration. Others have proposed local neighbourhood service centers for some areas of large cities with services such as family casework, group work, work with gangs, day care, homemakers. Some would add a mental hygiene clinic, employment center, and legal aid and housing services. If this cross between a settlement and multifunction treatment centre were created, it should obviously include integration and accountability devices of the sort already discussed. It should certainly encompass information and advice functions and a good referral service. The existence of a physical center would also facilitate its relationship to a "grass roots" self-help organization as well.

New York City has resumed experimentation with such an approach in a pilot Interdepartmental Neighbourhood Services Center created in the spring of 1960 on a directive from the mayor. Unlike the earlier "Department Store of Services," which concentrated on case finding, information, steering, and referral, the new unit, in an area of high rates of social breakdown, actually seeks to provide well integrated team services and accountability focused on families and their members. It includes a modest community organization programme. Service units of six workers each are assigned by two city departments (Education, Health) and the courts. In addition, the Youth Board assigns two Referral Units.

Defined as within the scope of the programme are the so-called multiproblem or hard core families, but it has been difficult to develop clear criteria for referral in the absence of a roster of the sort described. Case characteristics stated in Glueck "delinquency prediction" terms, rather than service ramifications of the case, were initially the basis for the referral system. Later, complex cases not worked with elsewhere on an intensive basis were accepted; the bulk come from schools and the Welfare Department.

The cornerstone of the plan is the designation of one rehabilitation caseworker per case (an "intensive" worker in the sense used above), even though the family may be on the rosters of such departments as welfare, schools, courts, and health. Although on the payrolls of various departments as probation officers, attendance teachers, youth guidance technicians, or social investigators, the Center's staff members become "general" social caseworkers. Only the minimum of core statutory responsibilities remains vested in the originating agencies (such as Department of Welfare relief eligibility or probation reporting responsibility), while the Center worker assumes the task of providing a broad range of "reaching out," supportive, protective, and rehabilitative services. Some of this help is very concrete and some is treatment through a relationship, in an effort to get a family back on its feet. Health consultation and guidance in access to the services of other city bureaus (housing, licenses, etc.) are provided by specialists although there is evidence that health ramifications of cases are so extensive as to demand a more complete health plan.

A specialist is also assigned to a community organization programme which has very modest objectives. The intent is to provide a bridge between the "below par" families and their neighbourhood by involving them in local activities of a constructive sort and exposing them to more stable people. Local resources which they require are developed (for example, exchange of baby sitting). The thought is that this type of community organization support of the casework may help make more normal the environment to which children are exposed and may generally strengthen family life.

Initial response to the programme has been encouraging. Of some interest is the fact that this particular three-year experiment is being conducted with some staff on the case-aide level and some who have full graduate social work training. All are experienced. In-service training and psychiatric consultation buttress the practice. A caseload of fifteen families per worker (several members may be seen regularly) is being experimented with; this permits one interview with a family member and two collateral contacts per week. The unit may serve 350-400 families at one time when fully staffed. Case turnover is very slow since extensive service is needed.

One might venture the suggestion that the creation of a neighbourhood services centre which also encourages local self-help activity and, inevitably, is staffed for intake provides an obvious opportunity to experiment with a broader "open door" citizens' advice and steering service. This would be a particularly strategic development should the three-year experiment be deemed successful and permanent operation and expansion be decided upon.

Hyde Park Youth Project. Many of the elements already described were also joined together in Chicago's three-year action research programme known as the Hyde Park Youth Project. Under the sponsorship of the city's Welfare Council and supported by a foundation grant the project undertook the following:

1. Services to individual "behaviour problem" children and their families.
2. Work with street clubs, corner groups, and street gangs.

3. Help to citizen groups and institutions in an effort to understand and alleviate community conditions considered the source of delinquency.
4. Coordination of all of this at the neighbourhood level.
5. Research and description designed to make the experience transferable.

The project was concentrated in a changing area of approximately two miles which included the University of Chicago. Its own staff was supplemented by a considerable amount of added support by "cooperating" agencies which accepted referrals or concentrated project cases into specific caseloads. The philosophy of reaching out was similar to that of the New York City Youth Board, the St. Paul project, and others. Great emphasis was placed on service integration and on bringing the programme to the neighbourhood level.

Rigorous measurement of total effectiveness against "controls" was not undertaken, but a variety of studies based on observation, judgments, and ratings were in a positive direction. The project's staff and sponsors urged that Chicago's Commission on Youth Welfare develop the type of programme demonstrated in Hyde Park in selective areas of the city and that this long-term endeavor be publicly financed.

Forms of Local Organization. To some extent, the question of whether and how case finding and accountability should be tied to neighbourhood organization must depend on the form which neighbourhood organization takes. New York City, for example, is actually organized in many ways and on many levels by local settlements and centres, health councils, school-based councils, block organizations, precinct coordinating councils, neighbourhood improvement groups, tenant organizations, parent organizations, social agency councils, the Youth Board, the urban renewal agency, the Commission on Human Bights. The pattern varies from area to area, functions both overlap and leave large gaps, and there are few means to interrelate these many efforts.

Several of the larger agencies see themselves as potentially able to coordinate local organization but none actually does. The Community Council lacks resources for direct operations but has served as a clearance and service centre for some of the many small, local groups.

It occasionally has been proposed that the schools serve as major local coordinating agencies in the delinquency field a role which would appear possible in relatively small communities. Schools have sometimes also taken initiative in promoting local neighbourhood self help efforts, as in the instance of New York where the school community relations programme has given a rather open-ended charge to its staff of school-community coordinators (teachers with relevant background). They have joined existing local councils or health councils and have represented the perspective of the schools, have created school-centered councils in order to increase and channel community interest in school problems, and have created block organizations. Recently they have done much to facilitate racial integration in schools. The premise is that citizen involvement in school and community problems is constructive and should be promoted. While many of these projects are noteworthy, community interests will ultimately require a somewhat more rational structure. The schools will want to relate their neighbourhood activity directly to school programmes while other provision is made for the sponsorship of general self-help developments.

Another type of local self-help effort with special focus on delinquency is represented by past efforts under the New York City Youth Board, through its Department of Borough Planning and Community Coordination. Trained community organizers in borough offices served as borough coordinators. They had assistants and clerical help. Within the structure there were actually two types of relatively separate efforts: (*a*) Borough committees, made up of citizens of considerable prestige, served as advisors to the borough office in its relationship to the Youth Board's city-wide planning and coordination machinery. These committees had no administrative functions or prerogatives; the projects they suggested were considered centrally. (*b*) A local community organization programme involved staff support and/or service to a variety of kinds of local and neighbourhood councils and their youth councils as well as a programme of frequent area meetings (in a variety of patterns) to tap neighbourhood needs and problems and initiate community actions. These neighbourhood councils and area meetings have been the center of substantial activity, the kind of local council organized depending in each instance upon the specific interests and resources of the particular community.

While the Youth Board programme is in transition, a very similar pattern of organization and vital activity is found in many other communities under the voluntary auspices of local community planning councils. New York's pattern developed as the consequence of a vacuum left by a Community Council with limited resources. Basic questions are raised about publicly conducted local community organization in the Youth Board pattern since a local neighbourhood organization must, perforce, direct its attention to public departments and local government from time to time. Are not staff limited by their status as public employees? Is such a structure not subject to political manipulation at some point in the future? The Youth Board's answer and the response of all those who see local organization as a legitimate public function was that councils which are organized by professional staff (whatever the salary source) are automonous councils. Moreover, public employees have knowledge of and easy access to public departments. Many of the concerns of local councils need to be addressed to such departments.

While the preponderance of opinion would tend at present to oppose publicly operated neighbourhood organization, conclusive evidence as to alleged dangers does not exist. Urban renewal, public housing, and public intergroup relations programmes are making more public resources available for such work. Some of these funds may be expanded through voluntary contracts, as when a local community council accepts a contract associated with urban renewal. Other funds will be expended publicly. Perhaps attention should be directed at providing necessary safeguards for public operation and at ensuring the coordination of local organization in appropriate fashion.

Possible Patterns

As large cities make their decisions about responsibility for local organization and the coordination of such organization, they should simultaneously consider provision for local accountability case integration and its possible ties to self-help and to coordination structures. For the present, several lines of experimentation rather than final decisions would seem to be in order.

1. Creation of public units (such as the Referral Units in New York) as centres of accountability and service integration. These units would organize case conferences. They would require central registers. They should be decentralized.
2. Creation of accountability—service integration units under voluntary auspices, tied to broader local self-help activities, on the pattern of LENA. The LENA area teams are especially suggestive.
3. Continued separation of the three levels of function: service integration and accountability, local self-help, city-wide coordination. This would be the "most natural" pattern and would continue present systems. It would not eliminate the urgent need to rationalize and simplify the relationships of city-wide planning and coordinating bodies to local self-help organizations.
4. Continued experimentation with neighbourhood-based treatment services staffed by "intensive" workers, on the pattern of the Interdepartmental Neighbourhood Services Centre. Experimentation in the use of community organization techniques as an adjunct to the casework should also continue. In

addition, it would be useful to experiment with assignment of an "advice bureau" role to such centers. There is need for more rigorous criteria for assignment of cases to special units and intensive workers under this and other patterns of organization.

The leadership in such experimentation and planning must come from planning and coordinating bodies on several levels.

❑❑❑

Bibliography

Alissi, A. (1980). Social group work: Commitments and perspectives. In A. Alissi (Ed.), *Perspectives on Social Group Work Practice: A Book of Readings* (pp. 5–33). New York: Free Press.

Andrews, J. (2001). Group work's place in social work: a historical analysis. *Journal of Sociology and Social Welfare.* Retrieved October 29, 2005.

Barclay, H.H. (1998). Validating tortured refugees: Reconnection in social work policy and practice. *International Social Work, 41*, 211-226.

Beattie, M. and Randell, J. (1997). Using refugee stories in social work. *Journal of Multicultural Social Work,* 6(1/2), 3-15.

Bemak, F. Chung, R.C. & Pedersen, P. (2002). *Counseling refugees: A psychosocial approach to innovative multicultural interventions.* Westport, CT: Greenwood Publishing.

Cariceo, C.M. (1998). Challenges in cross-cultural assessment: Counseling refugee survivors of torture and trauma. *Australian Social Work,* 51(2), 49-53.

Center for Victims of Torture. (2005). *Healing the hurt: A guide for developing services for torture survivors.* Minneapolis, MN: Center for Victims of Torture.

Cunningham, M. (2003). Impact of trauma work on social work clinicians: Empirical findings. *Social Work, 48(4),* 451-459.

DeJong, K. & Kleber, R. J. (2001). Early psychosocial interventions for war-affected populations. *Early Interventions.* Oxford: Oxford University.

Drachman, D. (1995). Immigration statuses and their influence on service provision, access and use. *Social Work, 40(2),* 188-197.

Drachman, D. (1992). A stage-of-migration framework for service to immigrant population. *Social Work, 37(1),* 68-72.

Engstrom, D.W. & Okamura, A. (2004). A plague of our time: Torture, human rights, and social work. *Families in Society, 85(3) , 291-300.*

Engstom, D.W. & Okamura, A. (2004). Working with survivors of torture: Approaches to helping. *Families in Society, 85(3),* 301-309.

Gangsei, D. (2004). Torture treatment and social work: Amplifying thoughts. *Families in Society, 85(3),* 313314.

Glassman, U. & Skolnik, L. (1984). The role of social group work in refugee resettlement. *Social Work with Groups, 7(1),* 45-62.

Gray, G. (2004). A perspective on "a plague of our time" and "working with survivors of torture." *Families in Society,* 85(3), 311-312.

Haenel, G. (1997). Aspects and problems associated with the use of interpreters in psychotherapy with victims of torture. *Torture, 7.* 68-71.

Hanscom, K.L. (2004). Torture: Why we can't call it something else. *Families in Society, 85(3),* 313.

Herman, J.L. (1992) *Trauma and recovery: The aftermath of violence.* New York: Basic.

Hirayama, H., and Cetingok, M. (1988). Empowerment: A social work approach for Asian immigrants. *Social-Casework, 69(1),* 41-47.

Hodge, D.R. (2005). Social work and the house of Islam: Orienting practitioners to the beliefs and values of Muslims in the United States. *Social Work, 50(2),* 162-172.

Hokenstad, M.C. and Midgley, J. (1997). *Issues in international social work.* Washington, D.C.: NASW Press.

Itzhaky, H. & Ribner, D.S. (1999). Gender, values and the workplace: Considerations of immigrant acculturation. *International Social Work, 42(2)*, 127-138.

Jaranson, J. & Popkin, M. (1998). *Caring for victims of torture.* Washington, D.C.: American Psychiatric Press, Inc.

Kaniasty, K. (2005). Social support and traumatic stress. *PTSD Research Quarterly, 16(2), 1-7.*

Kelly, P. (1994). Integrating systemic and postsystemic approaches to social work practice with refugee families. *Families in Society, 75(9)*, 541-549.

Levine, J. (2001). Working with victims of persecution: Lessons from Holocaust survivors. *Social Work, 46(4)*, 350-360.

Loutan, L. et al. (1999). Impact of trauma and torture on asylum seekers. *European Journal of Public Health, 9(2)*, 93-96.

Mupedziswa, R. (1997). Social work with refugees. *Issues in international social work.* Eds. M.C. Hokenstad and J. Midgley. Washington, D.C.: NASW Press, 110-124.

Ortiz, D. (2002). *The blindfold's eye: My journey from torture to truth.* New York: Orbis.

Padilla, Y.C. (1997). Immigration policy: Issues for social work practice. *Social Work*, 42(6), 595-606. Pipher, M. (2002). *The middle of everywhere: Helping refugees enter the American community.* New York: Harcourt.

Piwowarczyk, L. (2005). Engaging the sacred in treatment. *Torture, 15(1)*, 1-8.

Potocky, M. (1996). Refugee resettlement in the United States: Implications for international social welfare. *Journal of Sociology and Social Welfare, 23(2)*, 163-174.

Potocky, M. (1996). Toward a new definition of refugee. *International Social Work, 39(3)*, 245-256.

Ryan, A.S. (1992). Social work with immigrants and refugees. *Journal of Multicultural Social Work, 2(1).*

Smith, H.E. & Wilkinson, J. (2007). Social service provision. In H.E. Smith, A.S. Keller, & D.W. Lhewa (Eds.), *Like a refugee camp on First Avenue: Insights and experiences for the Bellevue/NYU Program for Survivors of Torture* (pp 272-298). New York: Bellevue/NYU Program for Survivors of Torture.

Strober, S.B. (1994). Social work interventions to alleviate Cambodian refugee psychological distress. *International Social Work, 37(1)*, 23-25.

Van der Veer, G. (200). Empowerment of traumatized refugees: A develop mental approach to prevention and treatment. *Torture, 10*, 8-21.

Weaver, H.N. & Burns, B.J. (2001). 'I shout with fear at night': Understanding the traumatic experiences of refugees and asylum seekers. *Journal of Social Work, 1*, 147-164.

Woodcock, J. (1997). Groupwork with refugees and asylum seekers. In T. Mistry & A. Brown (eds.), *Race and groupwork*, pp. 254-276. London: Whiting & Birch Ltd.

❑❑❑

Index

A

B

C

□□□